THE NEW FOLGER LIBRARY SHAKESPEARE

Designed to make Shakespeare's great plays available to all readers, the New Folger Library edition of Shakespeare's plays provides accurate texts in modern spelling and punctuation, as well as scene-by-scene action summaries, full explanatory notes, many pictures clarifying Shakespeare's language, and notes recording all significant departures from the early printed versions. Each play is prefaced by a brief introduction, by a guide to reading Shakespeare's language, and by accounts of his life and theater. Each play is followed by an annotated list of further readings and by a "Modern Perspective" written by an expert on that particular play.

Barbara A. Mowat was Director of Research *emerita* at the Folger Shakespeare Library, Consulting Editor of *Shakespeare Quarterly,* and author of *The Dramaturgy of Shakespeare's Romances* and of essays on Shakespeare's plays and their editing.

Paul Werstine is Professor of English at the Graduate School and at King's University College at Western University. He is a general editor of the New Variorum Shakespeare and author of *Early Modern Playhouse Manuscripts and the Editing of Shakespeare* and of many papers and articles on the printing and editing of Shakespeare's plays.

D0905843

The Folger Shakespeare Library

The Folger Shakespeare Library in Washington, D.C., a privately funded research library dedicated to Shakespeare and the civilization of early modern Europe, was founded in 1932 by Henry Clay and Emily Jordan Folger, and incorporated as part of Amherst College in Amherst, Massachusetts, one of the nation's oldest liberal arts colleges, from which Henry Folger had graduated in 1879. In addition to its role as the world's preeminent Shakespeare collection and its emergence as a leading center for Renaissance studies, the Folger Shakespeare Library offers a wide array of cultural and educational programs and services for the general public.

EDITORS

BARBARA A. MOWAT
Former Director of Research emerita
Folger Shakespeare Library

PAUL WERSTINE
Professor of English
King's University College
at Western University, Canada

Folger SHAKESPEARE LIBRARY

Shakespeare's Sonnets

EDITED BY BARBARA A. MOWAT
AND PAUL WERSTINE

Simon & Schuster Paperbacks
NEW YORK LONDON TORONTO SYDNEY NEW DELHI

Simon & Schuster
1230 Avenue of the Americas
New York, NY 10020

This Simon & Schuster trade paperback edition May 2020

SIMON & SCHUSTER and colophon are registered trademarks
of Simon & Schuster, Inc.

For information about special discounts for bulk purchases,
please contact Simon & Schuster Special Sales at 1-866-506-1949
or business@simonandschuster.com.

The Simon & Schuster Speakers Bureau can bring authors to your
live event. For more information or to book an event, contact the
Simon & Schuster Speakers Bureau at 1-866-248-3049 or visit our
website at www.simonspeakers.com.

Manufactured in the United States of America

10 9 8 7 6 5 4 3 2 1

ISBN 978-1-9821-5702-9
ISBN 978-1-5011-5033-3 (ebook)

From the Director of the Folger Shakespeare Library

It is hard to imagine a world without Shakespeare. Since their composition more than four hundred years ago, Shakespeare's plays and poems have traveled the globe, inviting those who see and read his works to make them their own.

Readers of the New Folger Editions are part of this ongoing process of "taking up Shakespeare," finding our own thoughts and feelings in language that strikes us as old or unusual and, for that very reason, new. We still struggle to keep up with a writer who could think a mile a minute, whose words paint pictures that shift like clouds. These expertly edited texts, presented here with accompanying explanatory notes and up-to-date critical essays, are distinctive because of what they do: they allow readers not simply to keep up, but to engage deeply with a writer whose works invite us to think, and think again.

These New Folger Editions of Shakespeare's plays are also special because of where they come from. The Folger Shakespeare Library in Washington, D.C., where the Editions are produced, is the single greatest documentary source of Shakespeare's works. An unparalleled collection of early modern books, manuscripts, and artwork connected to Shakespeare, the Folger's holdings have been consulted extensively in the preparation of these texts. The Editions also reflect the expertise gained through the regular performance of Shakespeare's works in the Folger's Elizabethan Theatre.

I want to express my deep thanks to editors Barbara Mowat and Paul Werstine for creating these indispensable editions of Shakespeare's works, which incorporate the best of textual scholarship with a richness of commentary that is both inspired and engaging. Readers who want to know more about Shakespeare and his plays can follow the paths these distinguished scholars have trod by visiting the Folger itself, where a range of physical and digital resources (available online) exists to supplement the material in these texts. I commend to you these words, and hope that they inspire.

Michael Witmore
Director, Folger Shakespeare Library

Contents

Editors' Preface

In recent years, ways of dealing with Shakespeare's texts and with the interpretation of his plays and poems have been undergoing significant change. This edition, while retaining many of the features that have always made the Folger Shakespeare so attractive to the general reader, at the same time reflects these current ways of thinking about Shakespeare. For example, modern readers, actors, and teachers have become interested in the differences between, on the one hand, the early forms in which Shakespeare's plays and poems were first published and, on the other hand, the forms in which editors through the centuries have presented them. In response to this interest, we have based our edition on what we consider the best early printed version of a particular play, poem, or collection of poems (explaining our rationale in a section called "An Introduction to This Text") and have marked our changes in the text—unobtrusively, we hope, but in such a way that the curious reader can be aware that a change has been made and can consult the "Textual Notes" to discover what appeared in the early printed version.

Current ways of looking at the plays and poems are reflected in our brief prefaces, in many of the commentary notes, in the annotated lists of "Further Reading," and especially in each edition's "Modern Perspective," an essay written by an outstanding scholar who brings to the reader his or her fresh assessment of the play, poem, or collection of poems in the light of today's interests and concerns.

As in the Folger Library General Reader's Shakespeare, which this edition replaces, we include explanatory notes designed to help make Shakespeare's language clearer to a modern reader, and we place the notes on the page facing the text that they explain. We also follow the earlier edition in including illustrations—of objects, of clothing, of mythological figures—from books and manuscripts in the Folger Library collection. We provide a brief account of the life of Shakespeare and an introduction to the text itself. We also include a section called "Reading Shakespeare's Language," in which we try to help readers learn to "break the code" of Elizabethan poetic language.

For each section of each volume, we are indebted to a host of generous experts and fellow scholars. The "Reading Shakespeare's Language" sections, for example, could not have been written had not Arthur King, of Brigham Young University, and Randall Robinson, author of *Unlocking Shakespeare's Language*, led the way in untangling Shakespearean language puzzles and shared their insights and methodologies generously with us. "Shakespeare's Life" profited by the careful reading given it by the late S. Schoenbaum. Our commentary notes in this volume were enormously improved through consultation of several of the more recent scholarly editions of the *Sonnets*. These editions are listed in our "Introduction to This Text," page xxxvii. We, as editors, take sole responsibility for any errors in our editions.

We are grateful to the authors of the "Modern Perspectives"; to Peter Hawkins, Steven May, and Marion Trousdale for helpful conversations about the *Sonnets;* to the Huntington and Newberry Libraries for fellowship support; to King's College for the grants it has provided to Paul Werstine; to the Social Sciences and Humanities Research Council of Canada, which provided him with a Research Time Stipend for 1990–91; to R. J. Shroyer of the University of Western Ontario for essential computer support; to the Folger Institute's Center for Shakespeare

Studies for its sponsorship of a workshop on "Shakespeare's Texts for Students and Teachers" (funded by the National Endowment for the Humanities and led by Richard Knowles of the University of Wisconsin), a workshop from which we learned an enormous amount about what is wanted by college and high-school teachers of Shakespeare today; to Alice Falk for her expert copyediting; and especially to Steve Llano, our production editor at Washington Square Press, whose expertise and attention to detail are essential to this project.

Our biggest debt is to the Folger Shakespeare Library—to Gail Kern Paster, Director of the Library, whose interest and support are unfailing, and to Werner Gundersheimer, the Library's Director from 1984 to 2002, who made possible our edition; to Deborah Curren-Aquino, who provides extensive editorial and production support; to Jean Miller, the Library's former Art Curator, who combs the Library holdings for illustrations, and to Julie Ainsworth, Head of the Photography Department, who carefully photographs them; to Peggy O'Brien, former Director of Education at the Folger and now Director of Education Programs at the Corporation for Public Broadcasting, who gave us expert advice about the needs being expressed by Shakespeare teachers and students (and to Martha Christian and other "master teachers" who used our texts in manuscript in their classrooms); to Allan Shnerson and Mary Bloodworth for their expert computer support; to the staff of the Academic Programs Division, especially Solvei Robertson (whose help is crucial), Mary Tonkinson, Kathleen Lynch, Carol Brobeck, Liz Pohland, Sarah Werner, Owen Williams, and Daniel Busey; and, finally, to the generously supportive staff of the Library's Reading Room.

Barbara A. Mowat and Paul Werstine

Shakespeare's Sonnets

Few collections of poems—indeed, few literary works in general—intrigue, challenge, tantalize, and reward as do Shakespeare's *Sonnets*. Almost all of them love poems, the *Sonnets* philosophize, celebrate, attack, plead, and express pain, longing, and despair, all in a tone of voice that rarely rises above a reflective murmur, all spoken as if in an inner monologue or dialogue, and all within the tight structure of the English sonnet form.

Individual sonnets have become such a part of present-day culture that, for example, Sonnet 116 ("Let me not to the marriage of true minds") is a fixture of wedding ceremonies today, and Sonnet 18 ("Shall I compare thee to a summer's day"), Sonnet 29 ("When in disgrace with fortune and men's eyes"), and Sonnet 73 ("That time of year thou mayst in me behold")—to name only a few—are known and quoted in the same way that famous lines and passages are quoted from *Hamlet* or *Romeo and Juliet* or *Macbeth*. Yet it is not just the beauty and power of individual well-known sonnets that tantalizes us, but also the story that the sequence as a whole seems to tell about Shakespeare's love life. The 154 sonnets were published in 1609 with an enigmatic dedication, presumably from the publisher Thomas Thorpe: "To The Onlie Begetter Of These Insuing Sonnets. Mr. W.H." Attempts to identify "Mr. W.H." have become inevitably entangled with the narrative that insists on emerging whenever one reads the *Sonnets* sequentially as they are ordered in the 1609 Quarto.

The narrative goes something like this: The poet (i.e., William Shakespeare) begins with a set of 17 sonnets advising a beautiful young man (seemingly an aristocrat, perhaps "Mr. W.H." himself) to marry and produce a child in the interest of preserving the family name and property but even more in the interest of reproducing the young man's remarkable beauty in his offspring. These poems of advice modulate into a set of sonnets which urge the poet's love for the young man and which claim that the young man's beauty will be preserved in the very poems that we are now reading. This second set of sonnets (Sonnets 18–126), which in the supposed narrative celebrate the poet's love for the young man, includes clusters of poems that seem to tell of such specific events as the young man's mistreatment of the poet, the young man's theft of the poet's mistress, the appearance of "rival poets" who celebrate the young man and gain his favor, the poet's separation from the young man through travel or through the young man's indifference, and the poet's infidelity to the young man. After this set of 109 poems, the *Sonnets* concludes with a third set of 28 sonnets to or about a woman who is presented as dark and treacherous and with whom the poet is sexually obsessed. Several of these sonnets seem also to involve the beautiful young man, who is, according to the *Sonnets'* narrative, also enthralled by the "dark lady."

The power of the narrative sketched above is so strong that counterevidence putting in doubt its validity seems to matter very little. Most critics and editors agree, for example, that it is only in specific clusters that the sonnets are actually linked, and that close attention to the sequence reveals the collection to be more an anthology of poems written perhaps over many years and perhaps to or about different men and women. Most are also aware that only about 25 of the 154 sonnets specify the sex of the beloved, and that in the century following the *Sonnets'* publication, readers who copied individual sonnets into their manuscript collections gave them titles that show, for example, that sonnets such as Sonnet 2 were seen as *carpe diem* ("seize the day") poems addressed "To one that would die a maid." Such facts, such recognitions, nevertheless, lose out to the narrative pull exerted by the 1609 collection. The complex and intriguing persona of the poet created by the language of the *Sonnets,* the pattern of emotions so powerfully sustained through the sequence, the sense of the presence of the aristocratic young man and the seductive dark lady—all are so strong that few editors can resist describing the *Sonnets* apart from their irresistible story. (Our own introduction to the language of the *Sonnets,* for example, discusses Sonnet 2 as a poem addressed to the beautiful young man, despite the fact that the sex of the poem's recipient is not specified and despite our awareness that in the seventeenth century, this extremely popular poem was represented consistently as being written to a young woman.) Individually and as a sequence, these poems remain more powerful than the mere mortals who read or study or edit them.

For a very helpful exploration of the *Sonnets* as they are read today, we invite you to read "A Modern Perspective" written by Professor Lynne Magnusson of the University of Toronto and printed at the back of this book.

Reading Shakespeare's Language: *The Sonnets*

The language of Shakespeare's *Sonnets,* like that of poetry in general, is both highly compressed and highly structured. While most often discussed in terms of its images and its metrical and other formal structures, the language of the *Sonnets,* like that of Shakespeare's plays, also repays close attention to such basic linguistic elements as words, word order, and sentence structure.

Shakespeare's Words

Because Shakespeare's sonnets were written four hundred years ago, they inevitably contain words that are unfamiliar today. Some are words that are no longer in general use—words that the dictionaries label *archaic* or *obsolete,* or that have so fallen out of use that dictionaries no longer include them. One surprising feature of the *Sonnets* is how rarely such archaic words appear. Among the more than a thousand words that make up the first ten sonnets, for instance, only eleven are not to be found in current usage: *self-substantial* ("derived from one's own substance"), *niggarding* ("being miserly"), *unfair* ("deprive of beauty"), *leese* ("lose"), *happies* ("makes happy"), *steep-up* ("precipitous"), *highmost* ("highest"), *hap* ("happen"), *unthrift* ("spendthrift"), *unprovident* ("improvident"), and *ruinate* ("reduce to ruins"). Somewhat more common in the *Sonnets* are words that are still in use but that in Shakespeare's day had meanings that are no longer current. In the first three sonnets, for example, we find *only* used where we might say "peerless" or "preeminent," *gaudy* used to mean "brilliantly fine," *weed* where we would say "garment," *glass* where we would say "mirror," and *fond* where we would say "foolish." Words of this kind—that is, words that are no longer used or that are used with unfamiliar meanings—will be defined in our facing-page notes.

The most significant feature of Shakespeare's word choice in the *Sonnets* is his use of words in which multiple meanings function simultaneously. In line 5 of the first sonnet, for example, the word *contracted* means "bound by contract, betrothed," but it also carries the sense of "limited, shrunken." Its double meaning enables the phrase "contracted to thine own bright eyes" to say succinctly to the young man that he has not only betrothed himself to his own good looks but that he has also thereby become a more limited person. In a later line in the same sonnet ("Within thine own bud buriest thy content" [s. 1.11]), the fact that *thy content* means both (1) "that which is contained within you, specifically, your seed, that with which you should produce a child," and (2) "your happiness" enables the line to say, in a highly compressed fashion, that by refusing to propagate, refusing to have a child, the young man is destroying his own future well-being.

It is in large part through choosing words that carry more than one pertinent meaning that Shakespeare packs into each sonnet almost incalculable richness of thought and imagery. In the opening line of the first sonnet ("From fairest creatures we desire increase"), each of the words *fairest, creatures,* and *increase* carries multiple relevant senses; when these combine with each other, the range of significations in this single line is enormous. In Shakespeare's day, the word *fair* primarily meant "beautiful," but it had recently also picked up the meaning of "blond" and "fair-skinned." In this opening line of Sonnet 1, the meaning "blond" is probably not operative (though it becomes extremely pertinent when the word *fair* is used in later sonnets), but the aristocratic (or upper-class) implications of "fair-skinned" are very much to the point (or so argues Margreta de Grazia; see Further Reading), since upper-class gentlemen and ladies need not work out of doors and expose their skins to wind and sun. (The negative class implications of outdoor labor carried in the sonnets by "dark" or "tanned" is carried today in the label "redneck.") The second word, *creatures,* had several meanings, referring, for example, to everything created by God, including the plant kingdom, while in some contexts referring specifically to human beings. When combined with the third word, *increase* (which meant, among its pertinent definitions, "procreation," "breeding," "offspring," "a child," "crops," and "fruit"), the word *creatures* takes the reader's mind to Genesis 1.28 and God's instructions to humankind to multiply and be fruitful, while the plant-life connotation of all three of the words provides a context for later words in the sonnet, such as *rose, famine, abundance, spring,* and *bud.* The words Shakespeare places in this first line ("From *fairest creatures* we desire *increase*")—with their undoubted link to concerns about upper-class propagation and inheritance—could well have alerted a contemporary reader to the sonnet's place in a familiar rhetorical tradition, that concerned with persuading a young gentleman to marry in order to reproduce and thus secure his family line and its heritable property. (See Erasmus's "Epistle to persuade a young gentleman to marriage," excerpted in the Appendix, pages 346–52.)

While almost every line of the 154 sonnets begs for a comparable unpacking of Shakespeare's words, we will here limit ourselves to two additional examples, these from lines 2 and 4 of the same sonnet (Sonnet 1). First, the word *rose* in the phrase *beauty's rose* (line 2) engages the reader's mind and imagination at many levels. Most simply, it refers simultaneously to the rose blossom and the rosebush; this double signification, as Stephen Booth points out (see Further Reading), enables the sonnet to acknowledge that although the individual person, like the rose blossom, inevitably withers and dies, the family line, like the rosebush, lives on through continual *increase.* But the *rose* signifies as well that which is most beautiful in the natural world. (See, e.g., Isaiah 35.1: "The desert and the wilderness shall rejoice; the waste ground shall be glad and flourish as the rose.") And *beauty's rose* not only meant youthful beauty but also inevitably called up memories of the *Romance of the Rose* (widely published in Chaucer's translation), in which the *rose* stands allegorically for the goal of the lover's quest. (The fact that the lover in the *Romance* desires a specific unopened rosebud, rather than one of the rosebush's opened flowers, may have implications for the word *bud* in line 11.)

The word *rose*, then, gains its multiple resonances by referring to both a flower and its bush and through meanings accumulated in cultural and poetic traditions. In contrast, the particular verbal richness of the word *his* in line 4, "*His* tender heir might bear *his* memory" (and in many of the other sonnets), exists because Shakespeare took advantage of a language change in process at the very time he was writing. Until around 1600 the pronoun *his* served double duty, meaning both *his* and *its*. However, in the late 1590s and early 1600s, the word *its* came into existence as possessive of *it,* and *his* began gradually to be limited to the meaning it has today as the possessive of *he.* Because of the emerging gender implications of *his,* the pronoun as used in line 4, while primarily meaning *its* and thus referring to *beauty's rose,* also serves as a link between the sonnet's first line, where the *fairest* creature is not yet a *rose,* and the young man, first directly addressed in line 5.

Because the diction of the *Sonnets* is so incredibly rich in meanings, and because space for our facing-page notes is limited, we have had to curtail severely our notes on words with multiple meanings. Where the primary meaning of a word is clear and where secondary meanings are readily available or are not essential to an understanding of the poem, we all too often have had to remain silent. When it seems possible that a given word might have more than one relevant meaning, the reader should test out possible additional meanings and decide if they add richness to the line. The only hazard here is that some words have picked up new meanings since Shakespeare's death; careful study of the diction of his *Sonnets* thus compels one to turn to a dictionary based on historical principles, such as the *Oxford English Dictionary.*

Shakespeare's Sentences

When Shakespeare made the decision to compose his *Sonnets* using the English (in contrast to the Italian) sonnet form, he seems at the same time to have settled on the shape of the *Sonnets'* sentences. The two forms are distinguished by rhyme scheme: in the Italian sonnet, the rhyme scheme in effect divides the poem into two sections, the eight-line *octave* followed by the six-line *sestet;* in the English, it sets three four-line quatrains in parallel, followed by the two-line rhyming couplet. While Shakespeare finds almost infinite ways to provide variety within the tightly controlled form of the English sonnet, and while the occasional sonnet is made up of a single sentence (e.g., Sonnet 29), his sentences tend to shape themselves within the bounds set by the quatrain and the couplet—that is, most quatrains and most couplets are each made up of one sentence or question, with occasional quatrains made up of two or more sentences or questions. (Quatrains that, in modern printed editions, end with a semicolon rather than a period or question mark are often so marked only to indicate that the thought continues into the next quatrain; syntactically, the clause is generally independent and could be completed with a period instead.) The reader therefore seldom finds in the *Sonnets* the long, complicated sentences often encountered in Shakespeare's plays. One does, though, find within the sentences the inversions, the interruptions of normal word order, and the postponements of essential sentence elements that are familiar to readers of the plays.

In the *Sonnets* as in the plays, for example, Shakespeare often rearranges subjects and verbs (i.e., instead of "He goes" we find "Goes he"); he frequently places the object before the subject and verb (i.e., instead of "I hit him," we might find "Him I hit"), and he puts adverbs and adverbial phrases before the subject and verb (i.e., "I hit fairly" becomes "Fairly I hit"). The first sonnet in the sequence, in fact, opens with an inversion, with the adverbial phrase "From fairest creatures" moved forward from its ordinary syntactical position after the verb. This transformation of the sentence "We desire increase from fairest creatures" into "From fairest creatures we desire increase" (s. 1.1) has a significant effect on the rhythm of the line and places the emphasis of the sentence immediately on the "fairest" creature who will be the topic of this and many sonnets to follow. In Sonnet 2 the sentence "Thy beauty's use would deserve much more praise" is transformed into "How much more praise deserved thy beauty's use" (s. 2.9), in large part through a double inversion: the transposing of the subject ("thy beauty's use") and the verb ("deserved") and the placing of the object before the inverted subject and verb. Again, the impact on the rhythm of the line is significant, and the bringing of the word *praise* toward the beginning of the line emphasizes the word's echo of and link to the preceding line ("Were an all-eating shame and thriftless praise") through its reiteration of the word *praise* and through repetition of the vowel sound in *shame.*

Occasionally the inversions in the *Sonnets* seem primarily to provide the poet with a needed rhyme word. In Sonnet 3, for example, the difference between *"she calls back /* In thee the lovely April of her prime" and *"she* in thee / *Calls back* the lovely April of her prime" (s. 3.9–10) seems largely to rest on the poet's choice of "thee" rather than "back" for the sonnet's rhyme scheme. However, Shakespeare's inversions in the *Sonnets* often create a space for ambiguity and thus for increased richness and compression. Sometimes the ambiguity exists only for a moment, until the eye and mind progress further along the line and the reader sees that one of the initially possible meanings cannot be sustained. For example, in Sonnet 5, the line "And that unfair which fairly doth excel" (s. 5.4) seems initially to present "that unfair" as the demonstrative adjective *that* followed by another adjective, *unfair,* until a reading of the whole line reveals that there is no noun for these apparent adjectives to modify, and that "that unfair" is more likely an inversion of the verb *to unfair* and its object, the pronoun *that.* The line thus means simply "deprive that of beauty which fairly excels"— though wordplay on *fairly* as (1) "completely," (2) "properly," and/or (3) "in beauty" makes the line far from simple.

Often the doubleness of meaning created by the inversion remains unresolved. In Sonnet 3, for example, the line "But if thou live remembered not to be" (s. 3.13) clearly contains an inversion in the words "remembered not to be"; however, it is unclear whether "remembered not to be" inverts "to be not remembered" (i.e., "[only] to be forgotten") or "not to be remembered" (i.e., "[in order] to be forgotten"). Thus, while the primary meaning of the line may well be "if you live in such a way that you will not be remembered," the reader cannot dismiss the line's simultaneous suggestion that the young man is living "with the intent of being forgotten" (Booth). The inversion, in other words, allows the line to carry two distinct tones, one of warning and the other of accusation.

Inversions are not the only unusual sentence structures in Shakespeare's language. Often in his *Sonnets* as in his plays, words that would in a normal English sentence appear together are separated from each other, usually in order to create a particular rhythm or to stress a particular word or phrase. In Sonnet 1, for example, in lines 5–6 ("But *thou,* contracted to thine own bright eyes, / *Feed'st* thy light's flame with self-substantial fuel"), the subject *thou* is separated from its verb *feed'st* by a phrase that, because of its placement, focuses sharp attention on the young man's looks and the behavior that the poet sees as defining him. A few lines later in the same sonnet,

> *Thou* that art now the world's fresh ornament
> And only herald to the gaudy spring
> Within thine own bud *buriest* thy content . . .
>
> (ll. 9–11)

the subject *Thou* is separated from its verb *buriest,* first by a clause that in its extreme praise ("that art now the world's fresh ornament / And only herald to the gaudy spring") is in interesting and direct contrast to the tone of accusation of the basic sentence elements within which the clause is set ("Thou buriest thy content"); the separation is further extended through the inversion that moves forward a prepositional phrase ("Within thine own bud") that would in ordinary syntax come after the verb. Line 12 of this same sonnet—"And, *tender churl*, mak'st waste in niggarding"—exemplifies a familiar kind of interruption in these poems, namely, an interjected compound vocative. Direct address to the beloved in the form of compound epithets, especially where one term of the compound ("tender") contradicts the other ("churl"), in meaning or in tone, is a device that Shakespeare uses frequently in the *Sonnets,* heightening the emotional tone and creating the kind of puzzle that makes the poems so intellectually intriguing. (Sonnet 4, for example, contains three such vocatives: "Unthrifty loveliness," "beauteous niggard," and "Profitless usurer.")

Sometimes, rather than separating basic sentence elements, Shakespeare simply holds back the subject and predicate, delaying them until other material to which he wants to give particular emphasis has been presented. The first quatrain of Sonnet 2 holds off until line 3 the

presentation of the subject of the sentence, and delays
the verb until line 4:

> When forty winters shall besiege thy brow
> And dig deep trenches in thy beauty's field,
> Thy youth's proud *livery,* so gazed on now,
> *Will be* a tattered weed of small worth held.

In this quatrain, the subject and predicate, "thy . . . liv-
ery . . . will be a tattered weed," are held back while for
two lines the poet draws a vivid picture of the young man
as he will look in middle age. Sonnet 2 is, in effect, an at-
tempt to persuade, an exhortation to the recipient to
change; the powerful description of youth attacked by
the forces of time gains much of its strength from its
placement in advance of the basic sentence elements.
(One need only reverse the order of the lines, placing
lines 3–4 before lines 1–2, to see how much power the
poem loses with that reversal.)

In addition to the delaying device, the quatrain con-
tains two further Shakespearean sentence strategies—a
subject/verb interruption in lines 3–4 followed by a com-
pression in line 4. The phrase "so gazed on now," which
separates the subject and verb ("livery . . . will be"),
stresses both the beauty of the young man and the brief-
ness of the moment for which that beauty will exist. The
last line, an example of the kind of compression that one
finds throughout the *Sonnets,* would, if fully unpacked
and its inversion reversed, read "[that will be] held [to
be] a tattered weed of small worth."

Metaphor and Metrical Effects

This first quatrain of Sonnet 2 can serve as a small exam-
ple not only of some of Shakespeare's sentence strategies

but also of how his word choice and word order operate to create the visual and musical effects that distinguish the *Sonnets*. While this topic is so large that we can only touch on it here, it seems appropriate to look at least briefly at two of the *Sonnets'* most important poetic techniques—metaphor and metrical effects.

The metaphor, a primary device of poetry, can be defined as a play on words in which one object or idea is expressed as if it were something else, something with which it is said to share common features. In the first quatrain of Sonnet 2 (quoted earlier), the young man's forehead, "so gazed on now," is imaged as a "field" that Time places under siege, digging "deep trenches" in its now youthful smoothness. The metaphor fast-forwards the aging process, turning the youth's smooth forehead in imagination into a furrowed, lined brow. While the word "field" could allude to any kind of open land or plain, the words "besiege" and "trenches" make it more specifically a battlefield ravaged by the armies of "forty winters." In line 3 the metaphor shifts, and the young man's youthful beauty is imaged as his "livery," a kind of uniform or splendid clothing that under the onslaught of time will become a "tattered weed" (*weed* having here the meaning "garment"). The quatrain seems, then, divided into two parts, with the metaphor shifting from that of the brow as a field to the brow (and other youthful features) as clothing. But the word *weed* carries its inevitable, though here secondary, meaning of an unwanted plant in a "field" of grass or flowers. This wordplay, which expands the scope of the word *field,* forces the reader to turn from line 4 back to lines 1 and 2, to visualize again the ravaged "field" of the once-smooth brow, and thus to experience with double force the quatrain's final phrase "of small worth held"—a phrase that syntactically belongs only to the tattered clothing but that, in the quatrain's overlapping metaphors, applies more broadly to the young man himself, now "so gazed on" but moving inevitably toward the day when he, no longer beautiful, will be considered "of small worth."

We mentioned at the outset that the language of the *Sonnets* is, like poetic language in general, highly structured. Nowhere is this fact more in evidence than in the rhythm of the *Sonnets'* lines. All of the *Sonnets* (except for Sonnet 145) are written in what is called "iambic pentameter" (that is, each line is composed of five metrical "feet," with each foot containing two syllables, usually with the first syllable unstressed and the second stressed). But within this general pattern, Shakespeare takes advantage of several features that characterize pronunciation in English—for example, the syllable stresses that inhere in all English words of more than one syllable, as well as the stress patterns in normal English sentences—and he arranges his words to create amazing metrical variety within the structure of the iambic pentameter line.

To return to the first quatrain of Sonnet 2: the first line of the sonnet ("When forty winters shall besiege thy brow") contains three two-syllable words; two carry stress on the first syllable ("forty" and "winter") and one is stressed on the second syllable ("besiege"). Shakespeare combines these words with four one-syllable words, three of which are unstressed in normal English sentences—a conjunction ("When"), an auxiliary verb ("shall"), and a possessive pronoun ("thy"). The resulting combination of words produces an almost perfect iambic pentameter (the only departure being the pyrrhic third foot, with its two unstressed syllables—"-ters shall"): "When *for'*ty *win'*ters shall be*siege'* thy *brow'*." After thus establishing the meter, the poet can depart radically from the iambic in line 2 without creating confusion about the poem's overall metrical structure. Line 2 ("And dig deep trenches in thy beauty's field") begins with an iamb ("And *dig'*") but then moves to a "spondee," a foot with two stressed syllables (*"deep' trench'-"*); the resulting rhythm for the opening of the line is the very strong series of three stressed syllables of *"dig' deep' trench'-."* The line then moves to the unstressed syllables in the pyrrhic foot ("-es in") before ending in iambic meter ("thy *beau'*ty's *field'"*)—a pattern that produces three unstressed syllables in mid-line. Line 3 ("Thy youth's proud livery, so gazed on now") echoes the opening rhythm of line 2—that is, an iamb followed by a spondee to create three stressed syllables ("Thy *youth's' proud' liv'-"*) again followed by three unstressed syllables ("-er-y so"); but then, instead of returning to the iambic, as did line 2, the line concludes with another group of three stressed syllables (*"gazed' on' now'"*). Line 4 seems to return us to the base of iambic pentameter ("Will *be'* a *tat'*tered *weed'* of *small'"*) only to end with a spondee (*"worth' held'"*), so that the beat of three stressed syllables (heard once in line 2 and twice in line 3) concludes the quatrain. It is to Shakespeare's skillful use of the unstressed pyrrhic foot that George Wright (see Further Reading, "An Art of Small Differences") credits much of the "softness and musical grace" of the *Sonnets.* "The strong iambs and spondees," he writes, rise from this pyrrhic base, a contrast that allows important spondaic and iambic syllables to gain special emphasis. In the lines we have been examining in Sonnet 2, one can see how the pyrrhics direct attention to such key words and phrases as "besiege" and "gazed on now."

With metaphors and metrics, as with word choice, word order, and sentence structure, every sonnet provides its own richness and its own variations, as well as occasional exceptions to any generalizations we have suggested. (Two of the *Sonnets,* for example, deviate even from the standard fourteen-line length, with Sonnet 99 having 15 lines and Sonnet 126 having only 12.) But each sonnet provides rich language, a wonderfully controlled tone, and an intellectual challenge sufficient to reward the most patient and dedicated reader.

Shakespeare's Life

Surviving documents that give us glimpses into the life of William Shakespeare show us a playwright, poet, and actor who grew up in the market town of Stratford-upon-Avon, spent his professional life in London, and returned to Stratford a wealthy landowner. He was born in April 1564, died in April 1616, and is buried inside the chancel of Holy Trinity Church in Stratford.

We wish we could know more about the life of the world's greatest dramatist. His plays and poems are testaments to his wide reading—especially to his knowledge of Virgil, Ovid, Plutarch, Holinshed's *Chronicles,* and the Bible—and to his mastery of the English language, but we can only speculate about his education. We know that the King's New School in Stratford-upon-Avon was considered excellent. The school was one of the English "grammar schools" established to educate young men, primarily in Latin grammar and literature. As in other schools of the time, students began their studies at the age of four or five in the attached "petty school," and there learned to read and write in English, studying primarily the catechism from the Book of Common Prayer. After two years in the petty school, students entered the lower form (grade) of the grammar school, where they began the serious study of Latin grammar and Latin texts that would occupy most of the remainder of their school days. (Several Latin texts that Shakespeare used repeatedly in writing his plays and poems were texts that schoolboys memorized and recited.) Latin comedies were introduced early in the lower form; in the upper form, which the boys entered at age ten or eleven, students wrote their own Latin orations and declamations, studied Latin historians and rhetoricians, and began the study of Greek using the Greek New Testament.

Since the records of the Stratford "grammar school" do not survive, we cannot prove that William Shakespeare attended the school; however, every indication (his father's position as an alderman and bailiff of Stratford, the playwright's own knowledge of the Latin classics, scenes in the plays that recall grammar-school experiences—for example, *The Merry Wives of Windsor* 4.1) suggests that he did. We also lack generally accepted documentation about Shakespeare's life after his schooling ended and his professional life in London began. His marriage in 1582 (at age eighteen) to Anne Hathaway and the subsequent births of his daughter Susanna (1583) and the twins Judith and Hamnet (1585) are recorded, but how he supported himself and where he lived are not known. Nor do we know when and why he left Stratford for the London theatrical world, nor how he rose to be the important figure in that world that he had become by the early 1590s.

We do know that by 1592 he had achieved some prominence in London as both an actor and a playwright. In that year was published a book by the playwright Robert Greene attacking an actor who had the audacity to write blank-verse drama and who was "in his own conceit [i.e., opinion] the only Shake-scene in a country." Since Greene's attack includes a parody of a line from one of Shakespeare's early plays, there is little doubt that it is Shakespeare to whom he refers, a "Shake-scene" who had aroused Greene's fury by successfully competing with university-educated dramatists like Greene himself. It was in 1593 that Shakespeare became a published poet. In that year he published his long narrative poem *Venus and Adonis;* in 1594, he followed it with *The Rape of Lucrece.* Both poems were dedicated to the young earl of Southampton (Henry Wriothesley), who may have become Shakespeare's patron.

It seems no coincidence that Shakespeare wrote these narrative poems at a time when the theaters were closed because of the plague, a contagious epidemic disease that devastated the population of London. When the theaters reopened in 1594, Shakespeare apparently resumed his double career of actor and playwright and began his long (and seemingly profitable) service as an acting-company shareholder. Records for December of 1594 show him to be a leading member of the Lord Chamberlain's Men. It was this company of actors, later named the King's Men, for whom he would be a principal actor, dramatist, and shareholder for the rest of his career.

So far as we can tell, that career spanned about twenty years. In the 1590s, he wrote his plays on English history as well as several comedies and at least two tragedies (*Titus Andronicus* and *Romeo and Juliet*). These histories, comedies, and tragedies are the plays credited to him in 1598 in a work, *Palladis Tamia,* that in one chapter compares English writers with "Greek, Latin, and Italian Poets." There the author, Francis Meres, claims that Shakespeare is comparable to the Latin dramatists Seneca for tragedy and Plautus for comedy, and calls him "the most excellent in both kinds for the stage." He also names him "Mellifluous and honey-tongued Shakespeare": "I say," writes Meres, "that the Muses would speak with Shakespeare's fine filed phrase, if they would speak English." Since Meres also mentions Shakespeare's "sugared sonnets among his private friends," it is assumed that many of Shakespeare's sonnets (not published until 1609) were also written in the 1590s.

In 1599, Shakespeare's company built a theater for

themselves across the river from London, naming it the Globe. The plays that are considered by many to be Shakespeare's major tragedies (*Hamlet, Othello, King Lear,* and *Macbeth*) were written while the company was resident in this theater, as were such comedies as *Twelfth Night* and *Measure for Measure.* Many of Shakespeare's plays were performed at court (both for Queen Elizabeth I and, after her death in 1603, for King James I), some were presented at the Inns of Court (the residences of London's legal societies), and some were doubtless performed in other towns, at the universities, and at great houses when the King's Men went on tour; otherwise, his plays from 1599 to 1608 were, so far as we know, performed only at the Globe. Between 1608 and 1612, Shakespeare wrote several plays—among them *The Winter's Tale* and *The Tempest*—presumably for the company's new indoor Blackfriars theater, though the plays seem to have been performed also at the Globe and at court. Surviving documents describe a performance of *The Winter's Tale* in 1611 at the Globe, for example, and performances of *The Tempest* in 1611 and 1613 at the royal palace of Whitehall.

Shakespeare wrote very little after 1612, the year in which he probably wrote *King Henry VIII.* (It was at a performance of *Henry VIII* in 1613 that the Globe caught fire and burned to the ground.) Sometime between 1610 and 1613 he seems to have returned to live in Stratford-upon-Avon, where he owned a large house and considerable property, and where his wife and his two daughters and their husbands lived. (His son Hamnet had died in 1596.) During his professional years in London, Shakespeare had presumably derived income from the acting company's profits as well as from his own career as an actor, from the sale of his play manuscripts to the acting company, and, after 1599, from his shares as an owner of the Globe. It was presumably that income, carefully invested in land and other property, which made him the wealthy man that surviving documents show him to have become. It is also assumed that William Shakespeare's growing wealth and reputation played some part in inclining the crown, in 1596, to grant John Shakespeare, William's father, the coat of arms that he had so long sought. William Shakespeare died in Stratford on April 23, 1616 (according to the epitaph carved under his bust in Holy Trinity Church) and was buried on April 25. Seven years after his death, his collected plays were published as *Mr. William Shakespeares Comedies, Histories, & Tragedies* (the work now known as the First Folio).

The years in which Shakespeare wrote were among the most exciting in English history. Intellectually, the discovery, translation, and printing of Greek and Roman classics were making available a set of works and worldviews that interacted complexly with Christian texts and beliefs. The result was a questioning, a vital intellectual ferment, that provided energy for the period's amazing dramatic and literary output and that fed directly into Shakespeare's plays. The Ghost in *Hamlet,* for example, is wonderfully complicated in part because he is a figure from Roman tragedy—the spirit of the dead returning to seek revenge—who at the same time inhabits a Christian hell (or purgatory); Hamlet's description of humankind reflects at one moment the Neoplatonic wonderment at mankind ("What a piece of work is a man!") and, at the next, the Christian disparagement of human sinners ("And yet, to me, what is this quintessence of dust?").

As intellectual horizons expanded, so also did geographical and cosmological horizons. New worlds—both North and South America—were explored, and in them were found human beings who lived and worshiped in ways radically different from those of Renaissance Europeans and Englishmen. The universe during these years also seemed to shift and expand. Copernicus had earlier theorized that the earth was not the center of the

The Globe

A stylized representation of the Globe theater.

cosmos but revolved as a planet around the sun. Galileo's telescope, created in 1609, allowed scientists to see that Copernicus had been correct; the universe was not organized with the earth at the center, nor was it so nicely circumscribed as people had, until that time, thought. In terms of expanding horizons, the impact of these discoveries on people's beliefs—religious, scientific, and philosophical—cannot be overstated.

London, too, rapidly expanded and changed during the years (from the early 1590s to around 1610) that Shakespeare lived there. London—the center of England's government, its economy, its royal court, its overseas trade—was, during these years, becoming an exciting metropolis, drawing to it thousands of new citizens every year. Troubled by overcrowding, by poverty, by recurring epidemics of the plague, London was also a mecca for the wealthy and the aristocratic, and for those who sought advancement at court, or power in government or finance or trade. One hears in Shakespeare's plays the voices of London—the struggles for power, the fear of venereal disease, the language of buying and selling. One hears as well the voices of Stratford-upon-Avon—references to the nearby Forest of Arden, to sheepherding, to small-town gossip, to village fairs and markets. Part of the richness of Shakespeare's work is the influence felt there of the various worlds in which he lived: the world of metropolitan London, the world of small-town and rural England, the world of the theater, and the worlds of craftsmen and shepherds.

That Shakespeare inhabited such worlds we know from surviving London and Stratford documents, as well as from the evidence of the plays and poems themselves. From such records we can sketch the dramatist's life. We know from his works that he was a voracious reader. We know from legal and business documents that he was a multifaceted theater man who became a wealthy landowner. We know a bit about his family life and a fair amount about his legal and financial dealings. Most scholars today depend upon such evidence as they draw their picture of the world's greatest playwright. Such, however, has not always been the case. Until the late eighteenth century, the William Shakespeare who lived in most biographies was the creation of legend and tradition. This was the Shakespeare who was supposedly caught poaching deer at Charlecote, the estate of Sir Thomas Lucy close by Stratford; this was the Shakespeare who fled from Sir Thomas's vengeance and made his way in London by taking care of horses outside a playhouse; this was the Shakespeare who reportedly could barely read but whose natural gifts were extraordinary, whose father was a butcher who allowed his gifted son sometimes to help in the butcher shop, where William supposedly killed calves "in a high style," making a speech for the occasion. It was this legendary William Shakespeare whose Falstaff (in *1* and *2 Henry IV*) so pleased Queen Elizabeth that she demanded a play about Falstaff in love, and demanded that it be written in fourteen days (hence the existence of *The Merry Wives of Windsor*). It was this legendary Shakespeare who reached the top of his acting career in the roles of the Ghost in *Hamlet* and old Adam in *As You Like It*—and who died of a fever contracted by drinking too hard at "a merry meeting" with the poets Michael Drayton and Ben Jonson. This legendary Shakespeare is a rambunctious, undisciplined man, as attractively "wild" as his plays were seen by earlier generations to be. Unfortunately, there is no trace of evidence to support these wonderful stories.

Perhaps in response to the disreputable Shakespeare of legend—or perhaps in response to the fragmentary and, for some, all-too-ordinary Shakespeare documented by surviving records—some people since the mid–nineteenth century have argued that William Shakespeare

Ptolemaic universe.

could not have written the plays that bear his name. These persons have put forward some dozen names as more likely authors, among them Queen Elizabeth, Sir Francis Bacon, Edward de Vere (earl of Oxford), and Christopher Marlowe. Such attempts to find what for these people is a more believable author of the plays is a tribute to the regard in which the plays are held. Unfortunately for their claims, the documents that exist that provide evidence for the facts of Shakespeare's life tie him inextricably to the body of plays and poems that bear his name. Unlikely as it seems to those who want the works to have been written by an aristocrat, a university graduate, or an "important" person, the plays and poems seem clearly to have been produced by a man from Stratford-upon-Avon with a very good "grammar-school" education and a life of experience in London and in the world of the London theater. How this particular man produced the works that dominate the cultures of much of the world almost four hundred years after his death is one of life's mysteries—and one that will continue to tease our imaginations as we continue to delight in his plays and poems.

An Introduction to This Text

A complete text of the Sonnets was first published in a 1609 Quarto titled *SHAKE-SPEARES SONNETS. Neuer before Imprinted.* The present edition is based directly on that printing.* The 1609 Quarto prints immediately

---

*We have also consulted the computerized text of the Quarto provided by the Text Archive of the Oxford University Computing Centre, to which we are grateful.

before its text of the poems a dedication page that reads as follows (each word printed entirely in capitals, except for "Mr.," and followed by a period): "TO. THE. ONLIE. BEGETTER. OF. | THESE. INSVING. SONNETS. | Mr. W.H. ALL. HAPPINESSE. | AND. THAT. ETER-NITIE. | PROMISED. | BY. | OVR.EVER-LIVING. POET. | WISHETH. | THE. WELL-WISHING. | AD-VENTVRER. IN. | SETTING. | FORTH. | T.T. [i.e., Thomas Thorpe, publisher of the Quarto]." Scholars have long speculated on the identity of "Mr. W.H." without arriving at any widely accepted conclusion. Following the Sonnets in the 1609 Quarto appears a poem of disputed authorship titled "A Louers complaint," which is not included in this edition.

In addition to providing an edited text of the 1609 Quarto version of the Sonnets, we include on pages 320–21 alternative texts of two of the sonnets (Sonnet 138 and Sonnet 144) that were first printed ten years before this quarto in a book titled *The Passionate Pilgrime. By W. Shakespeare.* The 1599 attribution of the entire *Passionate Pilgrime* to Shakespeare is misleading because much of the verse collected in it is not his; however, it does contain the earliest printing of the two sonnets in question, and for this reason those texts deserve consideration. There also exist a number of manuscript copies of particular sonnets, none of them thought to be in Shakespeare's own handwriting. Nonetheless, it has recently been argued that among these may lie an alternative Shakespearean version of Sonnet 2, as well as versions of other sonnets (8, 106, 128) that may derive from manuscript sources independent of that from which the 1609 Quarto was printed. We have, however, been persuaded by Katherine Duncan-Jones's argument in her 1997 Arden edition of the Sonnets, where she cogently refutes the claims for the authenticity of the Sonnet 2 manuscript version and also puts into serious question

the independent authority of the other surviving manu-
script texts. We thus have not included any manuscript
versions in this edition.

For the convenience of the reader, we have modern-
ized the punctuation and the spelling of the Quarto.
Whenever we change the wording of the Quarto or add
anything to it, we mark the change by enclosing it in su-
perior half-brackets (⌐ ¬). We want our readers to be im-
mediately aware when we have intervened. (Only when
we correct an obvious typographical error in the Quarto
does the change not get marked.) Whenever we change
the Quarto's wording or alter its punctuation so that
meaning changes, we list the change in the textual notes
at the back of the book, even if all we have done is fix an
obvious error.

The Explanatory Notes

The notes that appear on the pages facing the text are de-
signed to provide readers with the help that they may
need to enjoy the poems. Whenever the primary mean-
ing of a word in the text is not readily accessible in a good
contemporary dictionary, we offer the meaning in a note.
Sometimes we provide a note even when the relevant
meaning is to be found in the dictionary but when the
word has acquired since Shakespeare's time other poten-
tially confusing meanings. In our notes, we try to offer
modern synonyms for Shakespeare's words. We also try
to indicate to the reader the connection between the
word in the sonnet and the modern synonym. For exam-
ple, Shakespeare sometimes uses the word *glass* to mean
mirror, but, for modern readers, there may be no con-
nection evident between these two words. We provide
the connection by explaining Shakespeare's usage as fol-
lows: **"glass:** looking glass, mirror." Often in the *Sonnets,*
a phrase or clause needs explanation. Then, if space al-

lows, we rephrase in our own words the difficult passage, and add at the end synonyms for individual words in the passage. When scholars have been unable to determine the meaning of a word or phrase, we acknowledge the uncertainty. Biblical quotations are from the Geneva Bible (1560), modernized.

In the centuries since the publication of Shakespeare's *Sonnets*, many editors have worked at understanding and explaining the very condensed language of these poems. When we find the work of a particular editor especially helpful to the reader, we occasionally refer to that editor's notes. The following are editions that provide especially useful commentary:

> Booth, Stephen, ed. *Shakespeare's Sonnets* (New Haven, 1977)
> Duncan-Jones, Katherine, ed. *Shakespeare's Sonnets* (The Arden Shakespeare, 1997)
> Evans, G. Blakemore, ed. *The Sonnets* (The New Cambridge Shakespeare, 1996)
> Ingram, W. G., and Theodore Redpath, eds. *Shakespeare's Sonnets* (London, 1964, 1967)
> Kerrigan, John, ed. *The Sonnets and A Lover's Complaint* (The New Penguin Shakespeare, 1986)
> Orgel, Stephen, ed. *The Sonnets* (The Pelican Shakespeare, 2001)
> Vendler, Helen, ed. *The Art of Shakespeare's Sonnets* (Cambridge, Mass., 1997)

When an edition is mentioned in conjunction with a particular poem, the editor's remarks will be found in his or her commentary on that poem.

Illustrations are from the Folger archives. See "Index to Illustrations" (pp. 383–86) for information on the books or manuscripts in which the engravings or prints are found.

SHAKESPEARE'S SONNETS

In this first of many sonnets about the briefness of human life, the poet reminds the young man that time and death will destroy even the fairest of living things. Only if they reproduce themselves will their beauty survive. The young man's refusal to beget a child is therefore self-destructive and wasteful.

---

1. **increase:** reproduction, propagation

4. **tender:** i.e., young; **bear his memory:** i.e., carry its (or his) image as a living memorial

5. **contracted:** bound by contract, betrothed (but also with the sense of "limited, shrunken")

6. **Feed'st . . . fuel:** See longer note, p. 323. **self-substantial:** derived from one's own substance

10. **only:** peerless, preeminent; **herald:** forerunner, precursor; **gaudy:** brilliantly fine

11. **thy content:** (1) that which is contained within you—specifically, your seed, that with which you should produce a child; (2) your happiness

12. **churl:** miser (with wordplay on "lowbred fellow" or "villain"); **mak'st waste in niggarding:** i.e., diminishes or impoverishes through miserliness

13–14. **this glutton . . . thee:** i.e., be the kind of **glutton** who devours **the world's due** (the children one owes the world), first by refusing to reproduce and then by dying (See Erasmus's "Epistle" [B], in Appendix, p. 348.)

1

From fairest creatures we desire increase,
That thereby beauty's rose might never die,
But, as the riper should by time decease,
His tender heir might bear his memory.   4
But thou, contracted to thine own bright eyes,
Feed'st thy light's flame with self-substantial fuel,
Making a famine where abundance lies,
Thyself thy foe, to thy sweet self too cruel.   8
Thou that art now the world's fresh ornament
And only herald to the gaudy spring
Within thine own bud buriest thy content
And, tender churl, mak'st waste in niggarding.   12
    Pity the world, or else this glutton be—
    To eat the world's due, by the grave and thee.

The poet challenges the young man to imagine two different futures, one in which he dies childless, the other in which he leaves behind a son. In the first, the young man will waste the uninvested treasure of his youthful beauty. In the other, though still himself subject to the ravages of time, his child's beauty will witness the father's wise investment of this treasure.

---

2. **field:** i.e., the **brow** (imaged as a battlefield, besieged by Time, which digs **deep trenches**)

3. **proud:** magnificent, splendid; **livery:** distinctive clothing, military uniform

4. **weed:** garment (with possible wordplay on a **weed** in a **field**)

6. **lusty:** strong, vigorous (with possible wordplay on *lustful*)

7. **deep-sunken:** i.e., aged (literally, hollow, fallen in)

8. **all-eating shame:** (1) **shame** at having consumed everything; (2) **shame** that consumes you entirely; **thriftless praise:** (1) **praise** for having lived wastefully; (2) worthless **praise**

9. **use:** the act of holding land or other property so as to derive revenue or profit from it (but also with the sense of "employment for sexual purposes")

11. **sum my count:** i.e., provide a statement of reckoning for what I've received and spent; **make my old excuse:** i.e., justify me in my old age

12. **by succession thine:** i.e., inherited from you by legal right

2

When forty winters shall besiege thy brow
And dig deep trenches in thy beauty's field,
Thy youth's proud livery, so gazed on now,
Will be a tattered weed of small worth held.   4
Then being asked where all thy beauty lies,
Where all the treasure of thy lusty days,
To say within thine own deep-sunken eyes
Were an all-eating shame and thriftless praise.   8
How much more praise deserved thy beauty's use
If thou couldst answer "This fair child of mine
Shall sum my count and make my old excuse,"
Proving his beauty by succession thine.   12
    This were to be new made when thou art old
    And see thy blood warm when thou feel'st it cold.

The poet urges the young man to reflect on his own image in a mirror. Just as the young man's mother sees her own youthful self reflected in the face of her son, so someday the young man should be able to look at his son's face and see reflected his own youth. If the young man decides to die childless, all these faces and images die with him.

---

1. **glass:** looking glass, mirror

3. **fresh repair:** youthful condition

4. **beguile:** disappoint, cheat; **unbless some mother:** i.e., deprive someone of the blessings of motherhood

5. **fair:** beautiful; **uneared:** unplowed (The familiar metaphor that images copulation in agricultural terms continues in l. 6 with **tillage** and with wordplay on *husband* in **husbandry.**) See Erasmus's "Epistle" [D], in Appendix, pp. 349–50.

7. **fond:** foolish

7–8. **be . . . posterity:** i.e., out of his narcissism bury the generations that should succeed him

11. **windows . . . age:** i.e., your eyes when you are old

"Swift-footed Time." (s. 19.6)

3

Look in thy glass and tell the face thou viewest
Now is the time that face should form another,
Whose fresh repair if now thou not renewest,
Thou dost beguile the world, unbless some mother.　4
For where is she so fair whose uneared womb
Disdains the tillage of thy husbandry?
Or who is he so fond will be the tomb
Of his self-love, to stop posterity?　8
Thou art thy mother's glass, and she in thee
Calls back the lovely April of her prime;
So thou through windows of thine age shalt see,
Despite of wrinkles, this thy golden time.　12
　But if thou live remembered not to be,
　　Die single, and thine image dies with thee.

The poet returns to the idea of beauty as treasure that should be invested for profit. Here, the young man's refusal to beget a child is likened to his spending inherited wealth on himself rather than investing it or sharing it generously.

---

2. **thy beauty's legacy:** i.e., the beauty you have inherited

4. **frank:** generous; **are free:** i.e., who give freely

7. **Profitless usurer:** i.e., moneylender who makes no profit (The metaphor that links investment with the proper use of one's gifts recalls both the parable of the talents in Matthew 25 and Marlowe's *Hero and Leander.* See Appendix, pp. 344–46 and 352; see also p. 348 for Erasmus's "Epistle" [B].) **use:** expend, exhaust (with wordplay on "invest for profit")

8. **live:** (1) make a living; (2) survive

9. **traffic:** dealings, business

10. **deceive:** cheat, defraud

11–12. See Erasmus's "Epistle" [C], in Appendix, pp. 348–49.

A usurer. (s. 4.7)

4

Unthrifty loveliness, why dost thou spend
Upon thyself thy beauty's legacy?
Nature's bequest gives nothing but doth lend,
And being frank, she lends to those are free.   4
Then, beauteous niggard, why dost thou abuse
The bounteous largess given thee to give?
Profitless usurer, why dost thou use
So great a sum of sums yet canst not live?   8
For, having traffic with thyself alone,
Thou of thyself thy sweet self dost deceive.
Then how, when nature calls thee to be gone,
What acceptable audit canst thou leave?   12
    Thy unused beauty must be tombed with thee,
    Which usèd lives th' executor to be.

In this first of two linked sonnets, the poet compares the young man to summer and its flowers, doomed to be destroyed by winter. Even though summer inevitably dies, he argues, its flowers can be distilled into perfume. The beauty of the flowers, and thereby the essence of summer, are thus preserved.

---

1. **frame:** fashion, form
2. **gaze:** object gazed on
4. **that unfair:** i.e., deprive **that** of beauty; **fairly:** (1) completely; (2) properly; (3) i.e., in beauty
6. **confounds him:** i.e., destroys it, brings it to ruin
7. **lusty:** healthy, vigorous
9. **summer's distillation:** i.e., the essence of summer
10. **A liquid prisoner pent in walls of glass:** See Philip Sidney's *Arcadia:* "Have you ever seen a pure rosewater kept in a crystal glass, how fine it looks, how sweet it smells, while that beautiful glass imprisons it?" (1590 ed., p. 380).
11. **with beauty were bereft:** i.e., would be lost along with **beauty**
12. **Nor it nor no remembrance:** i.e., neither **it nor** any memory of
14. **Leese but:** lose only; **substance:** essence

5

Those hours that with gentle work did frame
The lovely gaze where every eye doth dwell
Will play the tyrants to the very same
And that unfair which fairly doth excel;   4
For never-resting time leads summer on
To hideous winter and confounds him there,
Sap checked with frost and lusty leaves quite gone,
Beauty o'er-snowed and bareness everywhere.   8
Then, were not summer's distillation left
A liquid prisoner pent in walls of glass,
Beauty's effect with beauty were bereft,
Nor it nor no remembrance what it was.   12
    But flowers distilled, though they with winter meet,
    Leese but their show; their substance still lives sweet.

Continuing the argument from s. 5, the poet urges the young man to produce a child, and thus distill his own summerlike essence. The poet then returns to the beauty-as-treasure metaphor and proposes that the lending of treasure for profit—i.e., usury—is not forbidden by law when the borrower is happy with the bargain. If the young man lends his beauty and gets in return enormous wealth in the form of children, Death will be helpless to destroy him, since he will continue to live in his offspring.

---

1. **ragged:** rough; **deface:** destroy, obliterate

3. **vial:** the "walls of glass" holding the perfume in s. 5 (but here also symbolizing the womb in which the young man's child should grow); **treasure:** enrich

5. **usury:** i.e., lending money for interest (also called **use**), which, while legal, was considered sinful (**forbidden**)

6. **happies:** makes happy; **pay the willing loan:** i.e., willingly **pay** back **the loan**

8–10. **Or ten times . . . thee:** These lines play with the interest rate of "one for ten"—i.e., 10 percent (here converted to "**ten for one,**" or 1000 percent)—and with the young man's prospect of reproducing himself tenfold through having ten children and then a thousandfold through his children's issue. **refigured:** duplicated

11–12. See Erasmus's "Epistle" [G], in Appendix, p. 352.

13. **self-willed:** wordplay on (1) obstinately selfish; (2) bequeathed to one's self

6

Then let not winter's ragged hand deface
In thee thy summer ere thou be distilled.
Make sweet some vial; treasure thou some place
With beauty's treasure ere it be self-killed.   4
That use is not forbidden usury
Which happies those that pay the willing loan;
That's for thyself to breed another thee,
Or ten times happier, be it ten for one.   8
Ten times thyself were happier than thou art
If ten of thine ten times refigured thee;
Then what could death do if thou shouldst depart,
Leaving thee living in posterity?   12
    Be not self-willed, for thou art much too fair
      To be death's conquest and make worms thine heir.

This sonnet traces the path of the sun across the sky, noting that mortals gaze in admiration at the rising and the noonday sun. When the sun begins to set, says the poet, it is no longer an attraction. Such is the path that the young man's life will follow—a blaze of glory followed by descent into obscurity—unless he begets a son.

---

2. **under eye:** (1) **eye** on the earth (and therefore below the sun); (2) subordinate **eye**

4. **with looks:** i.e., by gazing upon

5. **having:** i.e., the sun's **having; steep-up:** precipitous (Here, the sun moves around the earth, as in the Ptolemaic system. There is also an allusion to the sun-god driving his chariot up the hill toward its highest point at noon. See pictures, pp. xxxvi and 72.)

8. **Attending on:** (1) waiting on, serving; (2) paying attention to

9. **highmost pitch:** i.e., highest point, summit; **car:** chariot (See note to l. 5.)

11. **'fore duteous:** i.e, previously obedient or dutiful; **converted are:** are turned

12. **tract:** path

13. **thyself outgoing in thy noon:** (1) excelling yourself in this stage of early manhood; (2) outlasting the prime of your youth; (3) beginning to be extinguished even as the flame burns brightest

14. **get:** beget

14

7

Lo, in the orient when the gracious light
Lifts up his burning head, each under eye
Doth homage to his new-appearing sight,
Serving with looks his sacred majesty;   4
And having climbed the steep-up heavenly hill,
Resembling strong youth in his middle age,
Yet mortal looks adore his beauty still,
Attending on his golden pilgrimage.   8
But when from highmost pitch with weary car
Like feeble age he reeleth from the day,
The eyes, 'fore duteous, now converted are
From his low tract and look another way.   12
   So thou, thyself outgoing in thy noon,
   Unlooked on diest unless thou get a son.

The poet observes the young man listening to music without pleasure, and suggests that the young man hears in the harmony produced by the instrument's individual but conjoined strings an accusation about his refusing to play his part in the concord of "sire and child and happy mother."

---

1. **Music to hear:** i.e., you whose voice is like **music**

3. **lov'st thou:** perhaps, do you bother with, do you spend time on

4. **receiv'st . . . thine annoy:** i.e., do you enjoy being displeased

6. **unions:** combinations, conjunctions

7–8. **who confounds . . . bear:** i.e., **who,** by remaining single, destroy the potential harmony of marriage (and the **parts** of husband and father that you should play)

9–12. **Mark . . . sing:** Editors have suggested that these lines describe the tuning of lute strings, which are tuned in pairs; one string sets off sympathetic vibrations in its fellow, resulting in an enriched tone. (See picture, p. 82.)   **Mark:** notice, pay attention to **mutual ordering:** perhaps, harmony; perhaps, sympathetic tuning

14. **Thou . . . none:** The ancient mathematical dictum that "one is no number" became proverbial. (A *number* is [1] an "integer" and [2] an "aggregate or sum"; *one* is "a number" only in the first sense.)

16

8

Music to hear, why hear'st thou music sadly?
Sweets with sweets war not, joy delights in joy.
Why lov'st thou that which thou receiv'st not gladly,
Or else receiv'st with pleasure thine annoy?   4
If the true concord of well-tunèd sounds,
By unions married, do offend thine ear,
They do but sweetly chide thee, who confounds
In singleness the parts that thou shouldst bear.   8
Mark how one string, sweet husband to another,
Strikes each in each by mutual ordering,
Resembling sire and child and happy mother
Who, all in one, one pleasing note do sing;   12
    Whose speechless song, being many, seeming one,
    Sings this to thee: "Thou single wilt prove none."

The poet argues that if the young man refuses to marry for fear of someday leaving behind a grieving widow, he is ignoring the worldwide grief that will be caused if he dies single, leaving behind no heir to his beauty.

---

   3. **issueless:** childless; **hap:** happen
   4. **wail thee:** grieve for you; **makeless:** widowed
   5. **still:** unceasingly
   6. **form:** image, likeness
   7. **private:** ordinary, individual (This odd use of the word **private,** as Booth notes, may suggest its derivation from the Latin *privare,* "to bereave, deprive.")
   9. **Look what:** whatever; **unthrift:** spendthrift
   10. **Shifts but his:** i.e., merely changes its
   12. **user:** i.e., the possessor of the beauty (with wordplay on the meanings of **use** evoked in ss. 2, 4, and 6.)

"To give away yourself. . . ." (s. 16.13)

18

9

Is it for fear to wet a widow's eye
That thou consum'st thyself in single life?
Ah, if thou issueless shalt hap to die,
The world will wail thee like a makeless wife;   4
The world will be thy widow and still weep
That thou no form of thee hast left behind,
When every private widow well may keep,
By children's eyes, her husband's shape in mind.   8
Look what an unthrift in the world doth spend
Shifts but his place, for still the world enjoys it;
But beauty's waste hath in the world an end,
And, kept unused, the user so destroys it.   12
   No love toward others in that bosom sits
   That on himself such murd'rous shame commits.

This sonnet, expanding the couplet that closes s. 9, accuses the young man of a murderous hatred against himself and his family line and urges him to so transform himself that his inner being corresponds to his outer graciousness and kindness.

2. **unprovident:** improvident, heedless of the future

3. **Grant:** granted; or, I **grant,** I concede; **if thou wilt:** if you insist (Booth)

6. **stick'st not:** do not hesitate, are not reluctant

7. **roof:** i.e., house, family; **ruinate:** reduce to ruins (See Erasmus's "Epistle" [E], in Appendix, pp. 350–51.)

9. **thought:** i.e., way of thinking; **mind:** i.e., opinion (of you)

11. **presence:** bearing or appearance, outward demeanor

"Youth's proud livery." (s. 2.3)

20

10

For shame deny that thou bear'st love to any,
Who for thyself art so unprovident.
Grant, if thou wilt, thou art beloved of many,
But that thou none lov'st is most evident. 4
For thou art so possessed with murd'rous hate
That 'gainst thyself thou stick'st not to conspire,
Seeking that beauteous roof to ruinate
Which to repair should be thy chief desire. 8
O, change thy thought, that I may change my mind.
Shall hate be fairer lodged than gentle love?
Be as thy presence is, gracious and kind,
Or to thyself at least kind-hearted prove. 12
   Make thee another self for love of me,
     That beauty still may live in thine or thee.

The poet once again urges the young man to choose a future in which his offspring carry his vitality forward instead of one in which his natural gifts will be coldly buried. The very exceptionality of the young man's beauty obliges him to cherish and wisely perpetuate that gift.

---

1. **wane:** decrease in splendor (like the waning moon)

2. **one:** i.e., a child; **departest:** leave, forsake

3. **youngly:** in youth

4. **from youth convertest:** turn aside **from youth**

5. **Herein:** i.e., in the course of action here described

6. **Without this:** i.e., outside of **this** course of action **lives**

7. **minded so:** i.e., inclined (to choose **age and cold decay**); **the times should cease:** i.e., the **world** [l. 8] would end (See Revelation 10.5–6: "And the Angel . . . lift up his hand and sware . . . that time shall be no more.")

8. **threescore year:** i.e., a single lifespan (Psalm 90.10 says that "the time of our life is **threescore** years and ten.")

9. **for store:** (1) for purposes of breeding (normally applied to livestock); (2) to reserve for future use; (3) as something precious or valuable

10. **featureless:** ugly; **rude:** coarse, ill-shaped

11. **Look . . . more:** As in the parable of the talents, to him who has the most gifts will be given yet more (Matthew 25.29; see Appendix, p. 346.) **Look whom:** whomever

(continued)

22

11

As fast as thou shalt wane, so fast thou grow'st
In one of thine, from that which thou departest;
And that fresh blood which youngly thou bestow'st
Thou mayst call thine when thou from youth
    convertest.   4
Herein lives wisdom, beauty, and increase;
Without this, folly, age, and cold decay.
If all were minded so, the times should cease,
And threescore year would make the world away. 8
Let those whom nature hath not made for store,
Harsh, featureless, and rude, barrenly perish;
Look whom she best endowed she gave the more,
Which bounteous gift thou shouldst in bounty
    cherish.   12
    She carved thee for her seal, and meant thereby
    Thou shouldst print more, not let that copy die.

12. **in bounty cherish:** i.e., cultivate or care for by sharing generously

13. **seal:** engraved stamp used to make an impression in wax (As nature's **seal,** the young man shows nature's power and authority.)

14. **copy:** pattern, example (the original from which copies are made)

"This bloody tyrant Time." (s. 16.2)

11

As fast as thou shalt wane, so fast thou grow'st
In one of thine, from that which thou departest;
And that fresh blood which youngly thou bestow'st
Thou mayst call thine when thou from youth convertest.   4
Herein lives wisdom, beauty, and increase;
Without this, folly, age, and cold decay.
If all were minded so, the times should cease,
And threescore year would make the world away.   8
Let those whom nature hath not made for store,
Harsh, featureless, and rude, barrenly perish;
Look whom she best endowed she gave the more,
Which bounteous gift thou shouldst in bounty cherish.   12
　　She carved thee for her seal, and meant thereby
　　Thou shouldst print more, not let that copy die.

As he observes the motion of the clock and the movement of all living things toward death and decay, the poet faces the fact that the young man's beauty will be destroyed by Time. Nothing besides offspring, he argues, can defy Time's scythe.

---

1. **the clock:** i.e., the hours as struck by **the clock**
2. **brave:** splendid, glorious
6. **erst:** not long ago
7–8. **summer's . . . beard:** i.e., harvested wheat tied **in sheaves** and carried off the field on a cart (The words **bier** [the stand on which a corpse is carried to the grave] and **beard** [the bristly spines on wheat and the facial hair on men] conflate the harvested wheat with the dead body of a man.)
9. **of:** i.e., about; **question make:** (1) speculate; (2) entertain doubts
10. **wastes:** wilderness, deserts, desolate regions
11. **sweets:** pleasures, delights; **beauties:** beautiful things; **themselves forsake:** i.e., cease being **themselves** as they decay
12. **others:** i.e., other sweet and lovely things
13. **Time's scythe:** The familiar image of Time carrying an implement for cutting down grass suggests the biblical link between grass and man. See, e.g., 1 Peter 1.24: "For all flesh is as grass, and all the glory of man is as the flower of grass. The grass withereth and the flower falleth away." (See also, e.g., Psalm 103.15–16 and pictures, pp. 24 and 130.)
14. **breed:** generation; **brave:** defy (Note the conflation here of Time and Death.)

12

When I do count the clock that tells the time
And see the brave day sunk in hideous night,
When I behold the violet past prime
And sable curls ⌐all⌐ silvered o'er with white;   4
When lofty trees I see barren of leaves,
Which erst from heat did canopy the herd,
And summer's green all girded up in sheaves
Borne on the bier with white and bristly beard;   8
Then of thy beauty do I question make
That thou among the wastes of time must go,
Since sweets and beauties do themselves forsake
And die as fast as they see others grow;   12
    And nothing 'gainst Time's scythe can make defense
    Save breed, to brave him when he takes thee hence.

The poet argues that the young man, in refusing to prepare for old age and death by producing a child, is like a spendthrift who fails to care for his family mansion, allowing it to be destroyed by the wind and the cold of winter.

1. **your self:** perhaps, your soul (See longer note, pp. 323–25.)

3. **Against . . . end:** i.e., in anticipation of your death

5. **hold in lease:** possess for the limited period of time specified in a contract

6. **determination:** termination, ending; **were:** i.e., would be

9. **Who:** i.e., what kind of tenant or occupant (See Erasmus's "Epistle" [E], in Appendix, pp. 350–51.)

10. **husbandry:** careful household management (with probable wordplay on the word *husband*)

13. **unthrifts:** spendthrifts

"Methinks I have astronomy." (s. 14.2)

13

O, that you were your self! But, love, you are
No longer yours than you yourself here live;
Against this coming end you should prepare,
And your sweet semblance to some other give.   4
So should that beauty which you hold in lease
Find no determination; then you were
⌜Your⌝ self again after yourself's decease
When your sweet issue your sweet form should bear.   8
Who lets so fair a house fall to decay,
Which husbandry in honor might uphold
Against the stormy gusts of winter's day
And barren rage of death's eternal cold?   12
   O, none but unthrifts, dear my love, you know.
   You had a father; let your son say so.

As astrologers predict the future from the stars, so the poet reads the future in the "constant stars" of the young man's eyes, where he sees that if the young man breeds a son, truth and beauty will survive; if not, they die when the young man dies.

---

1. **judgment:** decision or conclusion about the future (an astrological term)

2. **I have astronomy:** i.e., I know astrology, I can read the future from the stars (See picture, p. 28.)

3–7. **But . . . well:** These lines list the kinds of predictions that astrologers claimed to make. **to brief minutes tell:** i.e., foretell to within the minute **Pointing to each his:** i.e., appointing **to each** minute its **say with:** i.e., **say with** regard to

8. **oft predict:** perhaps, frequent omens (The phrase is so uncommon that editors must simply speculate on its meaning.) **in heaven find:** i.e., read in the stars

10. **constant stars:** perhaps in contrast to the "wandering **stars**," the name given the planets, the "stars" read by astrologers

10–11. **such art / As:** i.e., learning **such as** that

12. **If . . . convert:** i.e., if you turn (your attention) from yourself to breeding

14. **end:** death; **doom:** final fate, destruction; **date:** end, limit (**End, doom,** and **date** all mean, in effect, death.)

14

Not from the stars do I my judgment pluck,
And yet methinks I have astronomy—
But not to tell of good or evil luck,
Of plagues, of dearths, or seasons' quality;   4
Nor can I fortune to brief minutes tell,
Pointing to each his thunder, rain, and wind,
Or say with princes if it shall go well
By oft predict that I in heaven find.   8
But from thine eyes my knowledge I derive,
And, constant stars, in them I read such art
As truth and beauty shall together thrive
If from thyself to store thou wouldst convert;   12
    Or else of thee this I prognosticate:
     Thy end is truth's and beauty's doom and date.

In the first of two linked sonnets, the poet once again examines the evidence that beauty and splendor exist only for a moment before they are destroyed by Time. Here the poet suggests—through wordplay on *engraft*—that the young man can be kept alive not only through procreation but also in the poet's verse.

---

3. **shows:** stage spectacles, plays (though with the suggestion of "illusions," "appearances")

4. **Whereon . . . comment:** The **stars** (i.e., the planets) are the audience to the **shows,** affecting them through occult **influence.** (See longer note, p. 325.)

5. **increase:** thrive, prosper; grow taller

6. **Cheerèd and checked:** (1) applauded and booed; (2) encouraged and restrained; **sky:** i.e., stars

7. **Vaunt:** i.e., rejoice (literally, swagger, boast)

8. **wear . . . memory:** This line holds in suspension several meanings that play against each other to describe the decline of **men** and **plants. wear:** (1) waste; (2) have on (as clothes) **brave state:** (1) splendid moment of **height** or zenith; (2) gorgeous display **out of memory:** (1) forgotten; (2) only in **memory**

9. **conceit:** idea, thought; **stay:** duration (though with overtones of "support" and of "pause")

14. **engraft you new:** i.e., renew your life through my poems (wordplay on **engraft,** with its root in the Greek for "to write" and its links to the creating of new life in plants through grafting) See picture, p. 36.

15

When I consider everything that grows
Holds in perfection but a little moment,
That this huge stage presenteth nought but shows
Whereon the stars in secret influence comment;   4
When I perceive that men as plants increase,
Cheerèd and checked even by the selfsame sky,
Vaunt in their youthful sap, at height decrease,
And wear their brave state out of memory;   8
Then the conceit of this inconstant stay
Sets you most rich in youth before my sight,
Where wasteful Time debateth with Decay
To change your day of youth to sullied night;   12
   And, all in war with Time for love of you,
   As he takes from you, I engraft you new.

Continuing the thought of s. 15, the poet argues that procreation is a "mightier way" than poetry for the young man to stay alive, since the poet's pen cannot present him as a living being.

1. **wherefore:** why
3. **in your decay:** i.e., as you decay
6. **unset:** unplanted
8. **liker:** i.e., more like you; **painted counterfeit:** (1) portrait; (2) feigned copy
9. **lines of life:** i.e., living children (The phrase alludes to various meanings of *line* that summon up such contexts as lineage, offspring, palmistry, and genealogy, along with portraiture and writing.)
10. **this time's pencil:** i.e., portraits drawn by artists of today (A **pencil** was a small artist's brush.) In the 1609 Quarto, l. 10 appears as "Which this (Times pensel or my pupill pen)." If one retains the Quarto's punctuation, "**this**" means "this sonnet" and "**time's pencil**" places the artist's brush in the hand of Time, which would here join the writer of the sonnets in preserving the young man's beauty.
11. **fair:** beauty
13. **give away yourself:** (1) marry; (2) produce children (See picture, p. 18.)

16

But wherefore do not you a mightier way
Make war upon this bloody tyrant Time,
And fortify yourself in your decay
With means more blessèd than my barren rhyme?   4
Now stand you on the top of happy hours,
And many maiden gardens, yet unset,
With virtuous wish would bear your living flowers,
Much liker than your painted counterfeit.   8
So should the lines of life that life repair
Which this time's pencil or my pupil pen
Neither in inward worth nor outward fair
Can make you live yourself in eyes of men.   12
   To give away yourself keeps yourself still,
   And you must live, drawn by your own sweet skill.

As further argument against mere poetic immortality, the poet insists that if his verse displays the young man's qualities in their true splendor, later ages will assume that the poems are lies. However, if the young man leaves behind a child, he will remain doubly alive—in verse and in his offspring.

2. **deserts:** excellent qualities

4. **parts:** attributes, gifts

6. **numbers:** lines or verses; **graces:** attractions, charms

11. **your true rights:** i.e., that which justly belongs to you; **poet's rage:** i.e., (the product of an) inspired frenzy (from the classical *furor poeticus*)

12. **stretchèd meter:** (1) i.e., poetic exaggeration; (2) strained **meter; antique song:** i.e., old-fashioned poem—or, perhaps, out-of-date poetic tradition

Grafting. (s. 15.14)

17

Who will believe my verse in time to come
If it were filled with your most high deserts?
Though yet, heaven knows, it is but as a tomb
Which hides your life and shows not half your parts.   4
If I could write the beauty of your eyes
And in fresh numbers number all your graces,
The age to come would say "This poet lies;
Such heavenly touches ne'er touched earthly faces."   8
So should my papers, yellowed with their age,
Be scorned, like old men of less truth than tongue,
And your true rights be termed a poet's rage
And stretchèd meter of an antique song.   12
    But were some child of yours alive that time,
    You should live twice—in it and in my rhyme.

In a radical departure from the previous sonnets, the young man's beauty, here more perfect even than a day in summer, is not threatened by Time or Death, since he will live in perfection forever in the poet's verses.

---

2. **temperate:** wordplay on weather that is **temperate** (i.e., not too hot) and on character that is gentle, not swayed by passion

4. **summer's . . . date:** i.e., summer is here for only a short time (In legal terms, a **lease** is temporary, expiring on a fixed **date.**)

5. **Sometime:** from time to time

6. **his:** i.e., its (the sun's)

7. **every . . . declines:** i.e., **every** thing of beauty will at some point diminish in beauty

8. **untrimmed:** i.e., changed in appearance (literally, stripped of ornament)

10. **Nor lose:** i.e., **nor** will you **lose; thou ow'st:** i.e., you own

11. **shade:** See Psalm 23.4: "though I should walk through the valley of the shadow of death," and see longer note, pp. 325–26.

12. **eternal lines:** immortal verse (though with an echo of the "**lines** of life" of s. 16); **to time thou grow'st:** i.e., you become grafted **to time** and thus will last as long as **time** lasts (Since a graft is bound by cords to the rootstock, **lines** here are also cords. See s. 15.14 and picture, p. 36.)

14. **this:** perhaps this sonnet, or perhaps the collection of sonnets

18

Shall I compare thee to a summer's day?
Thou art more lovely and more temperate.
Rough winds do shake the darling buds of May,
And summer's lease hath all too short a date.   4
Sometime too hot the eye of heaven shines,
And often is his gold complexion dimmed;
And every fair from fair sometime declines,
By chance or nature's changing course untrimmed.   8
But thy eternal summer shall not fade
Nor lose possession of that fair thou ow'st,
Nor shall Death brag thou wand'rest in his shade,
When in eternal lines to time thou grow'st.   12
   So long as men can breathe or eyes can see,
   So long lives this, and this gives life to thee.

The "war with Time" announced in s. 15 is here engaged in earnest as the poet, allowing Time its usual predations, forbids it to attack the young man. Should this command fail to be effective, however, the poet claims that the young man will in any case remain always young in the poet's verse.

---

1. **Devouring Time:** Proverbial: "**Time** devours all things." (See picture below.)

4. **burn . . . blood:** The **phoenix,** according to classical authors, at the end of a given period of time burned itself on a funeral pyre, and from its ashes the new **phoenix** arose. (See picture, p. 44.)

6. **swift-footed Time:** Proverbial: "**Time** flees away without delay." (See picture, p. 6.)

7. **sweets:** pleasures, delights

11. **course:** continuous process (but with wordplay on "running or galloping," "path," and "custom, habitual procedure"); **untainted:** i.e., unblemished

11–12. **allow / For:** i.e., permit (him to remain) as

"Devouring Time." (s. 19.1)

19

Devouring Time, blunt thou the lion's paws
And make the earth devour her own sweet brood;
Pluck the keen teeth from the fierce tiger's ⌈jaws,⌉
And burn the long-lived phoenix in her blood;   4
Make glad and sorry seasons as thou fleet'st
And do whate'er thou wilt, swift-footed Time,
To the wide world and all her fading sweets.
But I forbid thee one most heinous crime: 8
O, carve not with thy hours my love's fair brow,
Nor draw no lines there with thine antique pen;
Him in thy course untainted do allow
For beauty's pattern to succeeding men.   12
   Yet do thy worst, old Time; despite thy wrong,
   My love shall in my verse ever live young.

The poet fantasizes that the young man's beauty is the result of Nature's changing her mind: she began to create a beautiful woman, fell in love with her own creation, and turned it into a man. The poet, thus deprived of a female sexual partner, concedes that it is women who will receive pleasure and progeny from the young man, but the poet will nevertheless have the young man's love.

---

2. **master mistress:** perhaps, supreme **mistress;** or, perhaps, the **mistress** customarily addressed in sonnets, but here a man

5. **rolling:** i.e., wandering, roving

6. **Gilding . . . gazeth:** i.e., turning all that it looks upon to gold, as does the sun (See s. 33.4.)

7. **hue:** appearance, form (With **hues,** the meaning "colors, complexions" is added.) **in his controlling:** i.e., under his control

8. **Which:** perhaps refers to **hue,** but perhaps to his ability to control **all hues; amazeth:** i.e., astounds

9. **for:** i.e., to be, as

10. **wrought:** made; **fell a-doting:** i.e., became foolishly infatuated (but with overtones of "went out of her wits, began to act stupidly") See John Dickenson, *Arisbas* (1594; sig. E2): ". . . Nature in framing him hath wronged her own sex, bereaving it of so great a glory."

11. **by addition:** i.e., by adding a penis (but **addition** also meant something added to a coat of arms as a mark of honor, so that the phrase carries the meaning "by honoring you"); **of thee defeated:** cheated me out of you

(continued)

20

A woman's face with Nature's own hand painted
Hast thou, the master mistress of my passion;
A woman's gentle heart, but not acquainted
With shifting change, as is false women's fashion; 4
An eye more bright than theirs, less false in rolling,
Gilding the object whereupon it gazeth;
A man in hue all hues in his controlling,
Which steals men's eyes and women's souls amazeth. 8
And for a woman wert thou first created,
Till Nature as she wrought thee fell a-doting,
And by addition me of thee defeated
By adding one thing to my purpose nothing. 12
    But since she pricked thee out for women's pleasure,
    Mine be thy love, and thy love's use their treasure.

12. **to my purpose nothing:** i.e., that is of no use to me (with possible wordplay on **nothing** as a cant term for "vulva")

13. **pricked thee out:** selected you (with wordplay on "supplied you with male genitals")

14. **thy love's use:** wordplay on **use** as meaning "employment," "sexual enjoyment," "interest, profit" (The 1609 Quarto reads "and thy loues vse their treasure." As Orgel notes, if we retain Q's punctuation, the couplet might be understood to mean "since [Nature] selected you to experience pleasure as women do, mine be thy love, and may your lovers use their treasure.")

Phoenix. (s. 19.4)

20

A woman's face with Nature's own hand painted
Hast thou, the master mistress of my passion;
A woman's gentle heart, but not acquainted
With shifting change, as is false women's fashion;   4
An eye more bright than theirs, less false in rolling,
Gilding the object whereupon it gazeth;
A man in hue all hues in his controlling,
Which steals men's eyes and women's souls amazeth.   8
And for a woman wert thou first created,
Till Nature as she wrought thee fell a-doting,
And by addition me of thee defeated
By adding one thing to my purpose nothing.   12
    But since she pricked thee out for women's pleasure,
    Mine be thy love, and thy love's use their treasure.

The poet contrasts himself with poets who compare those they love to such rarities as the sun, the stars, or April flowers. His poetry will, he writes, show his beloved as a beautiful mortal instead of using the exaggerated terms of an advertisement.

---

1. **So . . . with:** i.e., I am not like; **muse:** i.e., poet (literally, the inspiring goddess of a poet)

2. **painted beauty:** i.e., one whose beauty is merely painted on

3. **Who . . . use:** i.e., **who** uses (comparisons with) **heaven itself**

4. **fair with his fair:** i.e., beautiful thing with the particular **beauty** he celebrates; **rehearse:** cite, mention (or recite, as an actor would in rehearsing lines written for him)

5. **Making . . . compare:** i.e., coupling (the beloved) proudly in a comparison (**compare**)

7. **rare:** splendid, excellent

8. **rondure:** i.e., sphere (literally, roundness, circle); **hems:** encloses

13. **like of hearsay well:** i.e., enjoy rumors or unsubstantiated reports

14. **that purpose not:** i.e., do not intend to (Proverbial: "He praises who wishes **to sell.**")

21

So is it not with me as with that muse
Stirred by a painted beauty to his verse,
Who heaven itself for ornament doth use
And every fair with his fair doth rehearse, 4
Making a couplement of proud compare
With sun and moon, with earth and sea's rich gems,
With April's firstborn flowers and all things rare
That heaven's air in this huge rondure hems. 8
O, let me, true in love, but truly write,
And then believe me, my love is as fair
As any mother's child, though not so bright
As those gold candles fixed in heaven's air. 12
    Let them say more that like of hearsay well;
    I will not praise that purpose not to sell.

This sonnet plays with the poetic idea of love as an exchange of hearts. The poet urges the young man to take care of himself, since his breast carries the poet's heart; and the poet promises the same care of the young man's heart, which, the poet reminds him, has been given to the poet "not to give back again."

---

1. **glass:** i.e., looking glass, mirror
2. **date:** age
4. **look I:** i.e., I expect; **expiate:** bring to an end
6. **seemly raiment of:** i.e., beautiful clothing that covers
9. **so wary:** as careful
10. **will:** i.e., **will** be careful (of myself)
11. **chary:** carefully (but with strong overtones of "cherished, precious")
12. **faring ill:** i.e., doing badly, not getting on well (though with possible overtones of the more specific "being badly fed")
13. **Presume not on:** i.e., do not count on reclaiming

22

My glass shall not persuade me I am old
So long as youth and thou are of one date,
But when in thee Time's furrows I behold,
Then look I death my days should expiate.   4
For all that beauty that doth cover thee
Is but the seemly raiment of my heart,
Which in thy breast doth live, as thine in me;
How can I then be elder than thou art?   8
O, therefore, love, be of thyself so wary
As I not for myself but for thee will,
Bearing thy heart, which I will keep so chary
As tender nurse her babe from faring ill.   12
    Presume not on thy heart when mine is slain.
    Thou gav'st me thine not to give back again.

The poet blames his inability to speak his love on his lack of self-confidence and his too-powerful emotions, and he begs his beloved to find that love expressed in his writings.

---

1. **As an unperfect actor:** i.e., like **an actor** who does not know his lines (or, perhaps, like an inexpert or unskilled **actor**)

2. **with:** i.e., by, through; **beside:** i.e., out of (The line can be read as "Whose **fear** makes him forget his lines.")

4. **Whose strength's abundance:** the excess power of which (i.e., the **rage**); **heart:** courage, spirit; purpose

5. **for fear of trust:** perhaps, not trusting myself (This ambiguous phrase links back to the fearful **actor** in l. 2.)

6. **perfect:** i.e., word perfect, exactly memorized (though with overtones of the word's more general meanings); **rite:** (1) ritual; (2) due (While the 1609 Quarto prints "loues right," *rite* was often spelled *right*.)

9. **my books:** perhaps, these poems (The word **books** is sometimes changed by editors to "looks.")

10. **dumb presagers:** perhaps, silent ambassadors (This would be a highly unusual meaning of *presager*.) **speaking breast:** i.e., heart's language

12. **more hath:** i.e., **more** often has

14. **wit:** intelligence

23

As an unperfect actor on the stage
Who with his fear is put beside his part,
Or some fierce thing replete with too much rage,
Whose strength's abundance weakens his own heart;   4
So I for fear of trust forget to say
The perfect ceremony of love's rite,
And in mine own love's strength seem to decay,
O'ercharged with burden of mine own love's might.   8
O, let my books be then the eloquence
And dumb presagers of my speaking breast,
Who plead for love and look for recompense
More than that tongue that more hath more
     expressed.   12
  O, learn to read what silent love hath writ.
  To hear with eyes belongs to love's fine wit.

This sonnet elaborates the metaphor of carrying the beloved's picture in one's heart. The poet claims that his eyes have painted on his heart a picture of the beloved. The poet's body is both the picture's frame and the shop where it is displayed. His only regret is that eyes paint only what they see, and they cannot see into his beloved's heart.

1. **stelled:** portrayed, drawn
2. **table:** a board or other flat surface on which a picture was painted
4. **perspective ... art:** i.e., seen perspectively (from the right angle or through a perspective glass— or, here, through the eyes of the poet), the lover's image in the poet's heart is the highest **art** (This line can be read in various ways, depending on different usages of **perspective** and of **art,** but the one proposed here seems to work best in context. **Perspective** is accented on the first and third syllables.)
7. **shop:** i.e., workshop
8. **That ... eyes:** i.e., for which your **eyes** provide the glass for its **windows his:** its **glazèd:** fitted with glass
11. **wherethrough:** through which
13. **this cunning want:** i.e., lack this skill or knowledge; **grace:** adorn

24

Mine eye hath played the painter and hath ⌜stelled⌝
Thy beauty's form in table of my heart;
My body is the frame wherein 'tis held,
And perspective it is best painter's art.   4
For through the painter must you see his skill
To find where your true image pictured lies,
Which in my bosom's shop is hanging still,
That hath his windows glazèd with thine eyes.   8
Now see what good turns eyes for eyes have done:
Mine eyes have drawn thy shape, and thine for me
Are windows to my breast, wherethrough the sun
Delights to peep, to gaze therein on thee.   12
  Yet eyes this cunning want to grace their art:
  They draw but what they see, know not the heart.

The poet contrasts himself with those who seem more fortunate than he. Their titles and honors, he says, though great, are subject to whim and accident, while his greatest blessing, his love, will not change.

1. **stars:** In astrological thinking, the wandering **stars** (i.e., planets) govern our good or bad fortune.

4. **Unlooked for:** (1) unexpectedly; (2) unregarded; **joy . . . most:** i.e., rejoice or delight in the person **I most honor** (Booth notes that **joy in** has astrological overtones, in that planets "**joy in**" being in signs of the zodiac where they are most powerful.)

5. **leaves:** i.e., petals

6. **marigold:** a flower described as opening and closing its petals in response to the presence or absence of the sun (See picture below.)

9. **painful:** (1) diligent; (2) suffering; **famousèd:** celebrated

10. **foiled:** overthrown, defeated

11. **razèd:** erased, obliterated

14. **remove . . . removed:** i.e., leave **nor be** forced to leave

"The marigold at the sun's eye." (s. 25.6)

25

Let those who are in favor with their stars
Of public honor and proud titles boast,
Whilst I, whom fortune of such triumph bars,
Unlooked for joy in that I honor most.   4
Great princes' favorites their fair leaves spread
But as the marigold at the sun's eye,
And in themselves their pride lies burièd,
For at a frown they in their glory die.   8
The painful warrior famousèd for worth,
After a thousand victories once foiled,
Is from the book of honor razèd quite,
And all the rest forgot for which he toiled.   12
   Then happy I, that love and am beloved
   Where I may not remove nor be removed.

The poet, assuming the role of a vassal owing feudal allegiance, offers his poems as a token of duty, apologizing for their lack of literary worth. He begs his liege lord to protect this expression of his duty until fortune allows him to boast openly of his love.

---

1. **vassalage:** the state of a devoted servant
2. **duty:** homage, due respect
3. **embassage:** message (of the kind delivered by an ambassador)
4. **wit:** poetic or linguistic facility
5. **wit:** intelligence, skill
6. **bare:** unadorned; paltry; naked; **wanting:** lacking
7. **conceit:** opinion, idea (though with wordplay on "literary **conceit,**" i.e., ingenious language)
8. **bestow:** lodge, place
9. **star:** See note to s. 25.1. **my moving:** i.e., the course of my life or my actions (with possible wordplay on the astrological meaning of **moving** as the name given the course followed by the planets)
10. **Points on:** i.e., directs its rays or influence on; **graciously with fair aspect:** i.e., auspiciously **aspect:** an astrological term meaning the relative position of the planets as observed from the earth
11. **loving:** wordplay on the word's secondary meaning, "expression of devotion"
12. **show me:** i.e., **show me** to be
14. **prove:** test

26

Lord of my love, to whom in vassalage
Thy merit hath my duty strongly knit,
To thee I send this written embassage
To witness duty, not to show my wit; 4
Duty so great, which wit so poor as mine
May make seem bare, in wanting words to show it,
But that I hope some good conceit of thine
In thy soul's thought, all naked, will bestow it; 8
Till whatsoever star that guides my moving
Points on me graciously with fair aspect,
And puts apparel on my tattered loving
To show me worthy of ⌜thy⌝ sweet respect. 12
    Then may I dare to boast how I do love thee;
    Till then, not show my head where thou mayst
       prove me.

In this first of two linked sonnets, the poet complains that the night, which should be a time of rest, is instead a time of continuing toil as, in his imagination, he struggles to reach his beloved.

2. **travel:** This word means both "**journey**" (l. 3) and "labor, travail." The spellings *travail* and *travel* were used interchangeably.

4. **work:** wordplay on "cause **my mind** to work" and "agitate"

6. **Intend:** set out on

9. **imaginary sight:** i.e., **sight** produced by the imagination

10. **shadow:** image, picture

12. **her old face: Night** is here represented as an **old** woman.

27

Weary with toil, I haste me to my bed,
The dear repose for limbs with travel tired,
But then begins a journey in my head
To work my mind when body's work's expired.   4
For then my thoughts, from far where I abide,
Intend a zealous pilgrimage to thee,
And keep my drooping eyelids open wide,
Looking on darkness which the blind do see;   8
Save that my soul's imaginary sight
Presents ⌈thy⌉ shadow to my sightless view,
Which like a jewel hung in ghastly night
Makes black night beauteous and her old face new.   12
   Lo, thus, by day my limbs, by night my mind,
   For thee and for myself no quiet find.

Continuing the thought of s. 27, the poet claims that day and night conspire to torment him. Though he has flattered both day and night by comparing them to beautiful qualities of his beloved, day continues to exhaust him and night to distress him.

---

1. **plight:** state, condition (perhaps, specifically, physical and/or mental condition)

7. **to complain:** i.e., to cause me (or give me the opportunity) to lament or bewail

9. **I tell . . . bright:** i.e., I flatter **the day** by saying you are **bright** (like daylight)

10. **dost him grace:** embellish or do honor to **the day**

12. **When:** i.e., by saying that **when; twire:** peep or peer; **even:** evening

"When I consider everything that grows. . . ." (s. 15.1)

28

How can I then return in happy plight
That am debarred the benefit of rest,
When day's oppression is not eased by night,
But day by night and night by day oppressed;   4
And each, though enemies to either's reign,
Do in consent shake hands to torture me,
The one by toil, the other to complain
How far I toil, still farther off from thee?   8
I tell the day to please him thou art bright
And dost him grace when clouds do blot the heaven;
So flatter I the swart complexioned night,
When sparkling stars twire not, thou ⌈gild'st⌉ the
      even.   12
   But day doth daily draw my sorrows longer,
   And night doth nightly make grief's length seem
      stronger.

The poet, dejected by his low status, remembers his friend's love, and is thereby lifted into joy.

---

2. **beweep:** weep over
6. **Featured like him:** i.e., having one man's (good) looks; **like . . . possessed:** i.e., being **like** another man in having **friends**
7. **art:** learning, skill
10. **Haply:** by chance (with wordplay on *happily*); **state:** i.e., mental or emotional condition
12. **sullen:** dull-colored, gloomy
14. **state:** position in life, status, wealth or possessions (though with wordplay on **state** as used in l. 10)

"Abundant issue." (s. 97.9)

29

When in disgrace with fortune and men's eyes,
I all alone beweep my outcast state,
And trouble deaf heaven with my bootless cries,
And look upon myself and curse my fate,   4
Wishing me like to one more rich in hope,
Featured like him, like him with friends possessed,
Desiring this man's art and that man's scope,
With what I most enjoy contented least;   8
Yet in these thoughts myself almost despising,
Haply I think on thee, and then my state,
Like to the lark at break of day arising
From sullen earth, sings hymns at heaven's gate;   12
    For thy sweet love remembered such wealth brings
    That then I scorn to change my state with kings.

The poet pictures his moments of serious reflection as a court session in which his memories are summoned to appear. As they come forward, he grieves for all that he has lost, but he then thinks of his beloved friend and the grief changes to joy.

---

1. **sessions:** wordplay on (1) judicial trial or investigation (emphasized in the word **summon** [l. 2]); (2) sitting together of a number of persons in conference (See John Dickenson, *Arisbas* [1594; sig. E2]: "Being in these dumps he held a session in his thoughts, whereto he assembled all his powers. . . .") In reading (1), **thought** is the judge; in reading (2), **thought** (regarded as plural) makes up the assembly.

2. **remembrance of things past:** See Wisdom of Solomon, 11.10: ". . . their grief was double with mourning and the **remembrance of things past**."

6. **dateless:** endless

10. **heavily:** sorrowfully, laboriously

10–11. **tell o'er . . . account:** (1) enumerate the distressing debts (see l. 12); (2) recite the sorrowful story

13. **the while:** i.e., in the meantime

30

When to the sessions of sweet silent thought
I summon up remembrance of things past,
I sigh the lack of many a thing I sought,
And with old woes new wail my dear time's waste;   4
Then can I drown an eye, unused to flow,
For precious friends hid in death's dateless night,
And weep afresh love's long since canceled woe,
And moan th' expense of many a vanished sight.   8
Then can I grieve at grievances foregone,
And heavily from woe to woe tell o'er
The sad account of fore-bemoanèd moan,
Which I new pay as if not paid before.   12
   But if the while I think on thee, dear friend,
   All losses are restored and sorrows end.

The poet sees the many friends now lost to him as contained in his beloved. Thus, the love he once gave to his lost friends is now given wholly to the beloved.

---

1. **endearèd with:** made more precious by
2. **by lacking:** i.e., not having; **dead.** i.e., lost forever "in death's dateless night" (s. 30.6)
5. **obsequious:** mournful (as befitting an obsequy or funeral)
6. **religious:** pious; conscientious
7. **interest of:** i.e., rightful or legal due (with wordplay on tears as coins paid as **interest** on a loan)
8. **removed:** i.e., moved (to another place), absent
9. **doth live:** i.e., (1) resides; (2) survives
10. **Hung . . . gone:** The image is of a mausoleum decorated with memorials to the dead.   **trophies:** memorials, but with the sense of "spoils of victory" **my lovers:** those who loved me   **gone:** dead
11. **their parts of me:** i.e., their shares in my love
12. **due of many:** i.e., debt owed to **many**

31

Thy bosom is endearèd with all hearts
Which I by lacking have supposèd dead,
And there reigns love and all love's loving parts,
And all those friends which I thought burièd.   4
How many a holy and obsequious tear
Hath dear religious love stol'n from mine eye,
As interest of the dead, which now appear
But things removed that hidden in ⌈thee⌉ lie.   8
Thou art the grave where buried love doth live,
Hung with the trophies of my lovers gone,
Who all their parts of me to thee did give;
That due of many now is thine alone.   12
   Their images I loved I view in thee,
   And thou, all they, hast all the all of me.

The poet imagines his poems being read and judged by his beloved after the poet's death, and he asks that the poems, though not as excellent as those written by later writers, be kept and enjoyed because of the love expressed in them.

---

1. **my well-contented day:** i.e., the **day** I am content to see

3. **shalt by fortune:** i.e., you shall perhaps; **resurvey:** reexamine, consider afresh; read again

5. **bett'ring of the time:** (literary) improvement or progress of the age

7. **Reserve:** keep

8. **happier:** more talented, more fortunate

10. **Had . . . age:** i.e., **had** my friend the poet lived to benefit from the superior style of **this age**

11. **dearer birth:** i.e., more worthy offspring; **brought:** i.e., given birth to

12. **march in ranks:** keep in step (as soldiers marching), with wordplay on **ranks** as lines or rows, including lines of poetry or of print; **of better equipage:** i.e. better equipped (another military term)

13. **since he died:** i.e., because **he died** (too soon); **better prove:** i.e., **prove** to be **better** (writers)

32

If thou survive my well-contented day
When that churl Death my bones with dust shall cover,
And shalt by fortune once more resurvey
These poor rude lines of thy deceasèd lover, 4
Compare them with the bett'ring of the time,
And though they be outstripped by every pen,
Reserve them for my love, not for their rhyme,
Exceeded by the height of happier men. 8
O, then vouchsafe me but this loving thought:
"Had my friend's muse grown with this growing age,
A dearer birth than this his love had brought
To march in ranks of better equipage. 12
    But since he died and poets better prove,
      Theirs for their style I'll read, his for his love."

The poet describes the sun first in its glory and then after its being covered with dark clouds; this change resembles his relationship with the beloved, who is now "masked" from him. But if even the sun can be darkened, he writes, it is no wonder that earthly beings sometimes fail to remain bright and unstained. (This is the first of a series of three poems in which the beloved is pictured as having hurt the poet through some unspecified misdeed.)

---

2. **Flatter:** (1) show honor to; (2) beguile; **sovereign:** superior (though with wordplay on royal flattery of courtiers)

4. **alchemy: Alchemy** sought to turn base metals to gold; the sun's rays make the **streams** appear to be "gilded," or covered with gold.

6. **rack:** mass of **clouds** driven by the wind in the upper air (but with wordplay on *wrack* as damage, ruin, devastation)

10. **all-triumphant:** glorious, magnificent

11. **out alack:** an exclamation of sorrow or anger; **but one hour:** i.e., only a moment

12. **region cloud:** i.e., the **rack** of l. 6 (The atmosphere was supposedly layered in "regions." The beloved is in a **region** above the poet, as are the clouds.)

14. **stain:** (1) lose color or brightness; (2) become discolored or marred; (3) become morally corrupt; **when . . . staineth:** i.e., if even the **sun** can be clouded over

33

Full many a glorious morning have I seen
Flatter the mountain tops with sovereign eye,
Kissing with golden face the meadows green,
Gilding pale streams with heavenly alchemy, 4
Anon permit the basest clouds to ride
With ugly rack on his celestial face,
And from the forlorn world his visage hide,
Stealing unseen to west with this disgrace. 8
Even so my sun one early morn did shine
With all-triumphant splendor on my brow,
But, out alack, he was but one hour mine;
The region cloud hath masked him from me now. 12
    Yet him for this my love no whit disdaineth;
    Suns of the world may stain when heaven's sun staineth.

In this sonnet the sun is again overtaken by clouds, but now the sun/beloved is accused of having betrayed the poet by promising what is not delivered. The poet writes that while the beloved's repentance and shame do not rectify the damage done, the beloved's tears are so precious that they serve as atonement.

---

3. **base:** dark, dingy; unworthy; **in:** on

4. **brav'ry:** splendor; **smoke:** fume or vapor

8. **heals . . . disgrace:** Proverbial: "Though **the wound** be healed yet the scar remains." **disgrace:** dishonor; disfigurement

9. **physic:** remedy; **grief:** (1) harm or injury; (2) sorrow

12. **cross:** adversity, misfortune

14. **rich:** valuable; powerful; **ill:** evil, bad

The sun-god in his chariot. (s. 7.5)

72

34

Why didst thou promise such a beauteous day
And make me travel forth without my cloak,
To let base clouds o'ertake me in my way,
Hiding thy brav'ry in their rotten smoke?   4
'Tis not enough that through the cloud thou break
To dry the rain on my storm-beaten face,
For no man well of such a salve can speak
That heals the wound and cures not the disgrace.   8
Nor can thy shame give physic to my grief;
Though thou repent, yet I have still the loss.
Th' offender's sorrow lends but weak relief
To him that bears the strong offense's ⌜cross.⌝   12
    Ah, but those tears are pearl which thy love sheds,
    And they are rich and ransom all ill deeds.

The poet excuses the beloved by citing examples of other naturally beautiful objects associated with things hurtful or ugly. He then accuses himself of being corrupted through excusing his beloved's faults.

2. **silver fountains mud:** i.e., silvery springs of water have **mud**

3. **stain:** (1) obscure; (2) blemish

4. **canker:** i.e., cankerworm (Proverbial: "The **canker** soonest eats the fairest rose.") See picture, p. 76.

5. **make faults:** commit wrongs, offend; **this:** i.e., **this** sonnet

6. **Authorizing:** sanctioning (though with possible wordplay on the root word *to author*) The accent falls on the second syllable. **with compare:** i.e., through comparisons

7. **Myself . . . amiss:** i.e., **corrupting myself** in the process of **salving** your faults   **corrupting:** debasing, defiling; infecting   **salving:** smoothing over; healing   **amiss:** error, fault

8. **Excusing . . . are:** There is almost no agreement about the meaning of this debated and variously emended line. See longer note, p. 326.

9. **to:** i.e., **to** the defense of; **sense:** i.e., reason

10. **advocate:** attorney

12. **civil war:** i.e., **war** within myself (in which **love** [for you] **and hate** [for what you have done] are the combatants)

13. **accessary:** accent on first syllable

14. **which:** i.e., who

35

No more be grieved at that which thou hast done.
Roses have thorns, and silver fountains mud;
Clouds and eclipses stain both moon and sun,
And loathsome canker lives in sweetest bud.   4
All men make faults, and even I in this,
Authorizing thy trespass with compare,
Myself corrupting salving thy amiss,
Excusing ⌐thy⌐ sins more than ⌐thy⌐ sins are.   8
For to thy sensual fault I bring in sense—
Thy adverse party is thy advocate—
And 'gainst myself a lawful plea commence.
Such civil war is in my love and hate   12
　　That I an accessary needs must be
　　To that sweet thief which sourly robs from me.

The poet accepts the fact that for the sake of the beloved's honorable name, their lives must be separate and their love unacknowledged.

1. **confess:** acknowledge; **twain:** (1) parted; (2) separate (with wordplay on "two")
3. **blots:** faults, blemishes
4. **borne:** (1) carried; (2) endured; **alone:** (1) by myself; (2) in solitude
5. **one respect:** See longer note, p. 326.
6. **separable spite:** (1) injurious or hateful separation; (2) outrage or injury that separates
9. **evermore:** at any future time; **acknowledge thee:** i.e., openly recognize you (as someone close to me)
10. **bewailèd:** i.e., bitter
12. **Unless . . . name:** i.e., without dishonoring yourself
13. **in such sort:** i.e., **in such** a manner
14. **thou . . . report:** i.e., since we are one in our love, your good reputation (**report**) also honors me

A cankerworm. (ss. 35.4, 70.7, and 95.2)

36

Let me confess that we two must be twain
Although our undivided loves are one;
So shall those blots that do with me remain,
Without thy help, by me be borne alone.   4
In our two loves there is but one respect,
Though in our lives a separable spite,
Which though it alter not love's sole effect,
Yet doth it steal sweet hours from love's delight. 8
I may not evermore acknowledge thee,
Lest my bewailèd guilt should do thee shame,
Nor thou with public kindness honor me
Unless thou take that honor from thy name.   12
    But do not so. I love thee in such sort
    As, thou being mine, mine is thy good report.

The poet feels crippled by misfortune but takes delight in the blessings heaped by nature and fortune on the beloved.

3. **dearest:** most grievous, direst
4. **of:** from
7. **Entitled . . . sit:** i.e., **sit crowned** among your virtues   **Entitled:** having a rightful claim or authority
8. **make . . . store:** i.e., attach **my love** to this abundance (**store**)
10. **shadow:** idea, conception
13. **Look what:** i.e., whatever

The nine muses. (s. 38.10)

37

As a decrepit father takes delight
To see his active child do deeds of youth,
So I, made lame by fortune's dearest spite,
Take all my comfort of thy worth and truth.   4
For whether beauty, birth, or wealth, or wit,
Or any of these all, or all, or more,
Entitled in ⌜thy⌝ parts do crownèd sit,
I make my love engrafted to this store.   8
So then I am not lame, poor, nor despised
Whilst that this shadow doth such substance give
That I in thy abundance am sufficed
And by a part of all thy glory live.   12
    Look what is best, that best I wish in thee.
    This wish I have, then ten times happy me.

The poet attributes all that is praiseworthy in his poetry to the beloved, who is his theme and inspiration.

1. **muse:** poetic gift or genius (This **muse,** which reappears in l. 13, is different from the **nine** mythological muses of l. 10, who inspire artists in the entire spectrum of human creativity; these are set in contrast to yet another **muse** [l. 9], that represented by the beloved as inspiration.) **want:** lack; **invent:** (1) write about; (2) find (from the Latin *invenio*)

2. **that:** i.e., **thou** who

3. **Thine own sweet argument:** i.e., yourself as the **subject** (l. 1)

4. **vulgar paper:** ordinary or commonplace writing; **rehearse:** repeat; say

6. **stand against thy sight:** i.e., withstand your scrutiny

8. **invention:** the act of poetic composition (See note to **invent,** l. 1.)

10. **nine:** See note to **muse,** l. 1, and picture, p. 78. **invocate:** invoke

12. **Eternal numbers:** immortal verses; **date:** period, duration

13. **muse:** the poetic gift cited in l. 1

38

How can my muse want subject to invent
While thou dost breathe that pour'st into my verse
Thine own sweet argument, too excellent
For every vulgar paper to rehearse?   4
O, give thyself the thanks if aught in me
Worthy perusal stand against thy sight,
For who's so dumb that cannot write to thee
When thou thyself dost give invention light?   8
Be thou the tenth muse, ten times more in worth
Than those old nine which rhymers invocate;
And he that calls on thee, let him bring forth
Eternal numbers to outlive long date.   12
    If my slight muse do please these curious days,
      The pain be mine, but thine shall be the praise.

As in s. 36, the poet finds reasons to excuse the fact that he and the beloved are parted. First, it is easier to praise the beloved if they are not a "single one"; and, second, absence from the beloved gives the poet leisure to contemplate their love.

---

1. **with manners:** politely, with propriety
2. **better:** superior; greater
5. **Even for this:** i.e., precisely **for this** reason
10. **not thy:** i.e., **not** that **thy**
13. **And that:** i.e., **and were it not that** (l. 10); **thou:** addressed to **absence; make one twain:** (1) divide **one** into two; (2) give **one** person an existence in two locations
14. **here:** (1) i.e., where I am; (2) in the poem; **remain:** abide, dwell

A lute. (s. 8.9–12)

39

O, how thy worth with manners may I sing
When thou art all the better part of me?
What can mine own praise to mine own self bring,
And what is 't but mine own when I praise thee?   4
Even for this let us divided live
And our dear love lose name of single one,
That by this separation I may give
That due to thee which thou deserv'st alone.   8
O absence, what a torment wouldst thou prove
Were it not thy sour leisure gave sweet leave
To entertain the time with thoughts of love,
Which time and thoughts so sweetly ⌜doth⌝ deceive,   12
    And that thou teachest how to make one twain
    By praising him here who doth hence remain.

This first of three linked sonnets accuses the young man of having stolen the poet's "love." The poet struggles to justify and forgive the young man's betrayal, but can go no farther than the concluding "we must not be foes." (While the word *love* is elaborately ambiguous in this sonnet, the following two sonnets make it clear that the theft is of the poet's mistress.)

---

6. **for . . . usest:** (1) if you make use of **my love;** (2) because you have intercourse with my mistress

7. **be blamed:** i.e., you are blameworthy

8. **taste:** (1) testing; (2) enjoyment; (3) savoring

10. **steal thee:** i.e., **steal** for yourself; **all my poverty:** i.e., the little bit that I have

11. **grief:** (1) suffering; (2) sorrow

12. **injury:** willful harm

13. **Lascivious grace:** i.e., attractiveness that is both lewd and seductive; **all ill well shows:** everything bad or evil looks good

14. **spites:** insults; **yet:** nevertheless

40

Take all my loves, my love, yea, take them all.
What hast thou then more than thou hadst before?
No love, my love, that thou mayst true love call;
All mine was thine before thou hadst this more.   4
Then, if for my love thou my love receivest,
I cannot blame thee for my love thou usest;
But yet be blamed if thou ⌜thyself⌝ deceivest
By willful taste of what thyself refusest.   8
I do forgive thy robb'ry, gentle thief,
Although thou steal thee all my poverty;
And yet love knows it is a greater grief
To bear love's wrong than hate's known injury.   12
    Lascivious grace, in whom all ill well shows,
    Kill me with spites, yet we must not be foes.

The poet again tries to forgive the young man, now on the grounds that the young man could hardly have been expected to refuse the woman's seduction. The attempt to forgive fails because the young man has caused a twofold betrayal: his beauty having first seduced the woman, both he and she have then been faithless to the poet.

---

1. **pretty wrongs:** i.e., little offenses (Proverbial: "Little things are **pretty.**") **liberty:** license

3. **befits:** i.e., befit

4. **still:** always

5–6. **Gentle . . . assailed:** a clever gender inversion of the proverb "All women may be won," which Shakespeare appropriated in *1 Henry VI* 5.3.78–79 as "She's beautiful, and therefore to be wooed; / She is a woman, **therefore to be won.**" **Gentle:** (1) well-born; (2) mild in disposition, kind, tender

8. **sourly:** peevishly; **he:** Note the unexpected and witty shift of responsibility here from the woman to the young man.

9. **my seat forbear:** i.e., keep away from a place belonging to me

11. **Who:** i.e., which; **riot:** debauchery

12. **truth:** i.e., troth, constancy, faithfulness

41

Those pretty wrongs that liberty commits
When I am sometime absent from thy heart,
Thy beauty and thy years full well befits,
For still temptation follows where thou art.   4
Gentle thou art, and therefore to be won;
Beauteous thou art, therefore to be assailed;
And when a woman woos, what woman's son
Will sourly leave her till he have prevailed?   8
Ay me, but yet thou mightst my seat forbear,
And chide thy beauty and thy straying youth,
Who lead thee in their riot even there
Where thou art forced to break a twofold truth: 12
    Hers, by thy beauty tempting her to thee,
    Thine, by thy beauty being false to me.

The poet attempts to excuse the two lovers. He first argues that they love each other only because of him; he then argues that since he and the young man are one, in loving the young man, the woman actually loves the poet. The poet acknowledges, though, that all of this is mere "flattery" or self-delusion.

---

3. **of my wailing chief:** i.e., is the **chief** cause of my sorrow

4. **touches:** (1) affects; (2) injures; **nearly:** (1) closely; (2) particularly

5. **excuse ye:** i.e., find an excuse for you

7. **for my sake:** out of regard for me; **even so:** i.e., in the same way; **abuse:** wrong

8. **Suff'ring:** allowing; **approve her:** wordplay on "commend her" and "try or experience her sexually"

9. **my love's:** i.e., my mistress's

10. **losing:** i.e., I **losing; that loss:** i.e., what I have lost

12. **lay on me this cross:** i.e., put this heavy burden on me

Woman wearing a carcanet. (s. 52.8)

42

That thou hast her, it is not all my grief,
And yet it may be said I loved her dearly;
That she hath thee is of my wailing chief,
A loss in love that touches me more nearly.   4
Loving offenders, thus I will excuse ye:
Thou dost love her because thou know'st I love her,
And for my sake even so doth she abuse me,
Suff'ring my friend for my sake to approve her.   8
If I lose thee, my loss is my love's gain,
And losing her, my friend hath found that loss;
Both find each other, and I lose both twain,
And both for my sake lay on me this cross.   12
    But here's the joy: my friend and I are one;
    Sweet flattery! then she loves but me alone.

The poet, separated from the beloved, reflects on the paradox that because he dreams of the beloved, he sees better with his eyes closed in sleep than he does with them open in daylight. His desire, though, is to see not the dream image but the actual person.

---

1. **wink:** close my eyes
2. **unrespected:** (1) not worth respect; (2) not heeded, not paid attention to
4. **darkly bright:** (1) luminous behind the eyelids' dark shutters; (2) blind but seeing; **are bright:** i.e., are brightly, clearly (See longer note, pp. 326–27.)
5. **shadow:** dream image; **shadows:** dark places; other dream images
6. **thy shadow's form:** i.e., your physical being; **form happy show:** create a joyful spectacle
8. **thy shade:** i.e., your (mere) image
11. **fair imperfect:** i.e., beautiful but deficient (because only a dream image)
12. **stay:** remain, linger, reside
13. **to see:** (1) in appearance; (2) as regards my ability **to see**
14. **show thee me:** i.e., **show** you to **me** (though the syntax insists on the more obvious "**show me** to you")

43

When most I wink, then do mine eyes best see,
For all the day they view things unrespected;
But when I sleep, in dreams they look on thee
And, darkly bright, are bright in dark directed.   4
Then thou whose shadow shadows doth make bright,
How would thy shadow's form form happy show
To the clear day with thy much clearer light
When to unseeing eyes thy shade shines so!   8
How would, I say, mine eyes be blessèd made
By looking on thee in the living day,
When in dead night ⌜thy⌝ fair imperfect shade
Through heavy sleep on sightless eyes doth stay!   12
   All days are nights to see till I see thee,
    And nights bright days when dreams do show
      thee me.

In this sonnet, which links with s. 45 to form, in effect, a two-part poem, the poet wishes that he were thought rather than flesh so that he could be with the beloved. The poet, being mortal, is instead made up of the four elements—earth, air, fire, and water. The dullest of these elements, earth and water, are dominant in him and force him to remain fixed in place, weeping "heavy tears."

---

1. **dull substance:** heavy material; **thought:** Proverbial: "As swift as **thought.**"
2. **stop my way:** block my path
4. **limits:** regions; **where:** i.e., to **where; stay:** reside, linger
6. **removed:** remote, separated
8. **he would be:** i.e., **thought** wished to **be**
9. **thought kills me:** i.e., reflection makes me despair; **thought:** i.e., (swift) imagination
11. **so . . . wrought:** i.e., composed to such an extent **of earth and water** (In the thinking of the time, all that was material was composed of **earth,** air, fire, and **water,** with air and fire the lighter and freer.)
12. **attend time's leisure:** (1) wait until time passes; (2) wait upon the powerful figure of Time until he is ready to hear me; **moan:** (1) lamentation; (2) expression of grief (in this poem)
14. **badges of either's woe:** Because **tears** are wet (like **water**) and **heavy** (like **earth**), they serve as insignia (**badges**) that tie the poet to the two heavier **elements** and their **woe.**

44

If the dull substance of my flesh were thought,
Injurious distance should not stop my way,
For then, despite of space, I would be brought
From limits far remote, where thou dost stay.   4
No matter then although my foot did stand
Upon the farthest earth removed from thee,
For nimble thought can jump both sea and land
As soon as think the place where he would be.   8
But, ah, thought kills me that I am not thought,
To leap large lengths of miles when thou art gone,
But that, so much of earth and water wrought,
I must attend time's leisure with my moan;   12
   Receiving ⌜nought⌝ by elements so slow
   But heavy tears, badges of either's woe.

This sonnet, the companion to s. 44, imagines the poet's thoughts and desires as the "other two" elements—air and fire—that make up "life's composition." When his thoughts and desires are with the beloved, the poet, reduced to earth and water, sinks into melancholy; when his thoughts and desires return, assuring the poet of the beloved's "fair health," the poet is briefly joyful, until he sends them back to the beloved and again is "sad."

---

1. **two:** i.e., **two** elements; **slight:** i.e., light; **purging:** purifying

4. **These:** i.e., **my thought** and **my desire; with . . . slide:** i.e., move without effort

5. **quicker:** livelier; swifter

6. **In . . . love:** i.e., on an ambassadorial mission (**embassy**) carrying my **love**

7. **four:** i.e., **four** elements

8. **melancholy:** a psychological and physiological condition caused by an excess of black bile, one of the four humors thought to govern man's emotional and physical state (**Melancholy** as a humor is, like **earth** [s. 44.11], considered cold and dry.) For a chart of humors and elements, see picture, p. 98.

9. **recured:** restored

11. **even but now:** i.e., at this very moment

12. **recounting it:** giving a detailed account of it

14. **straight:** immediately

45

The other two, slight air and purging fire,
Are both with thee, wherever I abide;
The first my thought, the other my desire,
These present-absent with swift motion slide.   4
For when these quicker elements are gone
In tender embassy of love to thee,
My life, being made of four, with two alone
Sinks down to death, oppressed with melancholy;   8
Until life's composition be recured
By those swift messengers returned from thee,
Who even but now come back again, assured
Of ⌜thy⌝ fair health, recounting it to me.   12
   This told, I joy; but then, no longer glad,
   I send them back again and straight grow sad.

In this first of another pair of sonnets (perhaps a witty thank-you for the gift of a miniature portrait), the poet's eyes and his heart are in a bitter dispute about which has the legal right to the beloved's picture. The case is brought before a jury made up of the poet's thoughts. This jury determines that the eyes have the right to the picture, since it is the beloved's outer image; the heart, though, has the right to the beloved's love.

---

1. **at a mortal:** i.e., in a deadly
2. **conquest:** (1) booty; (2) property acquired not through inheritance; **thy sight:** i.e., the **sight** of you
3. **my . . . bar:** i.e., **would** forbid **my heart** any glimpse of your picture (On the legal language that fills this sonnet, see longer note, p. 327.)
4. **mine . . . right:** i.e., **would** forbid **mine eye** to exercise its unrestrained **right** (to view the picture)
5. **thou:** i.e., the essential "you"
6. **closet:** either a small private room or a cabinet
7. **defendant:** i.e., the eyes
9. **impanelèd:** constituted
10. **quest:** jury
12. **moiety:** portion; **dear:** loving

46

Mine eye and heart are at a mortal war
How to divide the conquest of thy sight.
Mine eye my heart ⌐thy¬ picture's sight would bar,
My heart mine eye the freedom of that right.　　4
My heart doth plead that thou in him dost lie,
A closet never pierced with crystal eyes;
But the defendant doth that plea deny,
And says in him ⌐thy¬ fair appearance lies.　　8
To ⌐'cide¬ this title is impanelèd
A quest of thoughts, all tenants to the heart,
And by their verdict is determinèd
The clear eyes' moiety and the dear heart's part,　　12
　　As thus: mine eyes' due is ⌐thy¬ outward part,
　　And my heart's right, ⌐thy¬ inward love of heart.

After the verdict is rendered (in s. 46), the poet's eyes and heart become allies, with the eyes sometimes inviting the heart to enjoy the picture, and the heart sometimes inviting the eyes to share in its "thoughts of love." The beloved, though absent, is thus doubly present to the poet through the picture and through the poet's thoughts.

---

1. **league is took:** alliance or compact is made
4. **heart in love:** love-struck **heart; with ...
smother:** i.e., smothers itself **with sighs** (There is a possible allusion to the belief that sighs draw blood from the heart.)
10. **still:** continually
12. **still:** always

The four humors, with their related elements, planets, etc. (s. 44, s. 45)

47

Betwixt mine eye and heart a league is took,
And each doth good turns now unto the other.
When that mine eye is famished for a look,
Or heart in love with sighs himself doth smother,   4
With my love's picture then my eye doth feast
And to the painted banquet bids my heart.
Another time mine eye is my heart's guest
And in his thoughts of love doth share a part.   8
So, either by thy picture or my love,
Thyself away are present still with me;
For thou ⌐no⌐ farther than my thoughts canst move,
And I am still with them, and they with thee;   12
　　Or, if they sleep, thy picture in my sight
　　Awakes my heart to heart's and eye's delight.

The poet contrasts the relative ease of locking away valuable material possessions with the impossibility of safeguarding his relationship with the beloved. The beloved can be enclosed only in the poet's heart, which cannot block the beloved's egress nor protect against those who would steal the beloved away.

1. **took my way:** set out on my journey
2. **truest:** surest, securest
3. **to:** i.e., for
3–4. **stay / From:** i.e., remain out of
4. **hands of falsehood:** i.e., thieves (literally, treacherous **hands**); **in . . . trust:** i.e., as in a safely guarded fortress
5. **to whom:** i.e., in comparison **to whom**
6. **Most worthy comfort:** you who are my chief delight (but with the secondary sense "you who most deserve **comfort**"); **grief:** cause of distress
7. **mine only care:** i.e., all that I care about (**Care** could also mean "grief" or "concern.")
8. **vulgar:** common, ordinary
11. **closure:** confines, enclosure
12. **From . . . part:** i.e., which you may enter and leave whenever you please
14. **truth . . . dear:** See *Venus and Adonis* 724: "Rich preys make true men thieves"; and *As You Like It* 1.3.116: "Beauty provoketh thieves sooner than gold." **truth:** honesty **dear:** precious

48

How careful was I, when I took my way,
Each trifle under truest bars to thrust,
That to my use it might unusèd stay
From hands of falsehood, in sure wards of trust!   4
But thou, to whom my jewels trifles are,
Most worthy comfort, now my greatest grief,
Thou best of dearest and mine only care
Art left the prey of every vulgar thief.   8
Thee have I not locked up in any chest,
Save where thou art not, though I feel thou art,
Within the gentle closure of my breast,
From whence at pleasure thou mayst come and part;   12
    And even thence thou wilt be stol'n, I fear,
    For truth proves thievish for a prize so dear.

The poet tries to prepare himself for a future in which the beloved rejects him. When that day comes, he writes, he will shield himself within the knowledge of his own worth, acknowledging that he can cite no reason in support of their love.

---

1. **Against:** in preparation for, in anticipation of
3. **Whenas:** when; **cast his utmost sum:** i.e., made its final reckoning
4. **advised respects:** prudent considerations
5. **strangely:** coldly, distantly
7. **converted:** transformed
8. **of settled gravity:** i.e., for behaving with staid solemnity
9. **ensconce me:** take shelter (A *sconce* is a small fortification or earthwork.)
10. **mine own desert:** i.e., what I deserve, my worth
11. **against:** in front of (Some editors see ll. 11–12 as picturing the poet raising his hand as a witness against himself. In that reading, **against** means "in opposition to," and **guard** [l. 12] means "protect.")
12. **guard:** ward off, parry
14. **allege:** adduce, urge

49

Against that time, if ever that time come,
When I shall see thee frown on my defects,
Whenas thy love hath cast his utmost sum,
Called to that audit by advised respects;   4
Against that time when thou shalt strangely pass
And scarcely greet me with that sun thine eye,
When love, converted from the thing it was,
Shall reasons find of settled gravity;   8
Against that time do I ensconce me here
Within the knowledge of mine own desert,
And this my hand against myself uprear
To guard the lawful reasons on thy part.   12
   To leave poor me thou hast the strength of laws,
   Since why to love I can allege no cause.

In this first of two linked sonnets, the poet's unhappiness in traveling away from the beloved seems to him reproduced in the plodding steps and the groans of the horse that carries him.

---

1. **heavy:** i.e., heavily, sorrowfully

3. **that ease and that repose:** i.e., his **travel's end,** which is what he seeks (l. 2); **say:** remind me

4. **Thus . . . measured:** i.e., you are this many **miles**

6. **to bear that weight:** i.e., bearing **my weight** of **woe** (l. 5)

8. **being made from:** i.e., when that **speed** is **made** away **from**

A jade. (s. 51.12)

104

50

How heavy do I journey on the way,
When what I seek, my weary travel's end,
Doth teach that ease and that repose to say
"Thus far the miles are measured from thy friend." 4
The beast that bears me, tired with my woe,
Plods ⌜dully⌝ on, to bear that weight in me,
As if by some instinct the wretch did know
His rider loved not speed, being made from thee. 8
The bloody spur cannot provoke him on
That sometimes anger thrusts into his hide,
Which heavily he answers with a groan,
More sharp to me than spurring to his side; 12
    For that same groan doth put this in my mind:
    My grief lies onward and my joy behind.

The slow-moving horse (of s. 50) will have no excuse for his plodding gait on the return journey, for which even the fastest horse, the poet realizes, will be too slow. Returning to the beloved, desire and love will outrun any horse.

---

1. **slow offense:** i.e., **offense** of moving slowly
4. **Till I return:** i.e., until my return journey; **posting:** riding hard
6. **swift extremity:** i.e., extreme swiftness
8. **no motion shall I know:** perhaps, I will (still) feel as though not moving
11. **Shall neigh no dull flesh in his fiery race:** This puzzling line appears to set up an opposition between the **dull flesh** of the horse and the **fiery** nature of **desire.** (In s. 45, **desire** is said to be composed of the element of fire.)
12. **love for love:** i.e., my **love,** out of compassion (for the horse); **jade:** nag (See picture, p. 104.)
13. **thee:** the beloved; **willful slow:** i.e., deliberately slowly
14. **leave:** permission; **go:** wordplay on "depart" and "walk"

51

Thus can my love excuse the slow offense
Of my dull bearer when from thee I speed:
From where thou art, why should I haste me thence?
Till I return, of posting is no need.   4
O, what excuse will my poor beast then find
When swift extremity can seem but slow?
Then should I spur, though mounted on the wind;
In wingèd speed no motion shall I know.   8
Then can no horse with my desire keep pace;
Therefore desire, of ⌜perfect'st⌝ love being made,
Shall neigh no dull flesh in his fiery race.
But love for love thus shall excuse my jade: 12
   "Since from thee going he went willful slow,
    Towards thee I'll run, and give him leave to go."

The poet likens himself to a rich man who visits his treasures rarely so that they remain for him a source of pleasure. The poet's infrequent meetings with the beloved, he argues, are, like rare feasts or widely spaced jewels, the more precious for their rarity.

1. **So . . . rich:** i.e., **I am** like a wealthy man

3. **will not:** i.e., chooses not to

4. **For blunting:** lest he blunt; **seldom:** rare, infrequent (Proverbial: "A **seldom** use of pleasures maketh the same the more pleasant.")

5. **Therefore:** for that (same) reason; **feasts:** i.e., feast days; **solemn:** ceremonial; **rare:** splendid; exceptional

7. **stones of worth:** valuable gems; **thinly placèd:** i.e., **placed** at wide intervals

8. **captain:** chief; **carcanet:** jeweled collar (See picture, p. 88.)

9–10. **So . . . hide: Time,** which **keeps** the beloved from the poet, serves the function of the rich man's **chest** that holds rarely visited treasure, or the rich man's **wardrobe** (a room where valuable clothes are kept under "ward" or guard), hiding the beloved as if he were a fine **robe** taken out for rare occasions.

12. **new unfolding:** i.e., newly revealing; **his imprisoned pride:** i.e., that among its contents of which it is most proud   **his:** its

13–14. **gives scope . . . hope:** i.e., allows **the rich** (l. 1; here, the poet) the range of experience (**scope**) of glorying in your presence, and, in your absence, of entertaining the expectation of seeing you again

52

So am I as the rich whose blessèd key
Can bring him to his sweet up-lockèd treasure,
The which he will not ev'ry hour survey,
For blunting the fine point of seldom pleasure.   4
Therefore are feasts so solemn and so rare,
Since seldom coming in the long year set,
Like stones of worth they thinly placèd are,
Or captain jewels in the carcanet.   8
So is the time that keeps you as my chest,
Or as the wardrobe which the robe doth hide
To make some special instant special blessed
By new unfolding his imprisoned pride.   12
    Blessèd are you whose worthiness gives scope,
    Being had, to triumph, being lacked, to hope.

Using language from Neoplatonism, the poet praises the beloved both as the essence of beauty (its very Idea, which is only imperfectly reflected in lesser beauties) and as the epitome of constancy.

---

1. **substance:** (1) Platonic essence; (2) matter
2. **strange:** (1) alien (i.e., not yours); (2) unusual; **shadows:** images, reflections; **on you tend:** serve you, follow you
3. **shade:** shadow (wordplay that shifts from the image cast by a body in sunlight to Neoplatonic **shadows** [imperfect reflections of the Idea])
4. **but:** only; **every shadow lend:** perhaps, be the source of (or provide attributes for) **every shadow**
5. **Adonis:** the beautiful mythological youth loved by Venus; **counterfeit:** picture, portrait
7. **On . . . set:** i.e., portray **Helen's cheek** (1) with the highest artistic touch, or (2) with the best cosmetics (The mythological Helen of Troy was the most lovely of women. See picture, p. 114.)
8. **Grecian tires:** Greek costume or headdress
9. **spring and foison:** springtime and harvest
10. **shadow:** image
12. **And you:** i.e., **and you** are revealed
13. **external grace:** i.e., outward beauty
14. **you like none, none you:** i.e., **you** are **like none, none** are like **you**

53

What is your substance, whereof are you made,
That millions of strange shadows on you tend?
Since everyone hath, every one, one shade,
And you, but one, can every shadow lend.   4
Describe Adonis, and the counterfeit
Is poorly imitated after you;
On Helen's cheek all art of beauty set,
And you in Grecian tires are painted new.   8
Speak of the spring and foison of the year;
The one doth shadow of your beauty show,
The other as your bounty doth appear,
And you in every blessèd shape we know.   12
    In all external grace you have some part,
    But you like none, none you, for constant heart.

Here the beloved's truth is compared to the fragrance in the rose. As that fragrance is distilled into perfume, so the beloved's truth distills in verse.

2. **By:** i.e., through; **truth:** (1) integrity, virtue; (2) constancy (perhaps the "constant heart" of s. 53.14)

3. **fair:** beautiful

4. **For:** because of

5. **canker blooms:** the blossoms of the dog rose, a wild rose that has little fragrance; **dye:** color

6. **tincture:** hue, color

7. **such:** i.e., similar

8. **their maskèd buds discloses:** i.e., opens the **buds** (of the **canker blooms**), the beauty of which is **masked** or concealed until the flowers are open

9. **for their virtue only:** i.e., because **their only virtue; show:** visual appearance

10. **unrespected:** unregarded, unvalued

12. **Of . . . made:** i.e., when **roses** die, their fragrance is distilled into perfume (See s. 5.9–14.)

13. **And so of you:** i.e., **and** thus it is with **you; lovely:** lovable

14. **that:** i.e., beauty and youth; **vade:** (1) depart; (2) fade away; **by verse distils your truth:** i.e., **your truth** will distil itself in (my) **verse**

54

O, how much more doth beauty beauteous seem
By that sweet ornament which truth doth give.
The rose looks fair, but fairer we it deem
For that sweet odor which doth in it live.   4
The canker blooms have full as deep a dye
As the perfumèd tincture of the roses,
Hang on such thorns, and play as wantonly
When summer's breath their maskèd buds discloses;   8
But, for their virtue only is their show,
They live unwooed and unrespected fade,
Die to themselves. Sweet roses do not so;
Of their sweet deaths are sweetest odors made.   12
   And so of you, beauteous and lovely youth,
    When that shall vade, by verse distils your truth.

Continuing the idea of the beloved's distillation into poetry (in the couplet of s. 54), the poet now claims that his verse will be a "living record" in which the beloved will "shine . . . bright" until Doomsday.

1–2. **Not . . . rhyme:** These two lines restate a familiar classical motif. (See, e.g., Ovid, *Metamorphoses* [E], in Appendix, p. 344.) In l. 3, Shakespeare moves away from his models by having the beloved, rather than the poet, immortalized in his verse.

4. **with sluttish:** i.e., by disgustingly dirty

6. **broils:** tumults; **root out:** i.e., destroy

7. **Nor Mars his:** i.e., neither Mars's (**Mars** is the Roman god of war.) **quick:** strongly burning

9. **all oblivious enmity:** i.e., every hostile force that causes forgetfulness (or brings all to oblivion)

10. **your . . . still:** i.e., **praise** of you will always

12. **wear . . . doom:** i.e., survive until the world's end (**Doom** is Doomsday or **Judgment** Day [l. 13].) See picture, p. 180.

13. **that yourself:** i.e., when you **yourself** will

Helen of Troy. (s. 53.7)

55

Not marble nor the gilded ⌜monuments⌝
Of princes shall outlive this powerful rhyme,
But you shall shine more bright in these contents
Than unswept stone besmeared with sluttish time.   4
When wasteful war shall statues overturn,
And broils root out the work of masonry,
Nor Mars his sword nor war's quick fire shall burn
The living record of your memory.   8
'Gainst death and all oblivious enmity
Shall you pace forth; your praise shall still find room
Even in the eyes of all posterity
That wear this world out to the ending doom.   12
   So, till the judgment that yourself arise,
   You live in this, and dwell in lovers' eyes.

The poet addresses the spirit of love and then the beloved, urging that love be reinvigorated and that the present separation of the lovers serve to renew their love's intensity.

1. **love:** here, the spirit of **love**
4. **his:** its
5. **love:** here addressed to the beloved
6. **wink:** close
8. **dullness:** apathy, lack of interest
9. **Let . . . be:** i.e., let us view **this sad** interval of time as if it were an **ocean** (Although ll. 9–12 are difficult, the general image seems to be of two newly betrothed lovers standing **daily** on opposite shores of this **ocean,** awaiting a longed-for reunion.)
13–14. **Or . . . rare:** The **sad int'rim** is now imagined as **winter,** the difficulties of which make the return of summer even more **welcome.**

"The hungry ocean." (s. 64.5–7)

116

56

Sweet love, renew thy force. Be it not said
Thy edge should blunter be than appetite,
Which but today by feeding is allayed,
Tomorrow sharpened in his former might.   4
So, love, be thou. Although today thou fill
Thy hungry eyes even till they wink with fullness,
Tomorrow see again, and do not kill
The spirit of love with a perpetual dullness.   8
Let this sad int'rim like the ocean be
Which parts the shore where two contracted new
Come daily to the banks, that, when they see
Return of love, more blessed may be the view.   12
⌜Or⌝ call it winter, which being full of care
   Makes summer's welcome, thrice more wished,
      more rare.

In this and the following sonnet, the poet presents his relationship with the beloved as that of servant and master. As the beloved's servant, the poet describes himself (with barely suppressed bitterness) as having no life or wishes of his own as he waits like a "sad slave" for the commands of his "sovereign."

1. **slave:** a servant completely divested of freedom and personal rights

1–2. **tend / Upon:** wait for, await (with wordplay on "wait **upon,** serve")

3. **precious time . . . to spend:** i.e., **time to spend** that is **at all precious** or valuable

5. **world-without-end:** seemingly endless

7. **bitterness:** anguish; **sour:** distasteful

8. **bid . . . once adieu:** i.e., **once** said farewell to me   **your servant:** a phrase applied to an attendant, a lover, or a friend

10. **suppose:** imagine, form an idea of

12. **Save . . . those:** i.e., except **how happy you make those** who are **where you are**

13. **So true a fool:** (1) such a complete **fool;** (2) such a faithful, constant **fool**

14. **he:** i.e., **love; ill:** evil

57

Being your slave, what should I do but tend
Upon the hours and times of your desire?
I have no precious time at all to spend
Nor services to do till you require.   4
Nor dare I chide the world-without-end hour
Whilst I, my sovereign, watch the clock for you,
Nor think the bitterness of absence sour
When you have bid your servant once adieu.   8
Nor dare I question with my jealous thought
Where you may be, or your affairs suppose,
But, like a sad slave, stay and think of nought
Save where you are how happy you make those.   12
   So true a fool is love that in your will,
    Though you do anything, he thinks no ill.

This sonnet repeats the ideas and some of the language of s. 57, though the pain of waiting upon (and waiting for) the beloved and asking nothing in return seems even more intense in the present poem.

1–2. **That . . . control:** i.e., may the **god** who **made me your slave** protect me from trying to **control** (wordplay on the phrase "**God forbid** that **I should**") **in thought:** i.e., even in my imagination

3. **Or at your hand . . . crave:** i.e., **or should crave** an **account** of how you spend your time

4. **stay your leisure:** wait until you have time for me

5. **suffer:** allow; endure

6. **Th' imprisoned:** i.e., the imprisoning; **of your liberty:** i.e., that results from your freedom (or licentiousness)

7. **patience:** i.e., let **patience; tame to sufferance:** docile under suffering; **bide each check:** endure **each** rebuke or rebuff

9. **where you list:** wherever you please; **charter:** publicly acknowledged right

10. **privilege:** authorize

11. **To what you will:** i.e., **to** do whatever **you** wish

12. **self-doing crime:** offenses done by (or to) you

13. **I am to wait:** As in s. 57.1–2, there is rich wordplay on the concept of the servant who waits upon his master and the lover who waits for an absent beloved.

14. **ill:** bad, evil

58

That god forbid, that made me first your slave,
I should in thought control your times of pleasure,
Or at your hand th' account of hours to crave,
Being your vassal bound to stay your leisure.   4
O, let me suffer, being at your beck,
Th' imprisoned absence of your liberty,
And patience, tame to sufferance, bide each check
Without accusing you of injury.   8
Be where you list, your charter is so strong
That you yourself may privilege your time
To what you will; to you it doth belong
Yourself to pardon of self-doing crime.   12
    I am to wait, though waiting so be hell,
    Not blame your pleasure, be it ill or well.

The poet here plays with the idea of history as cyclical and with the proverb "There is nothing new under the sun." If he could go back in time, he writes, he could see how the beloved's beauty was praised in the distant past and thus judge whether the world had progressed, regressed, or stayed the same.

1–2. **If . . . before:** See Ecclesiastes 1.9–10: "What is it that **hath been**? that that shall be . . . : and there *is* no new thing under the sun. Is there any thing whereof one may say, Behold this, it is **new**? It **hath been** already in the old time that was before us."

2. **beguiled:** deceived, cheated

3. **invention:** a new creation; poetic originality

3–4. **bear . . . child:** i.e., produce a **child** who has lived before   **burden:** that which is borne in the womb

5. **record:** memory (accent on second syllable)

6. **courses of the sun:** i.e., years

8. **at . . . done:** i.e., **was first** expressed in writing

10. **To:** in response to; **composèd . . . frame:** elaborately constructed miracle of your form

11. **mended:** improved; **whe'er better they:** whether **they** were **better** than we

12. **revolution be the same:** i.e., the cycle of history keeps things **the same**

13. **wits:** geniuses, talented writers

14. **To . . . praise:** This faint praise of the beloved is probably ironic understatement.

59

If there be nothing new, but that which is
Hath been before, how are our brains beguiled,
Which, laboring for invention, bear amiss
The second burden of a former child.   4
O, that record could with a backward look,
Even of five hundred courses of the sun,
Show me your image in some antique book,
Since mind at first in character was done,   8
That I might see what the old world could say
To this composèd wonder of your frame;
Whether we are mended, or whe'er better they,
Or whether revolution be the same.   12
   O, sure I am the wits of former days
   To subjects worse have given admiring praise.

The poet meditates on life's inevitable course through maturity to death. Everything, he says, is a victim of Time's scythe. Only his poetry will stand against Time, keeping alive his praise of the beloved.

1–4. **Like . . . contend:** See Ovid, *Metamorphoses* [A], in Appendix, p. 341.   **Like as:** just as   **In sequent toil:** laboring one after another   **contend:** strive

5. **Nativity:** i.e., the newborn (with wordplay on birth considered astrologically); **once:** (1) at one time; (2) when **once; main:** broad expanse (with probable wordplay on **main** as open ocean)

7. **eclipses:** i.e., obscurations (Taken literally, this word calls attention to the metaphor [ll. 5–7] of a human life traced as a rising and then setting sun.)

8. **confound:** destroy (See Ovid, *Metamorphoses* [C], in Appendix, pp. 342–43.)

9. **transfix:** pierce through; **flourish:** bloom

10. **parallels:** i.e., wrinkles (literally, trenches)

11. **Feeds . . . truth:** See Ovid: "Thou time, the eater up of things, . . . / Destroy all things. . . . / You leisurely by ling'ring death consume them every whit" (*Metamorphoses* 15.258–60, Golding translation).

12. **his scythe:** See note to s. 12.13.

13. **to times in hope:** i.e., to ages that exist only in expectation (though with wordplay on "**stand . . . in hope**")

60

Like as the waves make towards the pebbled shore,
So do our minutes hasten to their end,
Each changing place with that which goes before;
In sequent toil all forwards do contend.   4
Nativity, once in the main of light,
Crawls to maturity, wherewith being crowned,
Crookèd eclipses 'gainst his glory fight,
And Time that gave doth now his gift confound.   8
Time doth transfix the flourish set on youth
And delves the parallels in beauty's brow,
Feeds on the rarities of Nature's truth,
And nothing stands but for his scythe to mow.   12
    And yet to times in hope my verse shall stand,
    Praising thy worth, despite his cruel hand.

The poet first wonders if the beloved is deliberately keeping him awake by sending dream images to spy on him, but then admits it is his own devotion and jealousy that will not let him sleep.

1. **Is it thy will:** i.e., do you wish that
4. **shadows like to thee:** i.e., dream images that look like you (with possible wordplay on "ghosts")
7. **shames:** shameful acts
8. **scope and tenor of thy jealousy:** i.e., aim and substance of your suspicions
12. **watchman:** one who keeps vigil
13. **watch I:** I stay awake

"Lofty towers . . . down-razed." (s. 64.3)

61

Is it thy will thy image should keep open
My heavy eyelids to the weary night?
Dost thou desire my slumbers should be broken
While shadows like to thee do mock my sight?   4
Is it thy spirit that thou send'st from thee
So far from home into my deeds to pry,
To find out shames and idle hours in me,
The scope and tenor of thy jealousy?   8
O, no. Thy love, though much, is not so great.
It is my love that keeps mine eye awake,
Mine own true love that doth my rest defeat
To play the watchman ever for thy sake.   12
    For thee watch I whilst thou dost wake elsewhere,
    From me far off, with others all too near.

The poet accuses himself of supreme vanity in that he thinks so highly of himself. He then admits that the "self" he holds in such esteem is not his physical self but his "other self," the beloved.

---

4. **inward in:** i.e., in the interior of

5. **Methinks:** it seems to me

8. **As . . . surmount:** i.e., so that I surpass everyone else in every merit or attainment

9. **glass:** looking glass, mirror

10. **Beated:** beaten, battered; **chopped:** chapped; **antiquity:** old age

11. **quite contrary I read:** i.e., **I** interpret in **quite** the opposite way

12. **Self so self-loving:** i.e., to love such a **self; were iniquity:** i.e., would (indeed) be sinful

13. **myself, that for myself:** i.e., my (real, or other) self, **that** as **myself**

14. **beauty of thy days:** i.e., **thy** youthful **beauty**

62

Sin of self-love possesseth all mine eye
And all my soul and all my every part;
And for this sin there is no remedy,
It is so grounded inward in my heart.   4
Methinks no face so gracious is as mine,
No shape so true, no truth of such account,
And for myself mine own worth do define
As I all other in all worths surmount.   8
But when my glass shows me myself indeed
Beated and chopped with tanned antiquity,
Mine own self-love quite contrary I read;
Self so self-loving were iniquity.   12
   'Tis thee, myself, that for myself I praise,
   Painting my age with beauty of thy days.

By preserving the youthful beauty of the beloved in poetry, the poet makes preparation for the day that the beloved will himself be old.

1. **Against:** before; in anticipation of (the time when)

5. **steepy:** precipitous

9. **fortify:** erect fortifications; build defenses

10. **confounding:** destructive, destroying; **age's cruel knife:** Here, age and Time become one destructive enemy, with the scythe blending into the **knife** that cuts wrinkles in the brow and finally kills.

11. **That he:** i.e., so that Time; **memory:** i.e., human **memory**

12. **lover's:** beloved's

14. **still green:** always young

"Time's injurious hand." (s. 63.2)

130

63

Against my love shall be, as I am now,
With Time's injurious hand crushed and o'erworn;
When hours have drained his blood and filled his brow
With lines and wrinkles; when his youthful morn   4
Hath traveled on to age's steepy night,
And all those beauties whereof now he's king
Are vanishing, or vanished out of sight,
Stealing away the treasure of his spring;   8
For such a time do I now fortify
Against confounding age's cruel knife,
That he shall never cut from memory
My sweet love's beauty, though my lover's life.   12
   His beauty shall in these black lines be seen,
    And they shall live, and he in them still green.

Signs of the destructive power of time and decay—such as fallen towers and eroded beaches—force the poet to admit that the beloved will also be lost to him and to mourn this anticipated loss.

---

1. **fell:** cruel, ruthless
2. **rich . . . age:** (1) ruins of antiquity, remnants of a formerly wealthy city or kingdom; (2) elaborate funeral monuments of once important figures **proud:** magnificent **cost:** luxurious objects
3. **sometime:** formerly (See picture, p. 126.)
4. **brass eternal:** (1) (supposedly) indestructible **brass;** (2) **brass** eternally; **mortal rage:** (1) human fury; (2) deadly destruction
6. **Advantage on:** superiority over (The image of the sea and land engaged in an ongoing battle is continued in **win of** [gain from], l. 7.) See Ovid, *Metamorphoses* [D] in Appendix, pp. 343–44, and picture, p. 116.
7. **wat'ry main:** ocean
8. **Increasing . . . store:** i.e., sea and land alternately winning and losing possession of plenty (**store**)
9. **state:** condition; territory
10. **state:** magnificence (with possible wordplay on the meaning "government, ruling power"); **confounded to decay:** utterly destroyed
14. **to have:** i.e., at having

64

When I have seen by Time's fell hand defaced
The rich proud cost of outworn buried age;
When sometime lofty towers I see down-razed
And brass eternal slave to mortal rage;   4
When I have seen the hungry ocean gain
Advantage on the kingdom of the shore,
And the firm soil win of the wat'ry main,
Increasing store with loss and loss with store;   8
When I have seen such interchange of state,
Or state itself confounded to decay,
Ruin hath taught me thus to ruminate,
That Time will come and take my love away.   12
   This thought is as a death, which cannot choose
   But weep to have that which it fears to lose.

In the face of the terrible power of Time, how, the poet asks, can beauty survive? And how can the beloved, most beautiful of all, be protected from Time's injury? The only protection, he decides, lies in the lines of his poetry.

---

1. **Since brass:** i.e., there is neither **brass**

3. **with:** against; **rage:** violence; **hold a plea:** plead its case

4. **action:** wordplay on (1) suit at law; (2) operation; (3) military engagement; **flower:** i.e., flower's

6. **wrackful:** destructive; **batt'ring days:** i.e., **days** that pound like battering rams in a **siege**

7. **stout:** sturdy

9. **fearful:** frightening

9–10. **Where . . . hid:** i.e., **where,** alas, can the beloved hide from **Time,** which would place him in a treasure **chest** or a coffin

11. **his:** i.e., Time's (See note to s. 19.6.)

12. **spoil:** destruction (with wordplay on the *spoils* of war and pillaging)

14. **my love may still:** **my** beloved **may** always

65

Since brass, nor stone, nor earth, nor boundless sea
But sad mortality o'ersways their power,
How with this rage shall beauty hold a plea,
Whose action is no stronger than a flower?   4
O, how shall summer's honey breath hold out
Against the wrackful siege of batt'ring days,
When rocks impregnable are not so stout
Nor gates of steel so strong, but Time decays?   8
O, fearful meditation! Where, alack,
Shall Time's best jewel from Time's chest lie hid?
Or what strong hand can hold his swift foot back,
Or who his spoil ⌜of⌝ beauty can forbid?   12
   O, none, unless this miracle have might,
   That in black ink my love may still shine bright.

The poet lists examples of the societal wrongs that have made him so weary of life that he would wish to die, except that he would thereby desert the beloved.

1. **all these:** i.e., **all** the following
2. **As:** as for instance; **desert:** a deserving person
3. **needy . . . jollity:** (1) perhaps, worthless fops; or, (2) perhaps, beggarly worthlessness dressed in tawdry finery (See longer note, p. 327.)
4. **unhappily forsworn:** (1) regrettably abandoned or betrayed; (2) maliciously perjured
5. **gilded honor:** golden honors or titles; **misplaced:** given to the wrong person
6. **strumpeted:** i.e., accused of being a strumpet
7. **right:** genuine, true
8. **limping sway:** i.e., authority that is slow or ineffectual
9. **art:** scholarship, learning, science (The line could also refer to censored literary works.)
10. **doctor-like:** i.e., in the guise of a learned professor
11. **miscalled simplicity:** maligned as ignorance
12. **attending:** serving, waiting on; **ill:** evil

66

Tired with all these, for restful death I cry:
As, to behold desert a beggar born,
And needy nothing trimmed in jollity,
And purest faith unhappily forsworn,   4
And gilded honor shamefully misplaced,
And maiden virtue rudely strumpeted,
And right perfection wrongfully disgraced,
And strength by limping sway disablèd,   8
And art made tongue-tied by authority,
And folly, doctor-like, controlling skill,
And simple truth miscalled simplicity,
And captive good attending captain ill.   12
    Tired with all these, from these would I be gone,
    Save that, to die, I leave my love alone.

In this first of two linked sonnets, the poet asks why the beautiful young man should live in a society so corrupt, since his very presence gives it legitimacy. He concludes that Nature is keeping the young man alive as a reminder of the world as it used to be.

---

1. **wherefore:** why; **with infection:** i.e., in a corrupt world

2. **grace:** (1) adorn; (2) countenance

3. **That sin by him:** i.e., so **that sin by** means of **him**

4. **lace itself:** adorn **itself** (with wordplay on "diversify its appearance as with streaks of color," a meaning picked up in l. 5)

5–6. **Why . . . hue:** The allusion is probably to the use of cosmetics, which borrow (**steal**) the mere appearance (**dead seeing**) from **his living hue.** (Editors often change **seeing** to "seeming," and many read the lines as referring to portrait **painting.**)

7. **poor:** inferior; **indirectly:** wrongfully; by means of an intermediary

8. **Roses of shadow:** imitation **roses; his rose:** i.e., the **rose** of **his** complexion

9. **bankrout:** bankrupt

10. **Beggared:** i.e., destitute; **blush:** i.e., show red

11. **For . . . his:** i.e., since **Nature** has **no exchequer** (treasury; source of revenue) **now** except for the beauty of the beloved

12. **many:** perhaps, **many** beauties (Editors sometimes change **proud** to "proved" or "'prived.")

13. **stores:** keeps, preserves

138

67

Ah, wherefore with infection should he live,
And with his presence grace impiety,
That sin by him advantage should achieve
And lace itself with his society?   4
Why should false painting imitate his cheek
And steal dead seeing of his living hue?
Why should poor beauty indirectly seek
Roses of shadow, since his rose is true?   8
Why should he live, now Nature bankrout is,
Beggared of blood to blush through lively veins,
For she hath no exchequer now but his,
And, proud of many, lives upon his gains?   12
    O, him she stores, to show what wealth she had
    In days long since, before these last so bad.

Continuing the argument of s. 67, the poet sets the natural beauty of the young man against the "false art" of those whose beauty depends on cosmetics and wigs.

---

1. **Thus:** For this reason (the reason given at the conclusion of s. 67); **map:** (1) embodiment; (2) epitome; **days outworn:** a former age

3. **bastard signs of fair:** counterfeit **signs** of beauty; **borne:** worn, displayed, presented

4. **durst inhabit:** dared take up residence

5–8. **Before . . . gay:** i.e., **before** people wore wigs made of hair **shorn** from **the dead** (See *The Merchant of Venice* 3.2.94–98: "**golden** locks . . . often known / To be the dowry of a **second head,** / The skull that bred them in the sepulcher.") **gay:** lovely; showily attractive

9. **those . . . are:** i.e., that blessed former age is

11. **of another's green:** i.e., from **another's** youth

13. **store:** preserve

68

Thus is his cheek the map of days outworn,
When beauty lived and died as flowers do now,
Before these bastard signs of fair were borne,
Or durst inhabit on a living brow;   4
Before the golden tresses of the dead,
The right of sepulchers, were shorn away
To live a second life on second head,
Ere beauty's dead fleece made another gay.   8
In him those holy antique hours are seen,
Without all ornament, itself and true,
Making no summer of another's green,
Robbing no old to dress his beauty new.   12
    And him as for a map doth Nature store,
      To show false art what beauty was of yore.

The poet tells the young man that while the world praises his outward beauty, those who look into his inner being (as reflected in his deeds) speak of him in quite different terms. They ground their accusations in his having become too "common."

---

1. **Those parts of thee:** i.e., your physical appearance (and, perhaps, your talents, gifts)

2. **Want:** lack; **thought of hearts:** deepest (most heartfelt) **thought; mend:** improve

4. **even so as foes commend:** i.e., giving you grudging praise

6. **give thee so thine own:** i.e., grant you that which clearly belongs to you

7. **In other accents:** i.e., with different language; **confound:** (1) confute; (2) confuse, complicate

9. **look into:** (1) view; (2) investigate

10. **in guess:** by conjecture; **measure:** estimate

13. **But why:** i.e., **but** the reason **why**

14. **soil:** wordplay on (1) earth, ground (so that **soil** becomes "basis, justification"); (2) stain, blemish (The word **soil** is an editorial construction from Q's "solye," a non-word believed to be a typographical error for "soyle," the usual spelling of **soil.** Some editors prefer "solve," "toil," or "sully.") **common:** (1) publicly accessible (like public pasture or prostitutes); (2) ordinary

69

Those parts of thee that the world's eye doth view
Want nothing that the thought of hearts can mend.
All tongues, the voice of souls, give thee that ⌜due,⌝
Utt'ring bare truth, even so as foes commend.   4
⌜Thy⌝ outward thus with outward praise is crowned,
But those same tongues that give thee so thine own
In other accents do this praise confound
By seeing farther than the eye hath shown.   8
They look into the beauty of thy mind,
And that, in guess, they measure by thy deeds;
Then, churls, their thoughts, although their eyes
    were kind,
To thy fair flower add the rank smell of weeds.   12
  But why thy odor matcheth not thy show,
  The soil is this, that thou dost common grow.

The poet tells the young man that the attacks on his reputation do not mean that he is flawed, since beauty always provokes such attacks. (This sonnet may contradict s. 69, or may simply elaborate on it.)

1. **shall not be:** (1) ought not be attributed to; (2) should not be considered; **thy defect:** a fault or flaw in you
2. **mark:** target; **fair:** beautiful
3. **suspect:** suspicion (accent on second syllable)
4. **crow:** a bird that was associated with malice
5. **So:** provided that; **but approve:** merely prove
6. **wooed of time:** (1) seduced by the present age (but remaining **good**); (2) given Time's gifts
7. **canker vice:** i.e., **vice** like a cankerworm (Proverbial: "The **canker** soonest eats the fairest rose." See picture, p. 76.)
8. **unstainèd prime:** unblemished early manhood
9. **ambush of young days:** i.e., traps laid for youth
10. **charged:** attacked
11. **so:** so much
12. **To tie up envy:** i.e., as to restrain or confine malice; **enlarged:** at large
13. **suspect of ill:** suspicion of evil; **masked not thy show:** i.e., did not mask your **beauty** (l. 3)
14. **owe:** own, possess

70

That thou ⌜art⌝ blamed shall not be thy defect,
For slander's mark was ever yet the fair.
The ornament of beauty is suspect,
A crow that flies in heaven's sweetest air.   4
So thou be good, slander doth but approve
⌜Thy⌝ worth the greater, being wooed of time,
For canker vice the sweetest buds doth love,
And thou present'st a pure unstainèd prime.   8
Thou hast passed by the ambush of young days,
Either not assailed, or victor being charged;
Yet this thy praise cannot be so thy praise
To tie up envy, evermore enlarged.   12
　　If some suspect of ill masked not thy show,
　　Then thou alone kingdoms of hearts shouldst owe.

In this first of a series of four sonnets in which the poet addresses his own death and its effect on the beloved, he here urges the beloved to forget him once he is gone.

2. **surly sullen bell:** i.e., the passing **bell** ("And when any is passing out of this life, a **bell** shall be tolled. . . . And after the party's death, . . . there shall be rung no more than one short peal, and one other before the burial, and one other after the burial." *Constitutions and Canons ecclesiastical . . .* [1603].) **surly:** gloomy, stern   **sullen:** solemn

3. **warning:** notice (though also with the sense of "cautionary sign": Kerrigan cites John Donne's "Never send to know for whom the bell tolls; it tolls for thee.")

5. **this line:** i.e., the present sonnet

8. **make you woe:** distress you

10. **compounded am with clay:** am mixed with the dust of the earth

11. **rehearse:** repeat

13–14. **Lest . . . gone:** These lines are expanded and explained in s. 72.   **look into your moan:** investigate your grief

71

No longer mourn for me when I am dead
Than you shall hear the surly sullen bell
Give warning to the world that I am fled
From this vile world with vilest worms to dwell.   4
Nay, if you read this line, remember not
The hand that writ it, for I love you so
That I in your sweet thoughts would be forgot,
If thinking on me then should make you woe.   8
O, if, I say, you look upon this verse
When I, perhaps, compounded am with clay,
Do not so much as my poor name rehearse,
But let your love even with my life decay,   12
    Lest the wise world should look into your moan
    And mock you with me after I am gone.

Continuing from s. 71, this sonnet explains that the beloved can defend loving the poet only by speaking falsely, by giving the poet more credit than he deserves. The beloved is urged instead to forget the poet once he is dead.

1. **task:** compel, challenge; **recite:** declare
6. **than mine own desert:** (1) than my merits can do; (2) than is warranted by what I deserve
7. **hang . . . I:** The image here is of a tomb hung with trophies. (In *Much Ado About Nothing* 5.3, Claudio hangs an epitaph of praise on Hero's tomb.) **I:** i.e., me
8. **niggard:** i.e., miserly
9. **your true love:** i.e., **your love,** which is honest
10. **speak . . . untrue:** i.e., say complimentary but **untrue** things about **me**
12. **nor me:** neither me
13. **shamed . . . forth:** The poet may here refer to his verse, or to himself. (The tone can be likened to that of Hamlet's "I could accuse me of such things that it were better my mother had not borne me" [3.1.133–34].) Those who read the sonnets biographically see the line as Shakespeare's admission of shame about writing plays.
14. **should you:** i.e., **should you** be ashamed

72

O, lest the world should task you to recite
What merit lived in me that you should love,
After my death, dear love, forget me quite,
For you in me can nothing worthy prove;   4
Unless you would devise some virtuous lie,
To do more for me than mine own desert,
And hang more praise upon deceasèd I
Than niggard truth would willingly impart.   8
O, lest your true love may seem false in this,
That you for love speak well of me untrue,
My name be buried where my body is
And live no more to shame nor me nor you.   12
    For I am shamed by that which I bring forth,
    And so should you, to love things nothing worth.

The poet describes himself as nearing the end of his life. He imagines the beloved's love for him growing stronger in the face of that death.

1. **time of year:** See Ovid, *Metamorphoses* [B], in Appendix, pp. 341–42.

3. **against the cold:** (1) in **the cold** autumn wind; (2) in anticipation of **the cold** of winter

4. **choirs:** The **boughs,** compared here to the part of the church set apart for choristers, are now **bare,** as if reduced to ruin. One thinks almost inevitably of the monasteries destroyed by Henry VIII, with their **bare ruined choirs** where once there were choristers. **late:** recently

5. **twilight:** See note to l. 1 (above).

8. **Death's second self:** a description of sleep here applied to **night; seals up:** wordplay on (1) encloses, as in a coffin; (2) seels up (sews shut, as was done to falcons' eyes when the birds were being trained); (3) places a seal on a finished document

10. **his youth:** i.e., its **youth**

12. **with:** (1) by; (2) along with

14. **leave:** part with

73

That time of year thou mayst in me behold
When yellow leaves, or none, or few, do hang
Upon those boughs which shake against the cold,
Bare ruined choirs where late the sweet birds sang.   4
In me thou see'st the twilight of such day
As after sunset fadeth in the west,
Which by and by black night doth take away,
Death's second self, that seals up all in rest.   8
In me thou see'st the glowing of such fire
That on the ashes of his youth doth lie,
As the death-bed whereon it must expire,
Consumed with that which it was nourished by.   12
   This thou perceiv'st, which makes thy love more
      strong,
   To love that well which thou must leave ere long.

In this sonnet, which continues from s. 73, the poet consoles the beloved by telling him that only the poet's body will die; the spirit of the poet will continue to live in the poetry, which is the beloved's.

1–2. **that fell arrest / Without all bail:** i.e., death **fell:** cruel (Compare Hamlet's reference to "this **fell** sergeant, Death, / [who] Is strict in his **arrest**" [5.2.368–69].)

3. **My . . . interest:** i.e., I have a legal right to (**interest in**) this verse

4. **Which . . . stay:** i.e., **which** will remain with you always as a (1) commemoration; (2) memorandum

5. **thou reviewest:** you reread; **review:** see again

6. **consecrate to:** (1) devoted to; (2) reserved for

7. **his:** its

11. **coward . . . knife:** The **body,** in its subjection to death, is both cowardly and the victim of a cowardly attack by a wretch. (See *Richard II* 3.2.173–75, where Death, having allowed the king to believe his flesh "were brass impregnable," "Comes at the last and with a little pin / Bores through" that flesh, "and farewell, king!")

12. **Too . . . rememberèd:** i.e., too worthless **to be remembered** by you

13. **The worth of that:** i.e., the body's value

74

But be contented when that fell arrest
Without all bail shall carry me away,
My life hath in this line some interest,
Which for memorial still with thee shall stay. 4
When thou reviewest this, thou dost review
The very part was consecrate to thee.
The earth can have but earth, which is his due;
My spirit is thine, the better part of me. 8
So then thou hast but lost the dregs of life,
The prey of worms, my body being dead,
The coward conquest of a wretch's knife,
Too base of thee to be rememberèd. 12
   The worth of that is that which it contains,
   And that is this, and this with thee remains.

The poet compares himself to a miser with his treasure. He finds the beloved so essential to his life that he lives in a constant tension between glorying in that treasure and fearing its loss.

---

1. **So . . . life:** i.e., **you are** (as necessary) **to my thoughts as food** is **to life**

2. **sweet-seasoned:** i.e., springtime

3. **for the peace of you:** i.e., because of **the peace you** bring me (with possible wordplay on *piece*—i.e., piece of money—leading to the **miser and his wealth**); **hold such strife:** i.e., suffer the kind of conflict (This line is subject to any number of readings.)

5. **as an enjoyer: as** one who enjoys (**his wealth**); **anon:** immediately

6. **Doubting:** fearing; **the filching age:** i.e., the pilfering time he lives in

7. **counting:** considering (with wordplay on a **miser counting** his gold)

8. **bettered:** i.e., considering it even better

10. **clean:** completely

12. **is had:** i.e., I already have

13. **pine:** starve; **surfeit:** glut myself

14. **Or:** either; **all away:** possessing nothing

75

So are you to my thoughts as food to life,
Or as sweet-seasoned showers are to the ground;
And for the peace of you I hold such strife
As 'twixt a miser and his wealth is found: 4
Now proud as an enjoyer, and anon
Doubting the filching age will steal his treasure;
Now counting best to be with you alone,
Then bettered that the world may see my pleasure.   8
Sometime all full with feasting on your sight,
And by and by clean starvèd for a look;
Possessing or pursuing no delight
Save what is had or must from you be took.   12
    Thus do I pine and surfeit day by day,
    Or gluttoning on all, or all away.

The poet poses the question of why his poetry never changes but keeps repeating the same language and technique. The answer, he says, is that his theme never changes; he always writes of the beloved and of love.

---

1. **pride:** adornment, ornamentation
2. **variation or quick change:** Since **quick change** is itself synonymous with **variation,** this line is itself an example of **variation** in choice of expression, and thus shows that this **verse** is **far from barren.**
3. **with the time:** i.e., as other poets do today; **glance:** move rapidly
4. **methods:** poetic rules and arrangements; **compounds:** words that combine other words (like the word *compound* itself, which combines the Latin *cum,* meaning "with," and *ponere,* meaning "to put")
5. **still all one:** always the same
6. **invention:** poetic creation; **in a noted weed:** i.e., in familiar clothing (but **noted** also means "famous, celebrated, distinguished")
8. **where:** i.e., from **where**
10. **still my argument:** always my theme
14. **still telling what is:** i.e., always **telling** that which has already been

76

Why is my verse so barren of new pride,
So far from variation or quick change?
Why with the time do I not glance aside
To new-found methods and to compounds strange?   4
Why write I still all one, ever the same,
And keep invention in a noted weed,
That every word doth almost ⌜tell⌝ my name,
Showing their birth and where they did proceed?   8
O, know, sweet love, I always write of you,
And you and love are still my argument;
So all my best is dressing old words new,
Spending again what is already spent.   12
    For as the sun is daily new and old,
      So is my love, still telling what is told.

This sonnet seems to have been written to accompany the gift of a blank notebook. The poet encourages the beloved to write down the thoughts that arise from observing a mirror and a sundial and the lessons they teach about the brevity of life.

1. **glass:** mirror; **wear:** waste away (The Quarto uses the variant spelling *were.*)

2. **dial:** sundial (See picture below.) **waste:** dwindle

3. **vacant leaves:** blank pages (of **this book** [l. 4], a notebook in which the beloved is to write)

4. **this learning:** i.e., the **learning** that follows

6. **mouthèd:** gaping; **memory:** a reminder

7. **dial's shady stealth:** i.e., the imperceptible movement of the shadow across the **dial** (with wordplay on **stealth** as "theft," or **thievish progress**)

9. **Look what:** whatever

10. **waste:** unused

11–12. **Those . . . mind:** The image is of thought as a child **delivered from** the **brain,** put out to a wet nurse (i.e., written down), and then later restored to the parent (i.e., reread) for renewed **acquaintance.**

13. **offices:** tasks, functions

A sundial. (s. 77.2, 7)

77

Thy glass will show thee how thy beauties wear,
Thy dial how thy precious minutes waste;
The vacant leaves thy mind's imprint will bear,
And of this book this learning mayst thou taste: 4
The wrinkles which thy glass will truly show,
Of mouthèd graves will give thee memory;
Thou by thy dial's shady stealth mayst know
Time's thievish progress to eternity.   8
Look what thy memory cannot contain
Commit to these waste ⌜blanks,⌝ and thou shalt find
Those children nursed, delivered from thy brain,
To take a new acquaintance of thy mind.   12
    These offices, so oft as thou wilt look,
    Shall profit thee and much enrich thy book.

In this first of a series of three sonnets in which the poet expresses his concern that others are writing verses praising the beloved, the other poets are presented as learned and skillful and thus in no need of the beloved, in contrast to the poet speaking here.

---

1. **So . . . muse:** See, e.g., s. 38.

3. **As:** that; **every alien pen:** i.e., pens belonging to other persons; **hath got my use:** has adopted my custom or practice

4. **under thee:** i.e., under your protection

5. **dumb:** mute; **on high:** loudly, aloud

7. **added . . . wing:** In falconry, **feathers** were **added to** a bird's wings to improve its power of flight. Here, the beloved's inspiration has **added feathers to** (i.e., improved the verse of) even the learned.

9. **compile:** compose

10. **Whose . . . thee:** i.e., which is determined by you and is your child (**Influence** is an astrological term. See longer note to s. 15.4, p. 325.)

12. **arts:** learning and poetic skill; **gracèd be:** are adorned

13. **advance:** lift up

78

So oft have I invoked thee for my muse
And found such fair assistance in my verse
As every alien pen hath got my use
And under thee their poesy disperse.   4
Thine eyes, that taught the dumb on high to sing
And heavy ignorance aloft to fly,
Have added feathers to the learnèd's wing
And given grace a double majesty.   8
Yet be most proud of that which I compile,
Whose influence is thine and born of thee.
In others' works thou dost but mend the style,
And arts with thy sweet graces gracèd be.   12
    But thou art all my art and dost advance
    As high as learning my rude ignorance.

In this sonnet, which follows directly from s. 78, the poet laments the fact that another poet has taken his place. He urges the beloved to recognize that all of the beauty, grace, and virtue found in the rival's praise is taken from the beloved, so that the rival deserves no thanks.

---

1. **call upon thy aid:** i.e., invoke you as my muse

2. **all . . . grace:** (1) **all** your favor; (2) **all** your charm

3. **gracious numbers:** verses filled with your grace; **are decayed:** have declined

4. **muse:** poetic powers (See note to s. 38.1.) **give another place:** yield to **another**

5. **thy lovely argument:** the **lovely** theme of you

6. **travail:** toil (accent on first syllable)

7. **of thee:** concerning you; **thy poet:** the **poet** writing your praises; **invent:** wordplay on (1) devise; (2) find out (Lines 8–14 show why a third customary meaning of **invent** as "create by original ingenuity" does not apply.)

11. **can afford:** is able to give

79

Whilst I alone did call upon thy aid,
My verse alone had all thy gentle grace;
But now my gracious numbers are decayed,
And my sick muse doth give another place.   4
I grant, sweet love, thy lovely argument
Deserves the travail of a worthier pen;
Yet what of thee thy poet doth invent
He robs thee of and pays it thee again.   8
He lends thee virtue, and he stole that word
From thy behavior; beauty doth he give
And found it in thy cheek. He can afford
No praise to thee but what in thee doth live.   12
    Then thank him not for that which he doth say,
    Since what he owes thee thou thyself dost pay.

The poet admits his inferiority to the one who is now writing about the beloved, portraying the two poets as ships sailing on the ocean of the beloved's worth—the rival poet as large and splendid and himself as a small boat that risks being wrecked by love.

---

1. **faint:** lose heart

2. **better spirit:** i.e., more inspired poet; **use your name:** (1) invoke you as muse; (2) claim your protection as his patron

4. **To make me:** i.e., with the result that I become (though with the implication of deliberate rivalry)

6. **humble as:** i.e., the small (boat) **as** well as

7. **saucy:** rashly venturing, presumptuous

8. **main:** ocean; **willfully:** obstinately; freely

9–10. **Your . . . ride:** Small ships float in shallow water; large ships need the **soundless deep** (water of such depth it cannot be sounded [measured]).

11. **being wracked:** if I should be wrecked

12. **He . . . pride:** i.e., he, in contrast, is a grandly and sturdily constructed ship (and/or a tall-masted ship) of great splendor

14. **my love was my decay:** (1) **my** affection **was my** ruin; (2) **my** beloved (as "**soundless deep**") caused **my** destruction

80

O, how I faint when I of you do write,
Knowing a better spirit doth use your name,
And in the praise thereof spends all his might,
To make me tongue-tied speaking of your fame.   4
But since your worth, wide as the ocean is,
The humble as the proudest sail doth bear,
My saucy bark, inferior far to his,
On your broad main doth willfully appear.   8
Your shallowest help will hold me up afloat
Whilst he upon your soundless deep doth ride,
Or, being wracked, I am a worthless boat,
He of tall building and of goodly pride.   12
    Then, if he thrive and I be cast away,
    The worst was this: my love was my decay.

The poet, imagining a future in which both he and the beloved are dead, sees himself as being completely forgotten while the beloved will be forever remembered because of the poet's verse.

---

1. **Or:** either
3. **hence:** i.e., the world; **your memory:** i.e., the **memory** of you
4. **in me each part:** i.e., every **part** of **me**
5. **from hence:** henceforth
7. **earth:** world; **common grave:** i.e., burial in the church ground with no marker to record the name
8. **entombèd in men's eyes:** i.e., buried in a prominent place (as in a sepulcher)
9. **monument:** wordplay on (1) sepulcher; (2) written document, record
10. **o'erread:** read over
11. **rehearse:** speak of
12. **this world:** i.e., today's **world**
13. **still:** always, forever; **live:** (1) continue to be alive; (2) dwell; **virtue:** power
14. **even in the mouths:** i.e., **in the** very **mouths** (**Breath,** in this line, is not only the air men breathe but also the articulated sounds that will recite the poet's verse and spread the beloved's fame.)

81

Or I shall live your epitaph to make
Or you survive when I in earth am rotten.
From hence your memory death cannot take,
Although in me each part will be forgotten.   4
Your name from hence immortal life shall have,
Though I, once gone, to all the world must die.
The earth can yield me but a common grave,
When you entombèd in men's eyes shall lie.   8
Your monument shall be my gentle verse,
Which eyes not yet created shall o'erread;
And tongues to be your being shall rehearse
When all the breathers of this world are dead.   12
    You still shall live—such virtue hath my pen—
    Where breath most breathes, even in the mouths
      of men.

In this first of two linked sonnets, the poet again addresses the fact that other poets write in praise of the beloved. The beloved is free to read them, but their poems do not represent the beloved truly.

---

1. **married to my muse:** i.e., under a vow to remain faithful to my poetry alone
2. **attaint:** dishonor; **o'erlook:** read
3. **dedicated words:** wordplay on (1) devoted **words;** (2) **words** of authors' dedications
4. **Of:** about; **blessing every book:** elaborate wordplay that includes (1) (dedications) gracing **every book;** (2) (**words** about the **fair subject**) making **every book** fortunate; and (3) (the beloved) showing favor to **every book**
5. **as fair . . . hue:** i.e., **as** just in comprehension **as** you are lovely in appearance
6. **Finding . . . praise:** i.e., in determining that your merits go beyond my ability to praise   **limit:** region
8. **stamp:** imprint or sign; **time-bettering days:** i.e., this progressive age
10. **What strainèd touches:** i.e., whatever artificial or ornamental details
11. **truly sympathized:** represented in a way that corresponds accurately to you
12. **plain:** unadorned
13. **their gross painting:** i.e., the overelaborate language of other poets   **gross:** flagrant; clumsy; thick   **painting:** description; flattery; application of cosmetics
14. **in thee:** i.e., on your face; **abused:** misused

82

I grant thou wert not married to my muse,
And therefore mayst without attaint o'erlook
The dedicated words which writers use
Of their fair subject, blessing every book.   4
Thou art as fair in knowledge as in hue,
Finding thy worth a limit past my praise,
And therefore art enforced to seek anew
Some fresher stamp of the time-bettering days.   8
And do so, love; yet when they have devised
What strainèd touches rhetoric can lend,
Thou, truly fair, wert truly sympathized
In true plain words by thy true-telling friend.   12
    And their gross painting might be better used
    Where cheeks need blood; in thee it is abused.

This sonnet continues from s. 82, but the poet has learned to his dismay that his plain speaking (and/or his silence) has offended the beloved. He argues that no words can match the beloved's beauty.

---

1. **painting:** See s. 82.13, and note.
2. **fair . . . set:** i.e., beauty applied **no painting**
3–4. **I . . . debt:** See s. 82.6.   **tender:** offer
5. **slept . . . report:** i.e., stopped writing (or, perhaps, written in an understated way) about you
6. **That:** so **that; extant:** alive
7. **modern:** (1) commonplace, ordinary; (2) up-to-date, present-day
8. **Speaking:** i.e., in **speaking; grow:** flourish
9. **for . . . impute:** i.e., **you** regarded as **my sin**
10. **being dumb:** i.e., I remaining silent
12. **would . . . tomb:** i.e., intending to **give life** instead memorialize
14. **both your poets:** i.e., **both** the poet of the *Sonnets* and the rival poet (or, perhaps, **your** two rival **poets**)

83

I never saw that you did painting need
And therefore to your fair no painting set.
I found, or thought I found, you did exceed
The barren tender of a poet's debt.   4
And therefore have I slept in your report,
That you yourself, being extant, well might show
How far a modern quill doth come too short,
Speaking of worth, what worth in you doth grow.   8
This silence for my sin you did impute,
Which shall be most my glory, being dumb,
For I impair not beauty, being mute,
When others would give life and bring a tomb.   12
   There lives more life in one of your fair eyes
   Than both your poets can in praise devise.

The poet reiterates his claim that poems praising the beloved should reflect the beloved's perfections rather than exaggerate them. He accuses the beloved of caring too much for praise.

---

1. **Who . . . more:** i.e., who is it that in praising you most extravagantly **can say more**

3. **In whose confine:** i.e., within whom; **immurèd is the store:** i.e., is enclosed the entire stock (of beauty and worth)

4. **Which . . . grew:** perhaps, **which** anyone held up as **your equal** would need to possess (The line cannot be paraphrased precisely.)

6. **his subject:** i.e., its **subject** (no matter how ordinary)

8. **so . . . story:** i.e., in this way ennobles his writing

9. **but copy:** only transcribe

10. **making worse:** debasing; **clear:** free of fault

11. **counterpart:** copy; **fame his wit:** make his poetic genius famous

13. **blessings:** gifts of nature, excellent qualities

14. **Being fond on:** (1) having a strong liking for; (2) **being** besotted or dazed by; **your praises:** presumably, "**praises** offered you" (though the more obvious reading of the phrase is "**praises** you give others"); **worse:** perhaps, more blatant

84

Who is it that says most, which can say more
Than this rich praise, that you alone are you,
In whose confine immurèd is the store
Which should example where your equal grew?   4
Lean penury within that pen doth dwell
That to his subject lends not some small glory,
But he that writes of you, if he can tell
That you are you, so dignifies his story.   8
Let him but copy what in you is writ,
Not making worse what nature made so clear,
And such a counterpart shall fame his wit,
Making his style admirèd everywhere.   12
    You to your beauteous blessings add a curse,
      Being fond on praise, which makes your praises
        worse.

In this first of two linked sonnets, the poet says that his silence in the face of others' extravagant praise of the beloved is only outward muteness. His thoughts are filled with love.

1. **in . . . still:** i.e., politely stays quiet
2. **comments of your praise:** i.e., poems praising you (literally, treatises **of praise** of you); **compiled:** composed
3. **Reserve . . . character:** i.e., keep their writings in store (This phrase is often emended.)
4. **phrase:** style, language; **filed:** polished smooth (For the nine muses, see note to s. 38.1, and picture, p. 78.)
5. **other:** others
6–8. **like . . . pen:** The poet, who simply says "yes" when others write in praise of the beloved, compares himself to an illiterate parish **clerk** who answers the priest's prayers with "**amen.**" Evans points out that "**'Tis so, 'tis true**" (l. 9) translates the Hebrew "**amen.**" **affords:** supplies
10. **most of:** utmost
11. **that is:** i.e., I **add** it
12. **holds . . . before:** i.e., (**my thought**) keeps its position in the front **rank**
13. **respect:** regard well, pay attention to
14. **dumb:** silent; **speaking in effect:** i.e., which in fact speak

85

My tongue-tied muse in manners holds her still
While comments of your praise, richly compiled,
Reserve their character with golden quill
And precious phrase by all the muses filed.   4
I think good thoughts whilst other write good words,
And like unlettered clerk still cry amen
To every hymn that able spirit affords
In polished form of well-refinèd pen.   8
Hearing you praised, I say " 'Tis so, 'tis true,"
And to the most of praise add something more;
But that is in my thought, whose love to you,
Though words come hindmost, holds his rank before. 12
　　Then others for the breath of words respect,
　　Me for my dumb thoughts, speaking in effect.

This final "rival poet" sonnet continues from s. 85 but echoes the imagery of s. 80. The poet explains that his silence is not from fear of his rival, but results from having nothing to write about, now that the rival's verse has appropriated the beloved's favor.

---

2. **Bound for the prize:** The image is of a privateer sailing off to capture booty. (For the rival poet as a large sailing ship, see s. 80.)

3. **ripe:** ready for birth; **inhearse:** bury

4. **Making . . . womb:** i.e., turning **my brain,** where the **thoughts** were conceived, into **their tomb**

5–11. **Was . . . boast:** See longer note, p. 328.

5. **spirit:** lively intelligence

6. **Above a mortal pitch:** i.e., in a style that transcends the reach of human talent (The **pitch** is the highest point in a falcon's flight.)

7. **compeers:** companions, associates

8. **astonishèd:** struck dumb

9. **He:** neither he

10. **gulls:** deludes; gorges; **intelligence:** reports

11. **cannot:** i.e., can

12. **sick of:** sickened or weakened by

13. **countenance:** face; favor; **line:** verse

14. **matter:** subject matter, something to write about; **that:** i.e., **that** lack; **mine:** my verse

86

Was it the proud full sail of his great verse,
Bound for the prize of all-too-precious you,
That did my ripe thoughts in my brain inhearse,
Making their tomb the womb wherein they grew? 4
Was it his spirit, by spirits taught to write
Above a mortal pitch, that struck me dead?
No, neither he, nor his compeers by night
Giving him aid, my verse astonishèd. 8
He, nor that affable familiar ghost
Which nightly gulls him with intelligence,
As victors of my silence cannot boast;
I was not sick of any fear from thence. 12
    But when your countenance filled up his line,
    Then lacked I matter; that enfeebled mine.

The poet writes as if his relationship with the beloved has ended—and as if that relationship had been a wonderful dream from which he has now waked.

---

1. **dear:** glorious; expensive (The relationship is here expressed in language that draws on that of economic or property rights but soon becomes legal.)

2. **like enough:** likely, probably; **estimate:** reputation; attributed value

3. **charter of thy worth:** document granting you your value or position; **releasing:** i.e., the right to set (yourself) free or transfer (yourself) to another

4. **My bonds in thee:** legal or emotional covenants binding you to me; **determinate:** no longer in force (a legal term)

5. **hold:** retain possession of; **granting:** bestowal; transfer (of yourself to me) by deed

7. **cause . . . gift:** i.e., reason I should be given **this fair gift; wanting:** lacking, missing

8. **patent:** title to possession; **back again is swerving:** i.e., is returning (to you)

10. **Or me . . . else mistaking:** i.e., **or else** you mistook my **worth** (or mistook **me**) when you gave it

11. **upon . . . growing:** i.e., **growing** out of an error

12. **on . . . making:** i.e., on (your) judging (you or me) more accurately

178

87

Farewell, thou art too dear for my possessing,
And like enough thou know'st thy estimate.
The charter of thy worth gives thee releasing;
My bonds in thee are all determinate.   4
For how do I hold thee but by thy granting,
And for that riches where is my deserving?
The cause of this fair gift in me is wanting,
And so my patent back again is swerving.   8
Thy self thou gav'st, thy own worth then not knowing,
Or me, to whom thou gav'st it, else mistaking;
So thy great gift, upon misprision growing,
Comes home again, on better judgment making.   12
   Thus have I had thee as a dream doth flatter,
   In sleep a king, but waking no such matter.

In this first of three linked sonnets in which the poet has been (or imagines himself someday to be) repudiated by the beloved, the poet offers to sacrifice himself and his reputation in order to make the now-estranged beloved look better.

1. **set me light:** consider me of small value
2. **place . . . scorn:** i.e., hold **my** merits up to scorn
4. **art forsworn:** i.e., have perjured yourself
6. **Upon thy part:** taking your side
7. **attainted:** (1) tainted; (2) accused
8. **losing:** (1) destroying; (2) being deprived of
12. **vantage:** benefit; **double-vantage:** doubly benefit
14. **for:** (1) on behalf of; (2) because of

"Till the judgment that yourself arise. . . ." (s. 55.13)

88

When thou shalt be disposed to set me light
And place my merit in the eye of scorn,
Upon thy side against myself I'll fight
And prove thee virtuous, though thou art forsworn.   4
With mine own weakness being best acquainted,
Upon thy part I can set down a story
Of faults concealed wherein I am attainted,
That thou, in losing me, shall win much glory;   8
And I by this will be a gainer too;
For bending all my loving thoughts on thee,
The injuries that to myself I do,
Doing thee vantage, double-vantage me.   12
    Such is my love, to thee I so belong,
      That, for thy right, myself will bear all wrong.

This sonnet is a detailed extension of the closing line of s. 88. The poet here lists the ways he will make himself look bad in order to make the beloved look good.

---

1. **Say:** announce, assert; **fault:** transgression
2. **comment upon:** i.e., enlarge on (literally, make remarks about)
3. **straight will halt:** will immediately limp
4. **reasons:** statements, claims
5. **ill:** badly
6. **set . . . change:** make the **change** you wish look more attractive
8. **acquaintance:** i.e., our familiarity; **look strange:** act as if we were strangers
9. **thy walks:** i.e., the places where you walk
11. **too much profane: too** impious or blasphemous
12. **haply:** perhaps
13. **For thee:** on your behalf; **debate:** i.e., combat
14. **For:** because

89

Say that thou didst forsake me for some fault,
And I will comment upon that offense;
Speak of my lameness and I straight will halt,
Against thy reasons making no defense.   4
Thou canst not, love, disgrace me half so ill,
To set a form upon desirèd change,
As I'll myself disgrace, knowing thy will;
I will acquaintance strangle and look strange,   8
Be absent from thy walks, and in my tongue
Thy sweet belovèd name no more shall dwell,
Lest I, too much profane, should do it wrong
And haply of our old acquaintance tell.   12
    For thee, against myself I'll vow debate,
      For I must ne'er love him whom thou dost hate.

Continuing from the final line of s. 89, this sonnet begs the beloved to deliver quickly any terrible blow that awaits the poet. Then the other blows being dealt by the world will seem as nothing.

---

1. **Then:** therefore (The line follows directly from the closing line of s. 89.)

2. **bent . . . cross:** determined to thwart all that I do

3. **the spite of fortune:** fortune's malice; **bow:** submit

4. **drop . . . afterloss:** i.e., fall (on me) after I'm already defeated

5. **'scaped this sorrow:** i.e., recovered from a present **sorrow** (The poem seems to imply that a new, rather devastating blow has struck the poet, something apart from the prospect of the beloved's repudiation.)

6. **in the . . . woe:** i.e., after I've overcome this **woe**

8. **linger out:** prolong; **a purposed overthrow:** an intended defeat

10. **griefs:** (1) injuries; (2) sorrows (**petty** in comparison to the beloved's treachery)

11. **in the onset:** at the beginning of the attack (military language, like **conquered** [l. 6] and **overthrow** [l. 8])

13. **strains:** sorts, kinds

184

90

Then hate me when thou wilt, if ever, now,
Now, while the world is bent my deeds to cross,
Join with the spite of fortune, make me bow,
And do not drop in for an afterloss.　　　　　　4
Ah, do not, when my heart hath 'scaped this sorrow,
Come in the rearward of a conquered woe;
Give not a windy night a rainy morrow,
To linger out a purposed overthrow.　　　　　　8
If thou wilt leave me, do not leave me last,
When other petty griefs have done their spite,
But in the onset come; so ⌜shall⌝ I taste
At first the very worst of fortune's might;　　　12
　　And other strains of woe, which now seem woe,
　　Compared with loss of thee will not seem so.

In this first of three linked sonnets, the poet sets the love of the beloved above every other treasure, but then acknowledges that that love can be withdrawn.

---

1. **birth:** rank, lineage; **skill:** knowledge; cleverness

3. **newfangled ill:** i.e., trendy and badly made

4. **horse:** i.e., horses (See picture below.)

5. **humor:** (1) whim; (2) temperament; **his:** its

7. **not my measure:** i.e., not what satisfy me

10. **prouder:** more splendid

12. **all men's pride:** i.e., (1) what **all** men would be proud to possess; (2) **all** the treasures men possess

13. **Wretched . . . that:** i.e., miserable only in the knowledge **that**

"Hawks, . . . hounds, . . . [and] horse." (s. 91.4)

91

Some glory in their birth, some in their skill,
Some in their wealth, some in their body's force,
Some in their garments, though newfangled ill,
Some in their hawks and hounds, some in their horse;   4
And every humor hath his adjunct pleasure,
Wherein it finds a joy above the rest.
But these particulars are not my measure;
All these I better in one general best.   8
Thy love is ⌈better⌉ than high birth to me,
Richer than wealth, prouder than garments' cost,
Of more delight than hawks or horses be;
And having thee, of all men's pride I boast.   12
   Wretched in this alone, that thou mayst take
   All this away, and me most wretched make.

Continuing the argument from s. 91, the poet, imagining the loss of the beloved, realizes gladly that since even the smallest perceived diminishment of that love would cause him instantly to die, he need not fear living with the pain of loss. But, he asks, what if the beloved is false but gives no sign of defection?

---

1. **But:** nevertheless; **do thy worst:** wordplay on the phrase "**do thy** best"
2. **term of life:** a legal phrase that means "during one's lifetime"; **assurèd:** (1) established securely; (2) pledged
3. **stay:** remain
4. **For it:** i.e., because (my) **life**
5. **worst of wrongs:** i.e., the **worst** the beloved can do (presumably the "stealing away" of l. 1)
6. **When . . . end:** i.e., since **my life** will **end** at the **least** rejection
7. **I see:** i.e., I perceive that
7–8. **a better . . . depend:** i.e., I am in possession of **a state** (of mind) that transcends any condition dependent on your whims or moods
10. **that my . . . lie:** i.e., (the end of) **my life** will be determined by your casting off allegiance to me
11. **happy title:** (1) fortunate legal **title;** (2) **title** to happiness
13. **blessèd-fair:** fortunate and lovely; **blot:** blemish
14. **mayst:** (1) i.e., may someday; (2) may already be; **yet:** (1) nevertheless; (2) as **yet**

188

92

But do thy worst to steal thyself away,
For term of life thou art assurèd mine,
And life no longer than thy love will stay,
For it depends upon that love of thine.   4
Then need I not to fear the worst of wrongs
When in the least of them my life hath end;
I see a better state to me belongs
Than that which on thy humor doth depend.   8
Thou canst not vex me with inconstant mind,
Since that my life on thy revolt doth lie.
O, what a happy title do I find,
Happy to have thy love, happy to die!   12
    But what's so blessèd-fair that fears no blot?
    Thou mayst be false, and yet I know it not.

The poet explores the implications of the final line of s. 92. It would be easy for the beloved to be secretly false, he realizes, because the beloved is so unfailingly beautiful and (apparently) loving.

1–2. **So . . . husband:** See s. 92.14.   **supposing:** believing, imagining

3. **altered new:** newly **altered**

4. **looks:** glances

6. **in that:** i.e., **in** your **looks, in** your **eye**

7. **looks:** appearances, faces

8. **writ:** written, transcribed

13. **How . . . grow:** i.e., your **beauty** grows seductive but deadly   **Eve's apple:** i.e., the fruit of the tree (described as "pleasant to the eyes") that was forbidden Adam and Eve by God, and that, once eaten, brought death into the world (See Genesis 3 and picture below.)

14. **answer not:** does not correspond to

Eve offering apple to Adam. (s. 93.13)

190

93

So shall I live, supposing thou art true,
Like a deceivèd husband; so love's face
May still seem love to me, though altered new;
Thy looks with me, thy heart in other place.   4
For there can live no hatred in thine eye;
Therefore in that I cannot know thy change.
In many's looks, the false heart's history
Is writ in moods and frowns and wrinkles strange.   8
But heaven in thy creation did decree
That in thy face sweet love should ever dwell;
Whate'er thy thoughts or thy heart's workings be,
Thy looks should nothing thence but sweetness tell.   12
    How like Eve's apple doth thy beauty grow,
    If thy sweet virtue answer not thy show.

This sonnet describes a category of especially blessed and powerful people who appear to exert complete control over their lives and themselves. These persons are then implicitly compared to flowers and contrasted with weeds, the poem concluding with a warning to such persons in the form of a proverb about lilies.

---

1. **will do none:** i.e., do not wish **to hurt** (Proverbial: "To be able to do harm and not to do it is noble.")

2. **the thing they most do show:** i.e., what their appearance indicates they will do

3. **moving:** affecting, rousing, stirring

4. **to temptation slow:** i.e., not easily tempted

5. **heaven's graces:** i.e., the blessings of fortune, perhaps the same as **nature's riches** in l. 6

6. **husband:** protect; **expense:** extravagance

7. **faces:** (1) visages, features; (2) appearance; aspect

8. **stewards:** managers, custodians

10. **to . . . die:** (1) it lives and dies alone; (2) it merely lives and dies

12. **outbraves:** surpasses in splendor; **his:** its (One can detect behind ll. 9–12 allusions to Matthew 6.28–29 ["Learn how the **lilies** of the field do grow: they labor not, neither spin; Yet I say unto you, That even Solomon in all his glory was not arrayed like one of these"]; the allusions lead to the word **lilies** in l. 14.)

14. **Lilies . . . weeds:** proverbial

94

They that have power to hurt and will do none,
That do not do the thing they most do show,
Who, moving others, are themselves as stone,
Unmovèd, cold, and to temptation slow,   4
They rightly do inherit heaven's graces
And husband nature's riches from expense;
They are the lords and owners of their faces,
Others but stewards of their excellence.   8
The summer's flower is to the summer sweet,
Though to itself it only live and die;
But if that flower with base infection meet,
The basest weed outbraves his dignity.   12
    For sweetest things turn sourest by their deeds;
    Lilies that fester smell far worse than weeds.

In this first of a pair of related poems, the poet accuses the beloved of using beauty to hide a corrupt moral center.

---

1. **shame:** morally disgraceful conduct
2. **canker:** i.e., cankerworm (See note to s. 35.4.)
3. **spot . . . name:** i.e., as a cankerworm leaves a small hole on the bud as it enters, so base conduct blemishes the **budding** reputation of the beloved
4. **sweets:** sweet fragrances
6. **on thy sport:** about your pastimes (especially sexual activity)
8. **blesses an ill report:** i.e., converts lewd rumors into something holy (with wordplay on **ill report** as "bad reputation")
9. **mansion:** lordly manor house
11. **beauty's veil:** i.e., beauty, which acts as a **veil**
12. **that eyes can see:** (1) **that** is visible; (2) **that** is mere appearance
13. **of this large privilege:** i.e., **of** (abusing) **this** advantage
14. **hardest:** most hardened, sharpest; **ill used:** badly employed; **his:** its (Booth calls this line "Shakespeare's homemade proverb.")

95

How sweet and lovely dost thou make the shame
Which, like a canker in the fragrant rose,
Doth spot the beauty of thy budding name!
O, in what sweets dost thou thy sins enclose!   4
That tongue that tells the story of thy days,
Making lascivious comments on thy sport,
Cannot dispraise but in a kind of praise;
Naming thy name blesses an ill report.   8
O, what a mansion have those vices got
Which for their habitation chose out thee,
Where beauty's veil doth cover every blot,
And all things turns to fair that eyes can see!   12
   Take heed, dear heart, of this large privilege;
   The hardest knife ill used doth lose his edge.

As in the companion s. 95, the beloved is accused of enjoying the love of many despite his faults, which youth and beauty convert to graces.

---

1. **wantonness:** lasciviousness; arrogance

2. **grace:** charm; **gentle:** gentlemanly, aristocratic (**Gentle sport** is a kind way of describing **wantonness.**)

3. **more and less:** i.e., higher and lower ranks

4. **mak'st . . . resort:** i.e. turn the **faults that resort to thee** into **graces**

8. **To:** into; **translated:** transformed; **for:** to be

10. **like:** i.e., into the **looks** of (Proverbial: "A wolf in sheep's clothing." See picture below.)

12. **wouldst . . . state:** i.e., chose to exert all your powers

13–14. **But . . . report:** This couplet repeats the couplet of s. 36. See longer note, p. 328.

A wolf disguised as a lamb. (s. 96.9–10)

96

Some say thy fault is youth, some wantonness;
Some say thy grace is youth and gentle sport.
Both grace and faults are loved of more and less;
Thou mak'st faults graces that to thee resort.   4
As on the finger of a thronèd queen
The basest jewel will be well esteemed,
So are those errors that in thee are seen
To truths translated and for true things deemed.   8
How many lambs might the stern wolf betray
If like a lamb he could his looks translate!
How many gazers mightst thou lead away
If thou wouldst use the strength of all thy state!   12
    But do not so. I love thee in such sort
    As, thou being mine, mine is thy good report.

In this first of three sonnets about a period of separation from the beloved, the poet remembers the time as bleak winter, though the actual season was warm and filled with nature's abundance.

---

5. **removed:** i.e., of (our) separation

6. **teeming:** pregnant, prolific (**Autumn** is throughout the poem pictured as a woman giving birth, or about to give birth. Autumn's relationship to **summer's time** is explained by editors in a variety of ways. See longer note, pp. 328–29.) **big:** pregnant; **increase:** abundance (See picture, p. 62.)

7. **wanton:** frolicsome; luxuriant (or lascivious, if modifying **the prime**); **burden of the prime:** i.e., offspring fathered by springtime

8. **widowed wombs:** i.e., the (pregnant) **wombs** of widows

10. **hope . . . fruit:** a bleak image (in that **orphans** and the fatherless [**unfathered**] look to a future with little **hope**)

11. **his:** i.e., its; **wait on thee:** i.e., are in attendance on you, serve you

13. **so dull a cheer:** i.e., such a heavy heart **cheer:** disposition, mood

14. **pale:** wordplay on (1) no longer bright green; (2) ashen (from dread)

97

How like a winter hath my absence been
From thee, the pleasure of the fleeting year!
What freezings have I felt, what dark days seen,
What old December's bareness everywhere!   4
And yet this time removed was summer's time,
The teeming autumn, big with rich increase,
Bearing the wanton burden of the prime,
Like widowed wombs after their lords' decease.   8
Yet this abundant issue seemed to me
But hope of orphans and unfathered fruit;
For summer and his pleasures wait on thee,
And thou away, the very birds are mute;   12
    Or if they sing, 'tis with so dull a cheer
    That leaves look pale, dreading the winter's near.

The poet here remembers an April separation, in which springtime beauty seemed to him only a pale reflection of the absent beloved.

---

2. **proud-pied:** gloriously many-colored; **his trim:** i.e., his finery (**April** is here a beautiful youth.)

4. **That:** i.e., so **that** even; **heavy Saturn:** As both the planet in its astrological context and the Roman god, **Saturn** is associated with melancholy, winter, and decrepitude. (See chart, p. 98.)   **heavy:** ponderous; sad

5. **nor the lays:** neither the songs

6. **different flowers in:** i.e., **flowers** differing **in**

7. **any summer's story tell:** i.e., narrate a cheerful **story** (See *The Winter's Tale* 2.1.33: "A sad tale's best for winter.")

8. **their proud lap:** (1) the splendid earth; (2) the earth **proud** of their beauty (See *Richard II* 3.3.49: "The fresh green **lap** of fair King Richard's land.")

9. **wonder:** express my astonishment; **white:** i.e., whiteness (Proverbial: "**White** as a lily.")

11. **but sweet:** merely pleasant; **but . . . delight:** i.e., mere representations of essential **delight**

12. **Drawn after:** copied from; **pattern:** model

14. **shadow:** possible wordplay on the Neoplatonic **shadow** (imperfect reflection of the Idea) and the image cast by a body in sunlight (See notes to s. 53.) **these:** perhaps the roses and lilies already mentioned; perhaps the flowers and herbs of s. 99 (Some editors end s. 98.14 with a colon to lead the reader's eye forward to the next poem.)

98

From you have I been absent in the spring,
When proud-pied April, dressed in all his trim,
Hath put a spirit of youth in everything,
That heavy Saturn laughed and leapt with him.　　4
Yet nor the lays of birds nor the sweet smell
Of different flowers in odor and in hue
Could make me any summer's story tell,
Or from their proud lap pluck them where they grew.　8
Nor did I wonder at the lily's white,
Nor praise the deep vermilion in the rose;
They were but sweet, but figures of delight,
Drawn after you, you pattern of all those.　　12
　Yet seemed it winter still, and, you away,
　As with your shadow I with these did play.

This third poem about the beloved's absence is closely linked to s. 98. In the present sonnet, the poet accuses spring flowers and herbs of stealing color and fragrance from the beloved. The sonnet is unusual in that the first "quatrain" has five lines; the poem therefore has 15 lines, the only such sonnet in the sequence. (See longer note, pp. 329–30.)

---

1. **forward:** (1) early, precocious; (2) bold, brash
2. **sweet that smells:** i.e., perfume
3. **purple:** a color that at the time included the spectrum from blood-red to deep violet
4. **for complexion:** as color or cosmetic
5. **grossly:** excessively; flagrantly
6. **for thy:** i.e., for stealing its whiteness from your
7. **stol'n thy:** i.e., stolen their fragrance from your
8. **fearfully:** in fear; **on thorns did stand:** i.e., were in a state of anxiety (with wordplay on the **thorns** of the rosebush)
10. **nor red:** i.e., neither **red; of both:** i.e., **both** colors (i.e., the **third** was a pink or damask rose)
11. **annexed:** added (**to his robb'ry** of colors)
12. **for:** because of; **pride . . . growth:** splendor of full bloom
13. **canker:** cankerworm (See note to s. 35.4.)
15. **But . . . thee:** i.e., that had not stolen its fragrance or **color** from you

99

The forward violet thus did I chide:
"Sweet thief, whence didst thou steal thy sweet
    that smells,
If not from my love's breath? The purple pride
Which on thy soft cheek for complexion dwells   4
In my love's veins thou hast too grossly dyed."
The lily I condemnèd for thy hand,
And buds of marjoram had stol'n thy hair;
The roses fearfully on thorns did stand,   8
⌜One⌝ blushing shame, another white despair;
A third, nor red nor white, had stol'n of both,
And to his robb'ry had annexed thy breath;
But, for his theft, in pride of all his growth   12
A vengeful canker ate him up to death.
    More flowers I noted, yet I none could see
    But sweet or color it had stol'n from thee.

In this first of a group of four sonnets about a period of time in which the poet has failed to write about the beloved, the poet summons his poetic genius to return and compose verse that will immortalize the beloved.

1. **muse:** poetic gift or genius (See s. 38.1.)
3. **Spend'st . . . fury:** i.e., do you waste your inspiration (Poetic inspiration was referred to as *furor poeticus,* or "poetic rage.")
4. **lend . . . light:** i.e., make lowly **subjects** luminous
5–6. **straight . . . spent:** i.e., immediately compensate for misspent **time** through noble verses
7. **lays:** songs, poems
8. **argument:** theme
9. **resty:** (1) sluggish, idle; (2) refractory, stubborn
10. **If:** i.e., (to see) whether; **graven:** carved
11. **satire to:** i.e., satirist of
12. **spoils:** acts of destruction (with wordplay on **spoils** as "booty")
13. **wastes:** destroys
14. **So thou prevent'st:** i.e., in that way you forestall

100

Where art thou, muse, that thou forget'st so long
To speak of that which gives thee all thy might?
Spend'st thou thy fury on some worthless song,
Dark'ning thy power to lend base subjects light? 4
Return, forgetful muse, and straight redeem
In gentle numbers time so idly spent;
Sing to the ear that doth thy lays esteem
And gives thy pen both skill and argument. 8
Rise, resty muse; my love's sweet face survey
If Time have any wrinkle graven there.
If any, be a satire to decay
And make Time's spoils despisèd everywhere. 12
    Give my love fame faster than Time wastes life;
    So thou prevent'st his scythe and crookèd knife.

Continuing from s. 100, this poem has the muse tell the poet that the beloved needs no praise. The poet responds that the poems are for the edification of future ages.

1. **truant:** lazy; wandering
2. **truth in beauty dyed:** i.e., **truth** steeped **in beauty** (an image of the beloved)
3. **my love:** i.e., the beloved; **depends:** i.e., depend
4. **therein dignified:** i.e., your dependence on my beloved is the source of your dignity and worth
5. **haply:** perhaps
6. **Truth needs no color:** a proverb in which **color** means "rhetorical heightening"; **with . . . fixed:** perhaps, since its complexion is natural and ingrained
7. **Beauty no pencil:** i.e., **Beauty** (needs) **no** artist's brush; **lay:** i.e., paint (literally, arrange colors on canvas)
8. **intermixed:** intermingled, mixed together
9. **he:** the beloved; **dumb:** mute, silent
11. **much:** i.e., long
12. **of ages:** i.e., by **ages**
13. **do thy office:** perform your duty
14. **long hence:** far in the future; **shows:** appears

101

O truant muse, what shall be thy amends
For thy neglect of truth in beauty dyed?
Both truth and beauty on my love depends;
So dost thou too, and therein dignified.   4
Make answer, muse. Wilt thou not haply say
"Truth needs no color with his color fixed,
Beauty no pencil beauty's truth to lay;
But best is best if never intermixed"?   8
Because he needs no praise, wilt thou be dumb?
Excuse not silence so, for 't lies in thee
To make him much outlive a gilded tomb
And to be praised of ages yet to be.   12
   Then do thy office, muse; I teach thee how
   To make him seem long hence as he shows now.

The poet defends his silence, arguing that it is a sign not of lessened love but of his desire, in a world where pleasures have grown common, to avoid wearying the beloved with poems of praise.

---

1. **love:** affection; **is strengthened:** i.e., has grown in strength; **in seeming:** i.e., to all appearance
2. **show:** i.e., outward manifestation
3. **merchandized:** bought and sold, bartered; **whose rich esteeming:** i.e., the **rich** worth of which
4. **publish:** make public
5. **in the spring:** i.e., in its early days
6. **lays:** songs, poems
7. **Philomel:** i.e., the nightingale (into which, in mythology, a woman named Philomela had been transformed); **in summer's front:** i.e., at the beginning of summer
8. **stops his pipe:** i.e., ceases to sing   **his:** i.e., the nightingale's (Most editors since 1835 have emended the Quarto's **his** to "her" in order to create greater clarity.) **in growth of riper days:** i.e., in the later, more abundant, **days** of summer
10. **her mournful hymns:** i.e., Philomel's sad tunes (Philomela's story was a tragic one.)
11. **But that:** i.e., **but** because; **wild . . . bough:** The image is of hosts of common birds singing in the trees. In conjunction with ll. 12–14, the image may be linked to earlier sonnets about rival poets.
12. **sweets:** pleasures
14. **dull:** i.e., bore (literally, render listless)

102

My love is strengthened, though more weak in seeming;
I love not less, though less the show appear.
That love is merchandized whose rich esteeming
The owner's tongue doth publish everywhere.   4
Our love was new, and then but in the spring,
When I was wont to greet it with my lays,
As Philomel in summer's front doth sing,
And stops his pipe in growth of riper days.   8
Not that the summer is less pleasant now
Than when her mournful hymns did hush the night,
But that wild music burdens every bough,
And sweets grown common lose their dear delight.   12
    Therefore, like her, I sometime hold my tongue,
    Because I would not dull you with my song.

In this fourth poem of apology for his silence, the poet argues that the beloved's own face is so superior to any words of praise that silence is the better way.

1. **poverty:** i.e., poor stuff; **muse:** poetic gift (See note to s. 38.1.)

2. **That:** i.e., in **that; her pride:** (1) her rhetorical splendor; (2) that of which she is proud (the beloved)

3. **argument all bare:** unadorned theme

4. **beside:** as well

6. **glass:** looking glass, mirror

7. **overgoes:** exceeds, excels; overpowers; **blunt invention:** dull creative powers

8. **Dulling:** removing the lustre of; **doing:** i.e., bringing, causing

9–10. **Were . . . well:** See *King Lear* 1.4.369: "Striving to better, oft we **mar** what's **well**" (cited in Kerrigan).   **Were it:** i.e., would it not be

11. **pass:** accomplishment

13. **sit:** have a place or location

103

Alack, what poverty my muse brings forth,
That, having such a scope to show her pride,
The argument all bare is of more worth
Than when it hath my added praise beside.   4
O, blame me not if I no more can write!
Look in your glass, and there appears a face
That overgoes my blunt invention quite,
Dulling my lines and doing me disgrace.   8
Were it not sinful, then, striving to mend,
To mar the subject that before was well?
For to no other pass my verses tend
Than of your graces and your gifts to tell.   12
   And more, much more, than in my verse can sit
   Your own glass shows you when you look in it.

The poet ponders the beloved's seemingly unchanging beauty, realizing that it is doubtless altering even as he watches. He warns that the epitome of beauty will have died before future ages are born.

2. **first your eye I eyed:** i.e., **I first** saw you

4. **pride:** splendor

6. **process:** i.e., the progression

8. **fresh, green:** These words may be synonyms, meaning "youthful, blooming"; or **fresh** may be linked to **April** and **green** to **June.** In any case, they mean young and vital, as opposed to **yellow autumn.**

9–10. **like . . . perceived:** Proverbial: "To move as the **dial hand,** which is not seen to move." **dial:** sundial or clock (See picture, p. 158.) **Steal from his figure:** wordplay on (1) (**beauty**) departs from its original form; (2) (time, as symbolized by the **dial hand**) steals (**beauty**) from the young man's appearance

11. **hue:** appearance; **still doth stand:** (1) i.e., remains unchanged or **still;** (2) continues to survive

13. **unbred:** unborn

14. **beauty's summer:** i.e., beauty at its peak

104

To me, fair friend, you never can be old,
For as you were when first your eye I eyed,
Such seems your beauty still. Three winters cold
Have from the forests shook three summers' pride,   4
Three beauteous springs to yellow autumn turned
In process of the seasons have I seen,
Three April perfumes in three hot Junes burned,
Since first I saw you fresh, which yet are green.   8
Ah, yet doth beauty, like a dial hand,
Steal from his figure, and no pace perceived;
So your sweet hue, which methinks still doth stand,
Hath motion, and mine eye may be deceived.   12
    For fear of which, hear this, thou age unbred:
    Ere you were born was beauty's summer dead.

Arguing that his poetry is not idolatrous in the sense of "polytheistic," the poet contends that he celebrates only a single person, the beloved, as forever "fair, kind, and true." Yet by locating this trinity of features in a single being, the poet flirts with idolatry in the sense of worshipping his beloved.

1. **idolatry:** The wit of the sonnet plays on the poet's pretense that **idolatry** means only polytheistic worship of idols (of which pagans and Roman Catholics alike were accused); the word also means "immoderate attachment to a person or thing."

2. **show:** seem, appear

4. **To . . . one:** i.e., **to** and **of** a single entity (the **belovèd**); **still . . . so:** i.e., (**my songs**) always the same

5. **my love:** i.e., **my belovèd**

6. **Still:** always

8. **difference:** variety, diversity (though with almost inevitable wordplay on "disagreement")

9. **argument:** topic, theme

10. **varying to:** i.e., (though sometimes) expressed in

11. **this change:** i.e., **this** varying of expression; **my invention spent:** i.e., my poetic creativity employed and/or exhausted

12. **Three . . . in one:** This reminder of the Christian Trinity, echoed in l. 14, suggests that the poet, like the Christian, worships a single "god" represented in three "persons" or attributes.

13. **lived alone:** i.e., inhabited separate individuals

14. **kept seat:** resided

214

105

Let not my love be called idolatry,
Nor my belovèd as an idol show,
Since all alike my songs and praises be
To one, of one, still such, and ever so.   4
Kind is my love today, tomorrow kind,
Still constant in a wondrous excellence;
Therefore my verse, to constancy confined,
One thing expressing, leaves out difference.   8
"Fair, kind, and true" is all my argument,
"Fair, kind, and true," varying to other words;
And in this change is my invention spent,
Three themes in one, which wondrous scope affords.   12
   "Fair," "kind," and "true" have often lived alone,
   Which three till now never kept seat in one.

The poet, in reading descriptions of beautiful knights and ladies in old poetry, realizes that the poets were trying to describe the beauty of the beloved, but, having never seen him, could only approximate it.

---

1. **wasted time: time** gone by (with wordplay on **wasted** as "ravaged")

2. **wights:** men and women (a term already archaic in Shakespeare's day)

3. **beauty:** perhaps the **beauty** of the described **wights,** or perhaps the beautiful poetic style of the **descriptions**

5. **blazon:** description of excellencies (in poetry, a catalogue of the body's beauties, as in l. 6)

6. **brow:** forehead

7. **their antique pen:** i.e., the **pen** of the old poets; **would have expressed:** i.e., were trying to depict

8. **master:** own, possess

9. **their praises:** (1) the **praises** of the beautiful **wights;** or, (2) the poems of praise by the old poets

10. **you prefiguring:** i.e., foreshadowing you (as, in traditional Christianity, events and figures in the earlier scriptures prefigure the life of Jesus Christ)

11. **for:** because; **divining eyes:** i.e., **eyes** of conjecture or prophecy

12. **skill:** understanding (The Quarto reads *still.*)

14. **wonder:** i.e., look on in amazement; **lack tongues:** i.e., **lack** (adequate) language (but with the suggestion of being struck dumb by the beloved's beauty)

106

When in the chronicle of wasted time
I see descriptions of the fairest wights,
And beauty making beautiful old rhyme
In praise of ladies dead and lovely knights,   4
Then in the blazon of sweet beauty's best,
Of hand, of foot, of lip, of eye, of brow,
I see their antique pen would have expressed
Even such a beauty as you master now.   8
So all their praises are but prophecies
Of this our time, all you prefiguring;
And, for they looked but with divining eyes,
They had not ⌜skill⌝ enough your worth to sing.   12
   For we, which now behold these present days,
   Have eyes to wonder, but lack tongues to praise.

This sonnet celebrates an external event that had threatened to be disastrous but that has turned out to be wonderful. The poet's love, in this new time, is also refreshed.

1. **Not:** i.e., neither

1–2. **prophetic . . . come:** i.e., prognostications of **the world** at large

3. **lease . . . control:** i.e., set limits to the length of time that I will love

4. **Supposed as forfeit:** i.e., which had been thought to be subject to; **confined doom:** restricted or limited fate (i.e., fate of being limited)

5. **The mortal . . . endured:** a much debated reference, accepted by most editors today as referring to the death of Queen Elizabeth, often imaged as Diana or **the moon** (See, e.g., Kerrigan.) **endured:** suffered

6. **sad augurs:** solemn or gloomy soothsayers; **presage:** i.e., warnings

7. **Incertainties:** events of which the outcome was uncertain; **assured:** i.e., as certain, safe (perhaps a reference to the peaceful accession of King James)

8. **olives of endless age:** i.e., olive branches that will last forever (The traditional link between the olive tree and **peace** may derive from the olive leaf brought Noah by the dove to signal the end of the flood [Genesis 8.11].)

9. **drops . . . time:** variously interpreted as springtime rain, as oil from the **olives,** and as the balm used in coronations

10. **subscribes:** submits

11. **spite of:** despite; **rhyme:** poem

(continued)

107

Not mine own fears nor the prophetic soul
Of the wide world dreaming on things to come
Can yet the lease of my true love control,
Supposed as forfeit to a confined doom.   4
The mortal moon hath her eclipse endured,
And the sad augurs mock their own presage;
Incertainties now crown themselves assured,
And peace proclaims olives of endless age.   8
Now with the drops of this most balmy time
My love looks fresh, and Death to me subscribes,
Since, spite of him, I'll live in this poor rhyme,
While he insults o'er dull and speechless tribes;   12
    And thou in this shalt find thy monument
      When tyrants' crests and tombs of brass are spent.

12. **insults:** triumphs; **dull . . . tribes:** i.e., persons without (poetic) language

13. **this:** i.e., **this** poem

14. **crests:** insignia on coats of arms (perhaps as displayed on **tombs**); **spent:** wasted away

Diana. (s. 107.5, s. 153)

107

Not mine own fears nor the prophetic soul
Of the wide world dreaming on things to come
Can yet the lease of my true love control,
Supposed as forfeit to a confined doom.   4
The mortal moon hath her eclipse endured,
And the sad augurs mock their own presage;
Incertainties now crown themselves assured,
And peace proclaims olives of endless age.   8
Now with the drops of this most balmy time
My love looks fresh, and Death to me subscribes,
Since, spite of him, I'll live in this poor rhyme,
While he insults o'er dull and speechless tribes;   12
    And thou in this shalt find thy monument
    When tyrants' crests and tombs of brass are spent.

The poet explains that his repeated words of love and praise are like daily prayer; though old, they are always new. True love is also always new, though the lover and the beloved may age.

1. **character:** write, inscribe
2. **figured:** portrayed, represented
3. **register:** record
5. **prayers divine:** probable allusion to the Anglican matins and evensong (morning and evening prayer) prescribed for daily reciting from the Book of Common Prayer
7. **no old thing old:** i.e., **no** familiar or often-repeated **thing** as worn out or stale
8. **hallowed:** made holy (Scholars link this line with the Lord's Prayer's "**hallowed** be Thy **name**" [Matthew 6.9].)
9. **So that:** i.e., in the same way; **case:** wordplay on (1) condition; (2) covering (as in the **case** of a book, or as in skin or clothing)
10. **Weighs not:** does not take into account
11. **gives . . . place:** i.e., yields to (or pays attention to) inevitable **wrinkles**
12. **for aye his page:** i.e., forever his servant (Several words connected with books—**page, case,** and **dust**—continue in ll. 9–12 the theme of the poet and his writing from ll. 1–8.)
13. **conceit:** understanding, idea; **there bred:** i.e., (still) being **bred there**
14. **would show it:** i.e., try to make it appear

108

What's in the brain that ink may character
Which hath not figured to thee my true spirit?
What's new to speak, what now to register,
That may express my love or thy dear merit? 4
Nothing, sweet boy; but yet, like prayers divine,
I must each day say o'er the very same,
Counting no old thing old, thou mine, I thine,
Even as when first I hallowed thy fair name. 8
So that eternal love in love's fresh case
Weighs not the dust and injury of age,
Nor gives to necessary wrinkles place,
But makes antiquity for aye his page, 12
    Finding the first conceit of love there bred,
    Where time and outward form would show it dead.

The poet defends his infidelities, arguing that his return washes away the blemish of his having left.

2. **my flame to qualify:** to diminish my passion

3. **depart:** separate, divide (with wordplay on "go away from")

5. **ranged:** wandered, strayed

7. **Just to the time:** i.e., exactly on **time; with the time exchanged:** i.e., changed by this interval

8. **myself . . . stain:** To "wash a **stain**" meant to remove a moral blemish. (Booth attacks the logic of the poet's excuse: "water can wash away a stain, but the periodic returns of a promiscuous lover do not wash away the crime of his infidelities.")

10. **all . . . blood:** i.e., every sort of temperament

11. **preposterously:** perversely, unnaturally

12. **nothing:** a thing or person not worth considering

14. **Save:** i.e., except for; **it:** i.e., the **universe**

A motley fool. (s. 110.2)

109

O, never say that I was false of heart,
Though absence seemed my flame to qualify;
As easy might I from myself depart
As from my soul, which in thy breast doth lie.   4
That is my home of love. If I have ranged,
Like him that travels I return again,
Just to the time, not with the time exchanged,
So that myself bring water for my stain.   8
Never believe, though in my nature reigned
All frailties that besiege all kinds of blood,
That it could so preposterously be stained
To leave for nothing all thy sum of good.   12
    For nothing this wide universe I call,
    Save thou, my rose; in it thou art my all.

The poet confesses to having been unfaithful to the beloved, but claims that his straying has rejuvenated him and made the beloved seem even more godlike.

---

2. **made . . . view:** i.e., played the fool, made a fool of myself   **motley:** i.e., motley fool (one dressed in the parti-colored clothing of the professional or theatrical Fool [See picture, p. 224.])   **to the view:** i.e., in the public eye

3. **Gored:** wounded; made filthy (with wordplay on *to gore* as "to make clothing parti-colored through the use of different colored gores or triangular patches")

4. **Made . . . new:** i.e., turned **new** loves into **old offenses** (perhaps, occasions for customary infidelity)

5. **truth:** constancy, veracity

6. **Askance:** sidewise (in scorn or contempt); **strangely:** coldly (like a stranger)

7. **blenches:** sideways glances; **gave . . . youth:** i.e., rejuvenated **my heart**

8. **worse essays:** i.e., experiments with the inferior

9. **have . . . end:** i.e., accept that which is undying

10. **grind:** sharpen (as in the metaphor "to whet or sharpen the **appetite**")

11. **proof:** experiment, experience; **try:** test; afflict

12. **in love:** i.e., in the capacity to love; **to . . . confined:** i.e., **to whom I** confine myself

13. **next . . . best:** i.e., **the best** (refuge, comfort) short of **heaven**

110

Alas, 'tis true, I have gone here and there
And made myself a motley to the view,
Gored mine own thoughts, sold cheap what is
     most dear,
Made old offenses of affections new.   4
Most true it is that I have looked on truth
Askance and strangely; but by all above,
These blenches gave my heart another youth,
And worse essays proved thee my best of love.   8
Now all is done, have what shall have no end.
Mine appetite I never more will grind
On newer proof, to try an older friend,
A god in love, to whom I am confined.   12
   Then give me welcome, next my heaven the best,
   Even to thy pure and most most loving breast.

In this first of two linked poems, the poet blames Fortune for putting him in a profession that led to his bad behavior, and he begs the beloved to punish him and to pity him.

---

1. **for . . . chide:** i.e., **chide** the **goddess Fortune** on my behalf (**Fortune** allotted good and bad luck.)
2. **guilty goddess of:** i.e., **goddess** responsible for
4. **public . . . breeds:** Editors generally read this line in terms of Shakespeare's life and suggest that he is here blaming his **public** life in the theater for whatever misdeeds or common behavior he is acknowledging in this group of sonnets.
5. **Thence:** from there; **brand:** mark of disgrace
6–7. **almost . . . To:** i.e., **my nature** is **almost** overpowered by
7. **like . . . hand:** i.e., as **the dyer's hand** is stained by the dye
8. **renewed:** regenerated, rejuvenated
10. **eisel:** vinegar; **'gainst:** i.e., to fight (This line may refer to the concoction of vinegar sometimes prescribed for the bubonic plague.)
11. **No:** i.e., there is no
12. **Nor:** i.e., **nor** will I consider **bitter** (l. 11); **double penance:** repeated or second punishment
13. **ye:** a form of *you*, here used in the singular
14. **Even that your pity:** i.e., **your pity** alone

111

O, for my sake do you ⌜with⌝ Fortune chide,
The guilty goddess of my harmful deeds,
That did not better for my life provide
Than public means which public manners breeds.   4
Thence comes it that my name receives a brand;
And almost thence my nature is subdued
To what it works in, like the dyer's hand.
Pity me, then, and wish I were renewed,   8
Whilst, like a willing patient, I will drink
Potions of eisel 'gainst my strong infection;
No bitterness that I will bitter think,
Nor double penance, to correct correction.   12
    Pity me, then, dear friend, and I assure ye
    Even that your pity is enough to cure me.

The pity asked for in s. 111 has here been received, and the poet therefore has no interest in others' opinions of his worth or behavior.

---

1. **impression:** indentation
2. **vulgar scandal:** public disgrace; base rumor; **stamped . . . brow:** Disgrace or rumor here becomes a branding iron that marks the poet as a felon. **brow:** forehead
3. **well or ill:** i.e., good or bad
4. **So you o'ergreen:** perhaps, as long as you cover over; **allow:** commend; grant
7. **to me:** i.e., is **alive to me**
8. **steeled sense:** hardened sensibility; **or changes right or wrong:** i.e., alters either to the good or to the bad (Editors agree that something like this is what these words may mean. See note to l. 14 below.)
9. **so:** such a
9–10. **care / Of:** concern with; consideration of
10. **adder's sense:** i.e., hearing (Proverbial: "Deaf as an adder.")
11. **critic:** faultfinder; **stoppèd are:** i.e., is closed
12. **neglect:** indifference; **dispense:** excuse
14. **besides:** i.e., other than you; **methinks:** it seems to me (This line and ll. 7 and 8 have led Booth to speculate that Shakespeare left this sonnet in an unfinished state. See Booth, pp. 364–70.)

112

Your love and pity doth th' impression fill
Which vulgar scandal stamped upon my brow;
For what care I who calls me well or ill,
So you o'ergreen my bad, my good allow?   4
You are my all the world, and I must strive
To know my shames and praises from your tongue;
None else to me, nor I to none alive,
That my steeled sense or changes right or wrong.   8
In so profound abysm I throw all care
Of others' voices that my adder's sense
To critic and to flatterer stoppèd are.
Mark how with my neglect I do dispense: 12
    You are so strongly in my purpose bred
    That all the world besides methinks ⌈are⌉ dead.

In this first of two linked sonnets, the poet confesses that everything he sees is transformed into an image of the beloved.

---

1. **mine . . . mind:** i.e., I see with **my** mind's **eye** (my imagination)
2. **that which governs:** i.e., the **eye** that guides
3. **Doth part his:** i.e., divides its (As ll. 5ff. explain, the **eye,** while continuing to see that which is exterior, fails to carry that image to the mind.)
4. **seeing:** i.e., to see; **effectually:** in fact; **out:** extinguished (The classical notion that the eye emits rays or beams of light was still generally believed.)
5. **form:** image, representation; **heart:** mind (For a similar use of **heart** to mean "mind," see, e.g., s. 46.10, where thoughts are called "tenants to the **heart.**")
6. **doth latch:** i.e., catches sight of
7. **his quick:** i.e., its (the eye's) quickly fleeting
8. **his . . . holds:** i.e., does its (the eye's) **own vision** retain
9. **rud'st:** roughest, coarsest; **gentlest:** tenderest
10. **sweet favor:** pleasant face (though Q's *sweet-favor* may have been a misprint for *sweet-favored,* in which case the compound would modify **creature**)
12. **shapes . . . feature:** turns them **to your** form
13. **Incapable of:** unable to receive or contain
14. **true:** loyal (though not reliable or truthful)

113

Since I left you, mine eye is in my mind,
And that which governs me to go about
Doth part his function, and is partly blind,
Seems seeing, but effectually is out;   4
For it no form delivers to the heart
Of bird, of flower, or shape which it doth ⌜latch;⌝
Of his quick objects hath the mind no part,
Nor his own vision holds what it doth catch.   8
For if it see the rud'st or gentlest sight,
The most sweet favor or deformèd'st creature,
The mountain or the sea, the day or night,
The crow or dove, it shapes them to your feature.   12
   Incapable of more, replete with you,
     My most true mind thus maketh mine ⌜eye⌝ untrue.

In a continuation of s. 113, the poet debates whether the lovely images of the beloved are true or are the mind's delusions, and he decides on the latter.

---

1. **Or whether doth:** The construction that begins with **Or whether** and continues with its repetition in l. 3 is best understood today by (1) taking l. 1 as beginning with **doth** and (2) omitting **whether** from l. 3. (**Doth my mind . . . , Or shall I . . . ?**)

2. **this flattery:** i.e., the gratifying delusions spelled out in s. 113.9–12 (with wordplay on **flattery** as insincere adulation given, e.g., to monarchs)

4. **your love:** i.e., my **love** for you; **alchemy:** power of transforming the base into the golden

5. **of monsters:** i.e., from unnatural creatures; **indigest:** shapeless, crude

6. **cherubins:** one of the second order of angels

7. **Creating:** i.e., making (from)

8. **to his beams assemble:** i.e., come within its (the eye's) gaze **beams:** eyebeams (See note to s. 113.4.)

9. **'tis flattery . . . seeing:** i.e., my eyes are deluding me (See l. 2 and note.)

11. **his gust:** i.e., its (the mind's) taste; **is greeing:** accords or agrees

12. **to his:** i.e., to suit its

13–14. **If . . . begin:** The image is of the eye as the kingly mind's taster; since the **poisoned cup** of flatteringly deceptive images is also loved by the eye/taster, the mind's (or the poet's) **sin** is lessened.

114

Or whether doth my mind, being crowned with you,
Drink up the monarch's plague, this flattery?
Or whether shall I say mine eye saith true,
And that your love taught it this alchemy, 4
To make of monsters and things indigest
Such cherubins as your sweet self resemble,
Creating every bad a perfect best
As fast as objects to his beams assemble? 8
O, 'tis the first: 'tis flattery in my seeing,
And my great mind most kingly drinks it up.
Mine eye well knows what with his gust is greeing,
And to his palate doth prepare the cup. 12
   If it be poisoned, 'tis the lesser sin
   That mine eye loves it and doth first begin.

The poet acknowledges that the very fact that his love has grown makes his earlier poems about the fullness and constancy of his love into lies.

1. **before have writ:** i.e., have written earlier
2. **Even:** precisely
4. **flame:** i.e., of love; **clearer:** more intensely
5. **reckoning time:** i.e., **Time,** which counts, or which settles up accounts (though possibly, instead, "considering what **time** can do"); **millioned:** counted in the millions; **accidents:** events; mishaps
6. **'twixt vows:** i.e., between making a promise and keeping it
7. **Tan:** turn into leather, turn brown; **sacred beauty:** i.e., **beauty** that should be inviolable
8. **course of alt'ring things:** (1) direction that changing **things** take; (2) current of changing situations (Lines 5–8 do not make a sentence. If, as has been suggested, **Divert** is an error for *Diverts*, the resulting sentence would read "... **time** ... diverts. ...")
9. **fearing of:** i.e., **fearing**
10. **then:** at that time
11. **o'er incertainty:** over uncertainty, i.e., beyond doubt
12. **Crowning the present:** i.e., making **the present** supreme; **rest:** remainder (of time), future
13. **Love:** i.e., Cupid, represented as **a babe** (See picture, p. 318.) **Then might I not:** i.e., therefore **I might not; say so:** i.e., say "**Now I love you best**"

115

Those lines that I before have writ do lie,
Even those that said I could not love you dearer;
Yet then my judgment knew no reason why
My most full flame should afterwards burn clearer.   4
But reckoning time, whose millioned accidents
Creep in 'twixt vows and change decrees of kings,
Tan sacred beauty, blunt the sharp'st intents,
Divert strong minds to th' course of alt'ring things—   8
Alas, why, fearing of time's tyranny,
Might I not then say "Now I love you best,"
When I was certain o'er incertainty,
Crowning the present, doubting of the rest?   12
   Love is a babe. Then might I not say so,
    To give full growth to that which still doth grow.

The poet here meditates on what he sees as the truest and strongest kind of love, that between minds. He defines such a union as unalterable and eternal.

---

1. **Let me not:** i.e., may I never
2. **Admit impediments:** wordplay on the **marriage** service in the Book of Common Prayer, where **impediments** ("obstacles" to, "just causes" impeding) the legality of the marriage are to be admitted (i.e., "confessed"), while in the sonnet, the word **impediments** (the "millioned accidents" of s. 115.5) suggests instead "impedimenta," things that impede or encumber progress, and **admit** means "concede the existence of" (with additional wordplay on "receive as valid or lawful or compatible with," "allow of the presence of," and "allow to enter")
4. **bends:** turns aside from its true course; **the remover:** i.e., (1) that which separates, takes away; (2) he or she who departs or disappears
5. **mark:** i.e., seamark (a lighthouse or beacon)
7. **the star:** i.e., the polestar or Polaris, used as a fixed point in navigation; **wand'ring bark:** lost ship
8. **worth's unknown:** i.e., value is (1) not mentally apprehended; (2) not attainable through inquiry; **his . . . taken:** i.e., its altitude be measured
11. **his:** i.e., its (**Time's**)
12. **bears it out:** endures; **doom:** i.e., Doomsday
13. **error:** (1) a fault in a legal judgment or the process to that judgment; (2) false belief; **proved:** demonstrated (to be **error**)

116

Let me not to the marriage of true minds
Admit impediments. Love is not love
Which alters when it alteration finds
Or bends with the remover to remove.   4
O, no, it is an ever-fixèd mark
That looks on tempests and is never shaken;
It is the star to every wand'ring bark,
Whose worth's unknown, although his height be taken. 8
Love's not Time's fool, though rosy lips and cheeks
Within his bending sickle's compass come;
Love alters not with his brief hours and weeks,
But bears it out even to the edge of doom.   12
   If this be error, and upon me proved,
   I never writ, nor no man ever loved.

In this first of a group of four sonnets of self-accusation and of attempts at explanation, the poet lists the charges that can be made against him, and then says he was merely testing the beloved's love.

1. **Accuse me thus:** i.e., indict me on the following charges (This courtroom language is continued in **Book . . . down, proof,** and **appeal.**)

2. **Wherein:** by which; **your . . . repay:** i.e., recompense **your great** worthiness or excellence

3. **upon . . . to call:** i.e., **to** invoke or appeal to **your dearest love**

4. **Whereto:** to which

5. **frequent been with:** i.e., **been** familiar or often in company **with; unknown minds:** i.e., strangers

6. **given to time:** i.e., wasted

8. **should:** i.e., would

9. **Book . . . down:** i.e., write **down,** record **errors:** wordplay on "mistakes" and "wanderings"

10. **on . . . accumulate:** i.e., **on** top of reliable **proof** (of my misdeeds) pile up conjecture

11. **level:** aim, line of fire

13. **appeal:** i.e., attempt to have the inevitable (negative) decision against me reversed; **did . . . prove:** i.e., was (simply) trying to test

14. **virtue:** goodness; strength

240

117

Accuse me thus: that I have scanted all
Wherein I should your great deserts repay,
Forgot upon your dearest love to call,
Whereto all bonds do tie me day by day;   4
That I have frequent been with unknown minds,
And given to time your own dear-purchased right;
That I have hoisted sail to all the winds
Which should transport me farthest from your sight.   8
Book both my willfulness and errors down,
And on just proof surmise accumulate;
Bring me within the level of your frown,
But shoot not at me in your wakened hate,   12
    Since my appeal says I did strive to prove
    The constancy and virtue of your love.

In this second sonnet of self-accusation, the poet uses analogies of eating and of purging to excuse his infidelities.

---

1. **Like as:** in the same way **as; appetites:** (1) craving for food; (2) lusts

2. **eager:** pungent; **urge:** stimulate

3. **As:** i.e., (and) just **as; prevent:** forestall, head off; **unseen:** i.e., not (yet) in evidence

4. **sicken:** i.e., make ourselves sick; **purge:** take drugs to empty the stomach or bowels

5. **Even so:** just **so**

6. **frame my feeding:** i.e., fashion my diet

7. **welfare:** doing (or being) well; **meetness:** appropriateness, suitableness

8. **To be:** i.e., in being; **needing:** need or want

9. **policy:** cunning, craftiness; **anticipate:** forestall

10. **faults assured:** i.e., real illnesses or disorders

12. **rank of:** overfed with; **ill:** badness; sickness

13. **thence:** i.e., from this experience

118

Like as to make our appetites more keen
With eager compounds we our palate urge;
As to prevent our maladies unseen
We sicken to shun sickness when we purge;   4
Even so, being full of your ne'er-cloying sweetness,
To bitter sauces did I frame my feeding;
And, sick of welfare, found a kind of meetness
To be diseased ere that there was true needing.   8
Thus policy in love, t' anticipate
The ills that were not, grew to faults assured,
And brought to medicine a healthful state
Which, rank of goodness, would by ill be cured.   12
    But thence I learn, and find the lesson true:
    Drugs poison him that so fell sick of you.

Filled with self-disgust at having subjected himself to so many evils in the course of his infidelity, the poet nevertheless finds an excuse in discovering that his now reconstructed love is stronger than it was before.

---

1. **siren:** Sirens were fabulous creatures (part woman, part bird, though also often identified with mermaids) whose singing lured sailors to destruction. See longer note, p. 330.

2. **limbecks:** alembics (See picture, p. 246.)

3. **Applying:** administering (as a remedy)

4. **Still:** always, constantly

5. **errors:** sins; mistakes

6. **so blessèd never:** i.e., blessed to an unlimited degree

7. **out . . . fitted:** wordplay on **eyes** (1) convulsed in their sockets by the fits of disease and (2) removed from their proper **spheres** (like stars or planets in the Ptolemaic system, and like men in their proper social **spheres**)

8. **distraction:** temporary madness; **madding:** i.e., delirium-producing

9. **ill:** evil

10. **still made better:** (1) **made** yet **better;** (2) always **made better**

11–12. **ruined . . . greater:** Proverbial: "A broken bone is the stronger when it is well set." **ruined love:** i.e., **love** like a building in ruins

13. **my content:** i.e., that which contents me

14. **ills:** i.e., **wretched errors** (l. 5)

119

What potions have I drunk of siren tears
Distilled from limbecks foul as hell within,
Applying fears to hopes and hopes to fears,
Still losing when I saw myself to win! 4
What wretched errors hath my heart committed,
Whilst it hath thought itself so blessèd never!
How have mine eyes out of their spheres been fitted
In the distraction of this madding fever! 8
O, benefit of ill! Now I find true
That better is by evil still made better;
And ruined love, when it is built anew,
Grows fairer than at first, more strong, far greater. 12
　So I return rebuked to my content,
　And gain by ills thrice more than I have spent.

In this fourth sonnet about his unkindness to the beloved, the poet comforts himself with the memory of the time the beloved was unkind to him.

2. **for:** because of, in exchange for
3. **Needs must:** of necessity, necessarily
4. **nerves:** sinews, tendons
7. **leisure:** opportunity
8. **in your crime:** i.e., as a result of your offense
9. **remembered:** reminded
11. **And . . . tendered:** i.e., so that I would quickly have offered (**tendered**) **you as you then** offered **me**
12. **humble salve:** i.e., healing ointment of humility (presumably, an apology); **fits:** befits
13. **that your trespass:** i.e., **that trespass** (i.e., **crime**) of yours; **fee:** payment
14. **ransoms:** pays for; **ransom:** redeem

Alchemy with her alembics. (s. 119.2)

120

That you were once unkind befriends me now,
And for that sorrow which I then did feel
Needs must I under my transgression bow,
Unless my nerves were brass or hammered steel.   4
For if you were by my unkindness shaken
As I by yours, you've passed a hell of time,
And I, a tyrant, have no leisure taken
To weigh how once I suffered in your crime.   8
O, that our night of woe might have remembered
My deepest sense how hard true sorrow hits,
And soon to you as you to me then tendered
The humble salve which wounded bosoms fits!   12
   But that your trespass now becomes a fee;
   Mine ransoms yours, and yours must ransom me.

The poet responds to slurs about his behavior by claiming that he is no worse (and is perhaps better) than his attackers.

1. **'Tis . . . esteemed:** This line extends and twists the proverb "There is small difference to the eye of the world in being nought (i.e., **vile**) and in being thought so."

2. **be:** i.e., **be (vile)**

3. **just pleasure:** i.e., (1) the **pleasure** that would have inhered in actually **being vile;** or (2) innocent **pleasure; so deemed:** i.e., **deemed vile**

4. **by others' seeing:** i.e., how others regard it

5. **adulterate:** corrupted; adulterous

6. **Give . . . to:** i.e., greet (as if in fellowship); **sportive blood:** i.e., lively (or amorous) nature

7. **are:** i.e., are there; **frailer:** morally weaker

8. **Which:** who; **in their wills:** i.e., willfully

9. **I . . . am:** i.e., I stand by my own actions and character (When Moses asks God's name, God responds with these words [Exodus 3.14].) **level:** aim; guess

11. **straight:** honest; **bevel:** i.e., dishonest (literally, oblique)

12. **By:** in terms of; **rank:** lustful; corrupt; **shown:** exhibited, displayed

13. **maintain:** assert

121

'Tis better to be vile than vile esteemed,
When not to be receives reproach of being,
And the just pleasure lost, which is so deemed
Not by our feeling but by others' seeing.   4
For why should others' false adulterate eyes
Give salutation to my sportive blood?
Or on my frailties why are frailer spies,
Which in their wills count bad what I think good?   8
No, I am that I am; and they that level
At my abuses reckon up their own.
I may be straight though they themselves be bevel;
By their rank thoughts my deeds must not be shown,   12
   Unless this general evil they maintain:
   All men are bad and in their badness reign.

This sonnet addresses the hard question of why the poet has given away the beloved's gift of a writing tablet. After several stumbling tries, the poet ends by claiming that for him to have kept the tables would have implied that he needed help in remembering the unforgettable beloved.

1. **tables:** i.e., writing tablet (probably the kind of tablet described by Peter Stallybrass and Roger Chartier as one or more pieces of coated vellum or paper, folded and stitched and sometimes elegantly bound, the coating allowing the vellum or paper to be written on with a stylus and then erased with a moistened cloth or by scraping)

2. **Full charactered:** fully inscribed or written

3. **idle rank:** perhaps (1) insignificant kind of object (the **tables** themselves); (2) trifling series or list (as were often, in printed form, bound with the **tables**)

6. **faculty:** physical capability, power

7. **razed oblivion:** i.e., **oblivion** that erases, obliterates; **his:** its

8. **record:** memory; writing; **missed:** lost, missing

9. **retention:** capacity for holding something (presumably referring to the **tables**)

10. **tallies:** pieces of wood on which to keep records; **score:** record (by cutting) (Both **tallies** and **score** would support the idea that these **tables** were the kind described in note 1, above, on which records were inscribed and then scraped away.)

11. **give . . . me:** i.e., **give** away the **tables**

13. **adjunct:** something connected but subordinate

14. **Were to import:** i.e., would be to imply

122

Thy gift, thy tables, are within my brain
Full charactered with lasting memory,
Which shall above that idle rank remain
Beyond all date, even to eternity—   4
Or, at the least, so long as brain and heart
Have faculty by nature to subsist;
Till each to razed oblivion yield his part
Of thee, thy record never can be missed.   8
That poor retention could not so much hold,
Nor need I tallies thy dear love to score;
Therefore to give them from me was I bold,
To trust those tables that receive thee more.   12
　　To keep an adjunct to remember thee
　　Were to import forgetfulness in me.

The poet repeats an idea from s. 59—that there is nothing new under the sun—and accuses Time of tricking us into perceiving things as new only because we live for such a short time. He reasserts his vow to remain constant despite Time's power.

---

2. **pyramids . . . might:** i.e., recently built spires, obelisks, or pinnacles (all of which resemble the great **pyramids** from ancient Egypt)

4. **dressings:** i.e., dressed-up versions; **a former sight:** i.e., something seen before

5. **Our dates are:** i.e., the term of (human) life is

5–6. **admire / . . . old:** i.e., wonder at some **old** thing that you (i.e., **Time**) fraudulently present (as new)

7. **make . . . desire:** i.e., consider these as objects created just for us

8. **before . . . told:** i.e., have heard about **them before**

9. **Thy registers and thee:** i.e., **Time** and its chronicles or records

10. **wond'ring at:** marveling over

11. **For . . . lie:** i.e., because Time's **records** (accent on the second syllable) and perceived experience are both liars

12. **Made more or less:** exaggerated and diminished; **thy . . . haste:** i.e., "swift-footed **Time**" (s. 19.6)

14. **true:** constant, unchanging; **scythe:** See note to s. 12.13.

123

No, Time, thou shalt not boast that I do change.
Thy pyramids built up with newer might
To me are nothing novel, nothing strange;
They are but dressings of a former sight.   4
Our dates are brief, and therefore we admire
What thou dost foist upon us that is old,
And rather make them born to our desire
Than think that we before have heard them told.   8
Thy registers and thee I both defy,
Not wond'ring at the present nor the past;
For thy records and what we see doth lie,
Made more or less by thy continual haste.   12
  This I do vow, and this shall ever be:
  I will be true despite thy scythe and thee.

In this difficult and much-discussed sonnet, the poet declares the permanence and wisdom of his love.

1. **my dear love:** i.e., the precious **love** that I feel; **were . . . state:** i.e., had been produced by circumstances (or by the beloved's privileged status)
2. **for:** i.e., as; **fortune's bastard:** i.e., offspring of whimsical forces; **unfathered:** made illegitimate, deprived of a father (and hence without support)
3. **time's . . . hate:** the favor or disfavor (1) of the present age, or (2) of Time
4. **Weeds . . . gathered:** (1) consigned to live among **weeds** or **gathered** into a bouquet; or (2) subject to a short, uncertain life, either as weed or flower
5. **it was builded:** i.e., **my love was** built; **accident:** i.e., (the forces of) chance or fortune
6. **suffers not in:** i.e., is not affected by
7. **thrallèd:** servile, enslaving
8. **our fashion calls:** i.e., (1) summons that which goes in and out of **fashion;** (2) bids the merely fashionable
9. **policy:** expediency; **heretic:** perhaps, heretical doctrine or practice
10. **on . . . hours:** i.e., as if on short-term contracts
11. **politic:** wise, judicious
12. **That it nor:** i.e., so **that it** neither
13. **I witness call:** i.e., **I call** as witnesses
13–14. **fools . . . crime:** a much-debated reference; perhaps "time-servers who repent at the last minute," or, perhaps "martyrs who **die for** their faith, despising that which is temporal and accused of criminal beliefs"

124

If my dear love were but the child of state,
It might for fortune's bastard be unfathered,
As subject to time's love or to time's hate,
Weeds among weeds, or flowers with flowers gathered. 4
No, it was builded far from accident;
It suffers not in smiling pomp, nor falls
Under the blow of thrallèd discontent,
Whereto th' inviting time our fashion calls. 8
It fears not policy, that heretic
Which works on leases of short-numbered hours,
But all alone stands hugely politic,
That it nor grows with heat nor drowns with showers. 12
    To this I witness call the fools of time,
      Which die for goodness who have lived for crime.

The poet, in apparent response to accusation, claims that his love (and, perhaps, his poetry of praise) is not basely motivated by desire for outward honor.

1. **Were 't aught:** i.e., would it matter; **I bore the canopy:** i.e., if I were publicly honored by serving majesty (It was a high honor to hold **the canopy** over the head of the dignitary at a public ceremony.)

2. **extern, outward:** external appearance, exterior

3. **great bases:** massive foundations; **for eternity:** to last forever (with wordplay on "to enshrine **eternity**")

4. **proves:** i.e., prove; **short:** short-lived; **waste:** destruction, decay

5. **dwellers on:** i.e., those who fix their attention on (with wordplay on "inhabitants," continued in l. 6 with **rent**)

7. **compound sweet:** i.e., **sweet** compounds

8. **Pitiful thrivers:** i.e., pathetic successes; **spent:** destroyed; used up

9. **obsequious . . . heart:** i.e., privately attentive

10. **oblation:** offering, gift

11. **seconds:** inferior stuff; **art:** artifice; skill

13. **suborned:** i.e., corrupt (The informant here abjured is apparently someone who claimed that the poet's attachment to [or verse in praise of] the beloved was basely motivated.)

14. **impeached:** discredited; **control:** power

125

Were 't aught to me I bore the canopy,
With my extern the outward honoring,
Or laid great bases for eternity,
Which proves more short than waste or ruining?   4
Have I not seen dwellers on form and favor
Lose all and more by paying too much rent,
For compound sweet forgoing simple savor,
Pitiful thrivers, in their gazing spent?   8
No, let me be obsequious in thy heart,
And take thou my oblation, poor but free,
Which is not mixed with seconds, knows no art
But mutual render, only me for thee.   12
    Hence, thou suborned informer; a true soul
    When most impeached stands least in thy control.

The poet acknowledges that the beloved young man grows lovelier with time, as if Nature has chosen him as her darling, but warns him that her protection cannot last forever—that eventually aging and death will come. (See longer note, pp. 330–31.)

---

1. **lovely:** lovable; beautiful
2. **glass:** hourglass (with its constantly flowing sand); **his sickle hour:** i.e., the **hour** when **Time's sickle** cuts down the living (See note to s. 12.13.)
3. **by waning grown:** i.e., become more lovely while aging; **show'st:** serve to exhibit or indicate
4. **Thy lover's:** i.e., the poet's (The 1609 Quarto's *louers* can also be read as "lovers" or "lovers'." In any of these renderings, the word can refer to paramour[s], friend[s], or "he/those who love you.")
5. **mistress over wrack:** ruler over decay
6. **onwards:** i.e., toward death; **still will:** i.e., continues to; **pluck:** pull, draw
7. **keeps:** holds onto; **to this:** i.e., for the following
8. **disgrace:** put to shame by outdoing; **wretched minutes kill:** i.e., destroy even the insignificant units of Time
9. **her:** Nature; **minion:** (1) darling; (2) servant
10. **still:** always, forever
11. **Her audit:** i.e., the accounting that Nature must render (to Time); **answered:** satisfied
12. **quietus:** clearing of accounts (with wordplay on its meaning as "death, or that which brings death"); **render:** (1) relinquish, surrender; (2) give back

126

O thou, my lovely boy, who in thy power
Dost hold Time's fickle glass, his sickle hour;
Who hast by waning grown, and therein show'st
Thy lover's withering as thy sweet self grow'st.   4
If Nature, sovereign mistress over wrack,
As thou goest onwards still will pluck thee back,
She keeps thee to this purpose, that her skill
May Time disgrace, and wretched ⌜minutes⌝ kill.   8
Yet fear her, O thou minion of her pleasure!
She may detain, but not still keep, her treasure.
Her audit, though delayed, answered must be,
And her quietus is to render thee.   12

The poet defends his love of a mistress who does not meet the conventional standard of beauty by claiming that her dark eyes and hair (and, perhaps, dark skin) are the new standard. The old version of beauty—blond hair and light skin—are so readily counterfeited that beauty in that form is no longer trusted.

---

1. **old age:** i.e., past; **black . . . fair:** wordplay on a set of meanings of both **black** and **fair** (**Fair** had long meant "beautiful," and had more recently come also to mean "blond-haired" and/or "light-skinned." **Black,** in reference to a person, meant "dark-skinned" and/or "having dark hair and eyes.")

2. **bore . . . name:** i.e., wasn't called "beauty" (with wordplay on **name** as a sign of legitimate birth)

3. **successive:** legitimate

4. **a bastard shame:** i.e., the **shame** of being (1) illegitimate, or (2) counterfeit, spurious

5. **put on:** assumed (with wordplay on "putting on makeup" or "donning a wig")

6. **Fairing:** beautifying; **art's:** artifice's

7. **hath no name:** i.e., has been bastardized

8. **But is profaned:** i.e., **beauty** has been desecrated, violated (because artificial **beauty** calls all **beauty** into question)

9. **Therefore . . . eyes:** i.e., because of this, (1) I have chosen a mistress whose **eyes;** or (2) my mistress has chosen **eyes** which; **raven black:** Proverbial: "**Black** as a **raven.**"

10. **eyes:** The repetition of **eyes** in ll. 9 and 10 leads many editors to emend to "brows" in l. 9 or 10. While the repetition is arguably a mistake, it is not clear which line is in error. **so suited, and:** i.e., **so** attired that

(continued)

127

In the old age, black was not counted fair,
Or, if it were, it bore not beauty's name;
But now is black beauty's successive heir,
And beauty slandered with a bastard shame.   4
For since each hand hath put on nature's power,
Fairing the foul with art's false borrowed face,
Sweet beauty hath no name, no holy bower,
But is profaned, if not lives in disgrace.   8
Therefore my mistress' eyes are raven black,
Her eyes so suited, and they mourners seem
At such who, not born fair, no beauty lack,
Sland'ring creation with a false esteem.   12
   Yet so they mourn, becoming of their woe,
   That every tongue says beauty should look so.

11. **At such:** i.e., at the behavior of those; **fair:** (1) beautiful; (2) blond and white-skinned; **no beauty lack:** i.e., make themselves beautiful (and white-skinned) artificially

12. **creation:** nature, natural **beauty; with . . . esteem:** i.e., by deeming it artificial

13. **so they mourn:** i.e., the way her eyes **mourn; becoming of:** i.e., so lovely in

The language of this sonnet is remarkably like that of Berowne's speeches in praise of Rosaline in *Love's Labor's Lost.* Having described her (3.1.206–7) as "a whitely [i.e., fair-skinned] wanton with a velvet brow, / With two pitch-balls stuck in her face for eyes," in 4.3 he responds to the King's "thy love is black as ebony" (267) by exclaiming

> Where is a book,
> That I may swear beauty doth beauty lack
> If that she learn not of her eye to look?
> No face is fair that is not full so black. . . .
> O, if in black my lady's brows be decked,
> It mourns that painting and usurping hair
> Should ravish doters with a false aspect:
> And therefore is she born to make black fair.
> Her favor turns the fashion of the days,
> For native blood [i.e., a naturally rosy
> complexion] is counted painting now.
> And therefore red [i.e., rosiness], that would avoid
> dispraise,
> Paints itself black to imitate her brow.
> (270–73, 278–85)

127

In the old age, black was not counted fair,
Or, if it were, it bore not beauty's name;
But now is black beauty's successive heir,
And beauty slandered with a bastard shame.   4
For since each hand hath put on nature's power,
Fairing the foul with art's false borrowed face,
Sweet beauty hath no name, no holy bower,
But is profaned, if not lives in disgrace.   8
Therefore my mistress' eyes are raven black,
Her eyes so suited, and they mourners seem
At such who, not born fair, no beauty lack,
Sland'ring creation with a false esteem.   12
   Yet so they mourn, becoming of their woe,
   That every tongue says beauty should look so.

This sonnet uses the conventional poetic idea of the poet envying an object being touched by the beloved. Here, the object is the keyboard of an instrument.

---

1. **oft:** often
2. **wood:** i.e., the keys of a virginal (a keyboard instrument in which the musician's fingers hitting the keys causes the strings to be plucked); **whose motion:** i.e., the movement of which; **sounds:** resounds; causes to sound (See picture, p. 284.)
3. **thou . . . sway'st:** you . . . control or wield
4. **concord:** harmony; **confounds:** overcomes
5. **jacks:** i.e., keys (The **jacks,** in fact, pluck the strings, but here the word is presumably used to mean the entire keyboard mechanism.)
8. **by:** i.e., beside
9. **tickled:** *To tickle* is "to play a keyboard instrument" and "to give pleasure or excitement."
9–10. **state / And situation:** status and location
13. **saucy jacks:** a phrase that meant "impudent fellows," here with the obvious wordplay; **happy:** fortunate; delighted

128

How oft, when thou, my music, music play'st
Upon that blessèd wood whose motion sounds
With thy sweet fingers when thou gently sway'st
The wiry concord that mine ear confounds, 4
Do I envy those jacks that nimble leap
To kiss the tender inward of thy hand,
Whilst my poor lips, which should that harvest reap,
At the wood's boldness by thee blushing stand. 8
To be so tickled they would change their state
And situation with those dancing chips,
O'er whom ⌈thy⌉ fingers walk with gentle gait,
Making dead wood more blest than living lips. 12
   Since saucy jacks so happy are in this,
   Give them ⌈thy⌉ fingers, me thy lips to kiss.

This sonnet describes what Booth calls "the life cycle of lust"—a moment of bliss preceded by madness and followed by despair.

---

1. **expense:** expenditure, using up; **spirit:** vital power; the vital **spirit** (thought to emanate from the heart and transform into clear bodily fluids such as semen), with possible wordplay on spiritual essence; **waste of shame:** i.e., shameful squandering (though with wordplay on **waste** as desert, or as common land, and on **shame** as disgrace, or guilt)

3. **full of blame:** culpable, blameworthy

4. **rude:** violent; **to trust:** i.e., to be trusted

5. **straight:** immediately (See Ben Jonson's translation of a poem by Petronius: "Doing, a filthy pleasure is, and short; / And done, we **straight** repent us of the sport.")

7–8. **as . . . mad:** In *Measure for Measure*, Claudio thus explains his sexual relations with Juliet: "Our natures do pursue, / Like rats that raven down [i.e., devour] their proper bane, / A thirsty evil, and when we drink, we die" (1.2.125–27).

11. **in proof:** i.e., in the experience itself; being tried; **proved:** i.e., having been tried or tested

12. **Before:** in prospect; **behind:** in retrospect; **a dream:** i.e., insubstantial, delusive (Tarquin, the rapist in *The Rape of Lucrece,* asks himself before the rape "What win I if I gain the thing I seek? / **A dream,** a breath, a froth of fleeting joy. / Who buys a minute's mirth to wail a week? / Or sells eternity to get a toy?" [211–14].)

266

129

Th' expense of spirit in a waste of shame
Is lust in action; and, till action, lust
Is perjured, murd'rous, bloody, full of blame,
Savage, extreme, rude, cruel, not to trust; 4
Enjoyed no sooner but despisèd straight;
Past reason hunted, and no sooner had,
Past reason hated as a swallowed bait
On purpose laid to make the taker mad. 8
⌐Mad¬ in pursuit and in possession so;
Had, having, and in quest to have, extreme;
A bliss in proof and ⌐proved a¬ very woe;
Before, a joy proposed; behind, a dream. 12
⠀⠀All this the world well knows, yet none knows well
⠀⠀To shun the heaven that leads men to this hell.

This sonnet plays with poetic conventions in which, for example, the mistress's eyes are compared with the sun, her lips with coral, and her cheeks with roses. (See picture, p. 312.) His mistress, says the poet, is nothing like this conventional image, but is as lovely as any woman.

3. **If snow be white:** Proverbial: "As **white** as **snow.**"

4. **wires:** The comparison of golden hair to gold wire (threads of beaten gold, used in embroidery and jewelry) dated back to the thirteenth century.

5. **roses damasked:** Ingram and Redpath note Barnabe Barnes's "Her cheeks to damask roses sweet / In scent and colour were so like, / That honey bees in swarms would meet / To suck!"

8. **reeks:** emanates (This word was somewhat more neutral in its connotations than it is today.)

11. **go:** walk (In *Venus and Adonis,* when Venus walks "The grass stoops not, she treads on it so light" [l. 1028].)

14. **she:** woman; **belied:** misrepresented, lied about; **false compare:** feigned or mendacious comparisons

130

My mistress' eyes are nothing like the sun;
Coral is far more red than her lips' red;
If snow be white, why then her breasts are dun;
If hairs be wires, black wires grow on her head.   4
I have seen roses damasked, red and white,
But no such roses see I in her cheeks;
And in some perfumes is there more delight
Than in the breath that from my mistress reeks.   8
I love to hear her speak, yet well I know
That music hath a far more pleasing sound.
I grant I never saw a goddess go;
My mistress, when she walks, treads on the ground.   12
    And yet, by heaven, I think my love as rare
    As any she belied with false compare.

The poet disagrees with those who say that his mistress is not beautiful enough to make a lover miserable. He groans for her as for any beauty. Only her behavior, he says, is ugly.

---

1. **so as thou art:** i.e., just **as** you are

2. **proudly . . . cruel:** Both pride and cruelty were attributes of the beautiful mistress of love poetry.

3. **dear:** wordplay on "loving" and "lovingly"; **doting:** infatuated; foolish

6. **groan:** That the lover should **groan** was a commonplace of the tradition. When surrendering to Cupid in *Love's Labor's Lost,* Berowne says "Well, I will love, write, sigh, pray, sue, **groan**" (3.1.214).

7. **say:** i.e., publicly assert

9. **to be sure:** i.e., as an assurance (that) (Booth: "in order to verify [that]," "to testify [that]"); **that . . . swear:** i.e, **that** what **I swear is not false**

10. **thinking on:** i.e., **thinking** of or about

11. **One on another's neck: one** after another

12. **black, fairest:** See notes to s. 127, esp. lines from *Love's Labor's Lost.*

13–14. **In . . . proceeds:** Booth calls this couplet "a single graceful razor stroke" that cuts the mistress apart. (Berowne, too, accuses Rosaline of being "the worst of all, . . . one that will do the deed / Though Argus were her eunuch and her guard" [*LLL* 3.1.205, 208–9]. The play does not support his accusation.) **black:** foul, iniquitous   **this slander:** i.e., the accusation in l. 6

131

Thou art as tyrannous, so as thou art,
As those whose beauties proudly make them cruel;
For well thou know'st to my dear doting heart
Thou art the fairest and most precious jewel.   4
Yet in good faith some say that thee behold,
Thy face hath not the power to make love groan;
To say they err I dare not be so bold,
Although I swear it to myself alone.   8
And, to be sure that is not false I swear,
A thousand groans, but thinking on thy face,
One on another's neck do witness bear
Thy black is fairest in my judgment's place.   12
    In nothing art thou black save in thy deeds,
    And thence this slander as I think proceeds.

The poet begs the mistress to model her heart after her eyes, which, because they are black as if dressed in mourning, show their pity for his pain as a lover.

---

1. **as:** i.e., **as** if

2. **torment:** i.e., torments (The words **pitying, torment, disdain,** and **pain** [ll. 1–4] recall the medieval love tradition in which the hard-hearted mistress looks with scorn upon the heart-struck lover. In *As You Like It,* the meeting of such a lover and his "proud disdainful" mistress is described as "a pageant truly played / Between the pale complexion of true love / And the red glow of scorn and proud **disdain**" (3.4.48, 51–53).

3. **Have ... be:** See s. 127.9–10, where the mistress's dark **eyes** are described as dressed in mourning.

4. **ruth:** compassion, pity

6. **Better becomes:** i.e., is more becoming to

7. **that full star:** i.e., Venus, called Hesperus when it ushers in the **even** (i.e., evening)

8. **sober:** solemn; subdued or muted in color

10. **as well:** i.e., just **as** properly; **beseem:** suit, fit (often applied to a person's appearance or clothing)

11. **mourning:** wordplay on (1) grieving; (2) wearing black as a sign of grief

12. **suit:** dress; **like:** i.e., the same way

13–14. **Then ... lack:** See notes to s. 127.

132

Thine eyes I love, and they, as pitying me,
Knowing thy heart torment me with disdain,
Have put on black, and loving mourners be,
Looking with pretty ruth upon my pain.   4
And truly not the morning sun of heaven
Better becomes the gray cheeks of the east,
Nor that full star that ushers in the even
Doth half that glory to the sober west   8
As those two mourning eyes become thy face.
O, let it then as well beseem thy heart
To mourn for me, since mourning doth thee grace,
And suit thy pity like in every part.   12
    Then will I swear beauty herself is black,
    And all they foul that thy complexion lack.

In this first of two linked sonnets, the pain felt by the poet as lover of the mistress is multiplied by the fact that the beloved friend is also enslaved by her.

---

1. **Beshrew:** a mild oath (literally, "curse")

2. **my friend and me:** It has been suggested that this sonnet and those linked to it were written at the same time as ss. 40–42, which are addressed to the **friend** seduced by the poet's mistress. (See s. 42.7–8.)

3. **torture:** torment (See note to s. 132.2.) **me alone:** i.e., just me

4. **to slavery:** i.e., to demeaning servitude (an extreme name for the abject situation of the obsessed lover)

6. **next:** i.e., nearest, closest (For the **friend** as the poet's other **self,** see, e.g., s. 62.13.) **harder:** more cruelly; **engrossed:** monopolized; possessed

7. **Of:** i.e., by

8. **crossed:** thwarted (with wordplay on "barred or precluded [from something desired]")

9. **Prison:** i.e., imprison

10. **bail:** confine (though at first reading the word appears to mean "free by becoming bail or security")

11. **keeps:** holds as prisoner; **guard:** guardroom; protector

12. **rigor:** harshness

13. **pent:** confined, imprisoned

14. **Perforce:** of necessity

133

Beshrew that heart that makes my heart to groan
For that deep wound it gives my friend and me.
Is 't not enough to torture me alone,
But slave to slavery my sweet'st friend must be?   4
Me from myself thy cruel eye hath taken,
And my next self thou harder hast engrossed;
Of him, myself, and thee I am forsaken,
A torment thrice threefold thus to be crossed.   8
Prison my heart in thy steel bosom's ward,
But then my friend's heart let my poor heart bail.
Whoe'er keeps me, let my heart be his guard;
Thou canst not then use rigor in my jail.   12
    And yet thou wilt, for I, being pent in thee,
    Perforce am thine, and all that is in me.

The poet continues to rationalize the young man's betrayal, here using language of debt and forfeit.

1. **now:** i.e., **now** that
2. **mortgaged:** pledged (The word picks up the meaning of "bail" as "security" in s. 133.10. For the set of financial/legal terms used in this poem—**forfeit, surety-like, bond, statute, usurer, sue, debtor**—see longer note, pp. 331–32.) **will:** intention; carnal desire
3. **forfeit:** pay as fine or penalty; **so:** in order that; on the condition that; **that other mine:** See s. 133.6 ("my next self") and note.
5. **will not be:** i.e., does not wish to be
7–8. **He . . . bind:** i.e., he signed a **bond** for me merely as my guarantor, but he is now bound as tightly by it as I
9. **statute . . . take:** i.e., you will **take** (everything allowed by) the **statute** your **beauty** enables (As Booth explains, **beauty** is a **bond** in that it is binding; a **bond** is often a **statute;** hence the wordplay: "**statute of thy beauty.**")
10. **put'st . . . use:** wordplay on "lay out for profit **all** your land or money" and "offer **all** of yourself for sexual purposes" **to:** i.e., for   **use:** See notes to ss. 2.9, 4.7, and 6.5.
11. **sue:** i.e., **(wilt) sue** (wordplay on "make a legal claim on" and "woo"); **came:** i.e., who became a
12. **my . . . abuse:** (1) my ill-usage (of my friend); (2) your mistreatment of me
14. **the whole:** i.e., the entire (sexual) debt

134

So, now I have confessed that he is thine
And I myself am mortgaged to thy will,
Myself I'll forfeit, so that other mine
Thou wilt restore to be my comfort still.   4
But thou wilt not, nor he will not be free,
For thou art covetous, and he is kind;
He learned but surety-like to write for me
Under that bond that him as fast doth bind.   8
The statute of thy beauty thou wilt take,
Thou usurer that put'st forth all to use,
And sue a friend came debtor for my sake;
So him I lose through my unkind abuse.   12
   Him have I lost; thou hast both him and me.
   He pays the whole, and yet am I not free.

In this first of two linked sonnets, the poet apparently begs his (promiscuous) mistress to allow him back into her bed.

---

1. **Whoever:** i.e., whatever (woman); **will:** Proverbial: "Women will have their wills." Wordplay on **will** dominates this and the following sonnet. For background on that wordplay, and for possible meanings of the word throughout these two sonnets, see longer note, pp. 332–33.

2. **to boot:** in addition; **overplus:** surplus

9. **sea . . . rain:** Proverbial: "**The sea** refuses no river." See also Ecclesiastes 1.7: "All the rivers run into **the sea,** yet **the sea** is not full."

10. **his store:** i.e., its **abundance**

13. **unkind:** perhaps, (1) **unkind** (person), or (2) unkindness; **fair:** handsome, honorable; **beseechers:** suitors, suppliants

14. **all but one:** i.e., **all** (of the **beseechers** and their **wills**) as only **one** lover; **me:** i.e., include me

135

Whoever hath her wish, thou hast thy will,
And will to boot, and will in overplus.
More than enough am I that vex thee still,
To thy sweet will making addition thus.   4
Wilt thou, whose will is large and spacious,
Not once vouchsafe to hide my will in thine?
Shall will in others seem right gracious,
And in my will no fair acceptance shine?   8
The sea, all water, yet receives rain still,
And in abundance addeth to his store;
So thou, being rich in will, add to thy will
One will of mine to make thy large will more.   12
    Let no unkind, no fair beseechers kill.
    Think all but one, and me in that one will.

In this second sonnet built around wordplay on the word *will,* the poet continues to plead for a place among the mistress's lovers.

1–3. **If . . . there:** For the relationship between the **soul** and the **will,** and for meanings of **will** in this sonnet, see longer note to s. 135.1, pp. 332–33. **check:** rebuke **come so near:** (1) approach you physically; (2) talk so bluntly **blind soul:** perhaps a reference to the belief that since the Rational Soul discerns the good through the light of Reason, if Reason is disabled, the **soul** is, in effect, **blind And will:** a specific quibble on (1) the faculty of the **will** as part of the Rational Soul, and (2) the poet's name **admitted:** (1) acknowledged; (2) allowed entrance

4. **for love:** i.e., out of charity

5. **treasure:** i.e., treasure chest

7. **In . . . receipt:** wordplay on **receipt** as a receptacle, as capacity, as size, and as amount (as of a sum received) **things:** As with **will,** the word *thing* was a slang term for both the penis and the vagina.

8. **Among . . . none:** i.e., **one** is insignificant when part of a large **number** (with wordplay on the proverb "**One** is no **number**"—see note to s. 8.14)

9. **number:** i.e., crowd (of lovers); **untold:** uncounted (i.e., as if I were **none**)

10. **thy store's account:** i.e., inventory of your accumulated possessions (See s. 135.9–12.)

11. **For:** i.e., as; **hold me:** consider me; **so:** i.e., **so** long as

12. **nothing me:** i.e., **nothing** (which is) **me**

13. **thy love:** i.e., that which you most desire

280

136

If thy soul check thee that I come so near,
Swear to thy blind soul that I was thy will,
And will, thy soul knows, is admitted there.
Thus far for love my love-suit, sweet, fulfill.   4
Will will fulfill the treasure of thy love,
Ay, fill it full with wills, and my will one.
In things of great receipt with ease we prove
Among a number one is reckoned none.   8
Then in the number let me pass untold,
Though in thy store's account I one must be.
For nothing hold me, so it please thee hold
That nothing me, a something, sweet, to thee.   12
    Make but my name thy love, and love that still,
    And then thou lovest me, for my name is Will.

The poet asks why both his eyes and his heart have fastened on a woman neither beautiful nor chaste.

---

1. **blind . . . Love:** "**Love** looks not with the **eyes** but with the mind; / And therefore is winged Cupid painted **blind**" (*A Midsummer Night's Dream* 1.1.240–41.) See picture below.

3. **lies:** resides

5. **corrupt:** i.e., corrupted; **overpartial:** unduly partial, biased

6. **ride:** (1) lie at anchor; (2) copulate

9. **that:** i.e., **that** place; **a several plot:** i.e., a privately owned piece of land

10. **knows:** i.e., **knows** to be; **common place:** i.e., land held in **common,** open to the community

11. **seeing this:** i.e., recognizing **this** truth (with wordplay on **seeing**)

12. **To put:** i.e., in order **to put**

13–14. **In . . . transferred:** These lines answer the questions posed in ll. 1–12. **false plague:** i.e., affliction of falseness **transferred:** handed over

Blind Cupid. (s. 137.1)

137

Thou blind fool, Love, what dost thou to mine eyes
That they behold and see not what they see?
They know what beauty is, see where it lies,
Yet what the best is take the worst to be.   4
If eyes, corrupt by overpartial looks,
Be anchored in the bay where all men ride,
Why of eyes' falsehood hast thou forgèd hooks,
Whereto the judgment of my heart is tied?   8
Why should my heart think that a several plot
Which my heart knows the wide world's common place?
Or mine eyes, seeing this, say this is not,
To put fair truth upon so foul a face?   12
   In things right true my heart and eyes have erred,
   And to this false plague are they now transferred.

The poet describes a relationship built on mutual deception that deceives neither party: the mistress claims constancy and the poet claims youth.

1. **love:** lover, mistress
3. **That:** i.e., so **that; untutored:** unsophisticated
4. **Unlcarnèd:** unskilled
5. **vainly:** fruitlessly; foolishly; conceitedly
7. **Simply:** i.e., like a simpleton; **credit:** trust
8. **suppressed:** hidden; not expressed
9. **wherefore:** why; **unjust:** faithless, dishonest
11. **habit:** (1) clothing, attire; (2) way of behaving
12. **age in love:** i.e., the infatuated elderly; **told:** (1) counted out; (2) spoken about
13. **lie with:** (1) make love with; (2) **lie** to
14. **in our faults:** i.e., through our failings and offenses; **flattered:** gratified; beguiled

A woman playing a virginal. (s. 128)

138

When my love swears that she is made of truth
I do believe her though I know she lies,
That she might think me some untutored youth,
Unlearnèd in the world's false subtleties.   4
Thus vainly thinking that she thinks me young,
Although she knows my days are past the best,
Simply I credit her false-speaking tongue;
On both sides thus is simple truth suppressed.   8
But wherefore says she not she is unjust?
And wherefore say not I that I am old?
O, love's best habit is in seeming trust,
And age in love loves not to have years told.   12
    Therefore I lie with her and she with me,
    And in our faults by lies we flattered be.

The poet, after refusing to make excuses for the mistress's wrongs, begs her not to flirt with others in his presence. He then excuses that wrong, only to ask her to direct her eyes against him as if they were mortal weapons.

---

1. **call not me:** i.e., do not ask me
4. **power with power:** i.e., your **power** strongly; **art:** cunning, artfulness
5. **elsewhere:** i.e., someone else
6. **glance thine eye:** turn your gaze
7. **What:** i.e., why; **might:** strength, **power** (l. 4)
8. **o'erpressed:** too burdened, overwhelmed; **bide:** withstand
9. **excuse thee:** i.e., **justify the wrong** (l. 1)
10. **looks:** glances
11. **my foes:** i.e., her eyes
13. **near:** almost
14. **Kill . . . looks:** a cliché in love poetry (Spenser's *Amoretti* 10 speaks of "the huge massacres which her eyes do make," and 49 asks "Is it because your eyes have power to kill?"); also, an allusion to mythological creatures (like the basilisk) whose looks could kill (See picture below.) **rid:** remove

A basilisk. (s. 139.14)

139

O, call not me to justify the wrong
That thy unkindness lays upon my heart;
Wound me not with thine eye but with thy tongue;
Use power with power, and slay me not by art.   4
Tell me thou lov'st elsewhere; but in my sight,
Dear heart, forbear to glance thine eye aside.
What need'st thou wound with cunning when thy might
Is more than my o'erpressed defense can bide?   8
Let me excuse thee: ah, my love well knows
Her pretty looks have been mine enemies;
And therefore from my face she turns my foes,
That they elsewhere might dart their injuries.   12
    Yet do not so; but since I am near slain,
      Kill me outright with looks, and rid my pain.

The poet warns the mistress that she would be wiser to pretend to love him and thus avoid driving him into a despair that would no longer hold its tongue.

---

1. **wise as:** i.e., as **wise as**

1–2. **press . . . patience:** i.e., put too much pressure on my patient silence (with an allusion to the method of torture in which the body of a prisoner who refused to speak was crushed under a mass of stone until he or she spoke or died [See picture below.])

4. **manner:** state of the case; **pity-wanting:** i.e., (1) unpitied; (2) pity-desiring

5. **wit:** i.e., the prudent way to proceed

6. **not to love:** i.e., you don't love me; **so:** i.e., that you do (love me)

7. **As:** i.e., just **as**

10. **speak ill of:** i.e., say ugly things about

11. **ill-wresting:** i.e., twisting (words) adversely

13. **so:** slanderous; **belied:** (1) slandered; (2) called false

14. **go wide:** i.e., go astray (a term from archery)

Torture by pressing. (s. 140.1–2)

140

Be wise as thou art cruel; do not press
My tongue-tied patience with too much disdain,
Lest sorrow lend me words, and words express
The manner of my pity-wanting pain.   4
If I might teach thee wit, better it were,
Though not to love, yet, love, to tell me so,
As testy sick men, when their deaths be near,
No news but health from their physicians know.   8
For if I should despair, I should grow mad,
And in my madness might speak ill of thee.
Now this ill-wresting world is grown so bad,
Mad slanderers by mad ears believèd be.   12
   That I may not be so, nor thou belied,
   Bear thine eyes straight, though thy proud heart
     go wide.

The poet describes his heart as going against his senses and his mind in its determination to love.

1. **In faith:** i.e., truly
2. **errors:** wordplay on (1) flaws; (2) wrongdoings
4. **Who . . . view:** i.e., which in spite of what the eyes see; **is pleased:** chooses; deigns; is happy; **dote:** (1) love excessively; (2) be deranged
5. **Nor:** neither
6. **tender feeling:** In *Love's Labor's Lost* 4.3.331–32, Berowne, describing the senses of the lover, says of the sense of touch: "Love's **feeling** is more soft and sensible / Than are the **tender** horns of cockled snails." **base:** degrading, low
7. **Nor:** i.e., **nor** does
8. **sensual feast:** i.e., **feast** of the senses; **alone:** exclusively
9. **But my:** i.e., **But** neither **my; five wits:** i.e., the imagination, common wit (i.e., common sense), fantasy, estimation, memory (Burton reduces such **wits** to three and describes them, along with the **five** [outward] **senses,** as part of the Sensible Soul, which is seated in the brain [*Anatomy of Melancholy*, 1.1.2.6–7].)
11. **Who . . . unswayed:** i.e., which **leaves** without a ruler or governor
12. **Thy:** i.e., in order thy
13. **my plague:** (1) the sickness of love; (2) the mistress; **count:** consider
14. **awards me pain:** (1) legally determines my punishment; (2) i.e., puts me in hell

141

In faith, I do not love thee with mine eyes,
For they in thee a thousand errors note;
But 'tis my heart that loves what they despise,
Who in despite of view is pleased to dote.   4
Nor are mine ears with thy tongue's tune delighted,
Nor tender feeling to base touches prone,
Nor taste, nor smell, desire to be invited
To any sensual feast with thee alone.   8
But my five wits nor my five senses can
Dissuade one foolish heart from serving thee,
Who leaves unswayed the likeness of a man,
Thy proud heart's slave and vassal wretch to be.   12
    Only my plague thus far I count my gain,
    That she that makes me sin awards me pain.

The poet accuses the woman of scorning his love not out of virtue but because she is busy making adulterous love elsewhere.

---

1. **Love:** i.e., **love** of you; **sin:** See s. 141.14. **virtue:** i.e., (1) chastity; (2) essential nature
2. **sinful loving:** perhaps, (1) my **sinful** love for you; or, perhaps, (2) your **sinful loving** (ll. 5–8)
3. **but:** only, merely
4. **it:** i.e., my **own state**
6. **profaned their scarlet ornaments:** Her **lips** are here treated as if somehow holy in their redness.
7. **sealed . . . love:** i.e., kissed others illicitly
8. **Robbed:** i.e., and **robbed; others' . . . rents:** i.e., the **beds** of other women of the pleasures and offspring that marriage grants them **revenues:** profits (accent on second syllable) **rents:** i.e., sexual dues (literally, fees paid by tenants)
9. **Be . . . I:** i.e., let it **be lawful** for me to; **as:** (1) in the same way that; (2) while
11. **Root pity:** i.e., implant **pity** deeply (**Pity** in the medieval love tradition referred to the lady's granting the lover her favors.)
12. **Thy pity:** i.e., your pitiable condition
13. **to have . . . hide:** i.e., to receive **pity** when you yourself refuse to **pity** (continuing the wordplay on **pity** as sexual favors and as compassion)
14. **By . . . be:** i.e., (I hope that) your own example will cause you to be

142

Love is my sin, and thy dear virtue hate,
Hate of my sin, grounded on sinful loving.
O, but with mine compare thou thine own state,
And thou shalt find it merits not reproving.   4
Or if it do, not from those lips of thine,
That have profaned their scarlet ornaments
And sealed false bonds of love as oft as mine,
Robbed others' beds' revenues of their rents.   8
Be it lawful I love thee as thou lov'st those
Whom thine eyes woo as mine importune thee;
Root pity in thy heart, that, when it grows,
Thy pity may deserve to pitied be.   12
    If thou dost seek to have what thou dost hide,
    By self-example mayst thou be denied.

The poet expands on s. 142.9–10 (where he pursues a mistress who pursues others) by presenting a picture of a woman who chases a barnyard fowl while her infant chases after her.

---

1. **careful:** heedful, attentive; anxious, distressed; **huswife:** housewife (pronounced "hussif")
2. **broke:** i.e., that has broken
3. **swift dispatch:** i.e., haste, speed
4. **pursuit:** accent on first syllable
5. **holds her in chase:** i.e., chases her
6–7. **bent / To follow:** i.e., intent on following
7. **flies:** flees (with wordplay on the fowl's attempts at flight)
11. **thy hope:** i.e., what you hope for
12. **be kind:** wordplay on showing maternal kindness and granting sexual favors
13. **will:** See longer note to s. 135.1, pp. 332–33. (This line has led some commentators to believe that "the young man" was also named William.)
14. **still:** soothe, pacify

143

Lo, as a careful huswife runs to catch
One of her feathered creatures broke away,
Sets down her babe, and makes all swift dispatch
In pursuit of the thing she would have stay,   4
Whilst her neglected child holds her in chase,
Cries to catch her whose busy care is bent
To follow that which flies before her face,
Not prizing her poor infant's discontent;   8
So runn'st thou after that which flies from thee,
Whilst I, thy babe, chase thee afar behind.
But if thou catch thy hope, turn back to me
And play the mother's part: kiss me, be kind.   12
 So will I pray that thou mayst have thy will,
 If thou turn back and my loud crying still.

The poet's three-way relationship with the mistress and the young man is here presented as an allegory of a person tempted by a good and a bad angel.

---

1. **loves:** objects of love; beloveds; **comfort:** support; delight; solace

2. **suggest me still:** i.e., constantly prompt me

3. **better angel:** This phrase suggests that the **spirits** are "good" and "bad" angels such as those in Marlowe's *Doctor Faustus,* where the good **angel** continually urges the hero toward a virtuous life and the bad **angel** encourages choices that lead to hell.

4. **colored ill:** i.e., dark (See notes to s. 127.)

5–8. **To . . . pride:** This version of the temptation has the "bad angel" proceeding only indirectly against the "hero" by tempting his "good angel" to desert him and become evil.   **foul pride:** evil allure

9. **whether:** i.e., **whether** it is the case

10. **directly:** rightly; immediately

11. **being . . . me:** i.e., since **both** are away **from me; to each friend:** i.e., (**both**) friends **to each** other

12. **hell:** Editors propose a reference to a couples' game called "barley break," which includes an area called "**hell,**" but the allegorical/theological language of the poem and the links to such scenes as those in *Doctor Faustus* make it more likely that the term refers to more than a party game.

14. **fire . . . out:** i.e., drive **my good one out** with flames, with probable allusion to (1) infection with venereal disease and (2) the flames of **hell**

144

Two loves I have, of comfort and despair,
Which like two spirits do suggest me still.
The better angel is a man right fair,
The worser spirit a woman colored ill.   4
To win me soon to hell my female evil
Tempteth my better angel from my ⌐side,⌐
And would corrupt my saint to be a devil,
Wooing his purity with her foul pride.   8
And whether that my angel be turned fiend
Suspect I may, yet not directly tell;
But being both from me, both to each friend,
I guess one angel in another's hell.   12
    Yet this shall I ne'er know, but live in doubt,
    Till my bad angel fire my good one out.

In this sonnet, perhaps written when Shakespeare was very young, the poet plays with the difference between the words "I hate" and "I hate not you." (Note that the lines of the sonnet are in tetrameter instead of pentameter.)

1. **Love's:** The reference could be to Venus, goddess of love, or to Cupid, her son.
3. **her:** i.e., the woman whose **lips** said **"I hate"**
5. **Straight in:** wordplay on "directly into" and "immediately into"
7. **used in:** (1) employed in; (2) accustomed to; **doom:** sentence, judgment
11. **who:** i.e., which
13. **from hate:** i.e., from hatred (i.e., she separated the words **"I hate"** from any intention of hating) See longer note on **hate away,** pp. 333–34.
14. **saying:** i.e., adding the words

Cupid torturing a lover.

145

Those lips that Love's own hand did make
Breathed forth the sound that said "I hate"
To me that languished for her sake;
But when she saw my woeful state,   4
Straight in her heart did mercy come,
Chiding that tongue that ever sweet
Was used in giving gentle doom,
And taught it thus anew to greet: 8
"I hate" she altered with an end
That followed it as gentle day
Doth follow night, who, like a fiend,
From heaven to hell is flown away.   12
    "I hate" from hate away she threw,
    And saved my life, saying "not you."

The poet here meditates on the soul and its relation to the body, in life and in death.

---

1. **Poor:** wordplay on (1) unfortunate; (2) ill-fed; (3) poverty-stricken; **earth:** i.e., body (See Genesis 2.7: "And the Lord God formed man of the dust of the ground, and breathed into his nostrils the breath of life; and man became a living **soul.**")

2. **Pressed with:** i.e., assailed by, beset by (See longer note, p. 334, and also note to s. 140.1–2.) **rebel powers:** i.e., the body and the passions, which refuse to be governed by the **soul; array:** (1) afflict, trouble; (2) clothe; (3) defile

4. **outward walls:** i.e., body; **costly:** sumptuously; **gay:** outwardly attractive, showy

5. **so . . . cost:** i.e., such a **large** outlay; **having:** i.e., since you have

6. **thy fading mansion:** The word **mansion** was often used for the body as the enclosure for the **soul.**

7. **excess:** wordplay on (1) extravagance; (2) intemperance in eating and drinking

8. **Eat up thy charge:** wordplay on literal and figurative meanings of **eat up** (i.e., consume) and on **thy charge** as (1) your outlay; (2) that which has been entrusted to you; (3) that which burdens you; **end:** fate; purpose; termination

9. **live thou upon:** (1) subsist on; (2) gain eternal life through; **servant's:** i.e., body's

10. **that:** i.e., the servant; **aggravate:** increase

11. **terms divine:** i.e., eternity (literally, **divine** portions of time)

146

Poor soul, the center of my sinful earth,
⌜Pressed with⌝ these rebel powers that thee array,
Why dost thou pine within and suffer dearth,
Painting thy outward walls so costly gay?   4
Why so large cost, having so short a lease,
Dost thou upon thy fading mansion spend?
Shall worms, inheritors of this excess,
Eat up thy charge? Is this thy body's end?   8
Then, soul, live thou upon thy servant's loss,
And let that pine to aggravate thy store.
Buy terms divine in selling hours of dross;
Within be fed, without be rich no more.   12
    So shalt thou feed on Death, that feeds on men,
    And Death once dead, there's no more dying then.

The poet describes his love for the lady as a desperate sickness.

1. **still:** constantly, incessantly
2. **longer nurseth:** i.e., prolongs
3. **ill:** sickness, **disease;** disaster, calamity
4. **uncertain:** unreliable; **sickly appetite:** word-play on (1) wish for food by someone in ill-health; (2) unhealthy (sexual) will or **desire** (l. 8) (For "will" and "**reason**" [l. 5], see longer note to s. 135.1, pp. 332–33.)
6. **prescriptions:** instructions; restrictions
7. **desperate:** (1) in despair; (2) given up as hopeless; **approve:** (1) demonstrate (that); (2) find through experience (that)
8. **physic:** i.e., (reason's) medicine; **except:** protest against, object to (The phrase **which physic did except** describes reason's opposition to **desire,** with possible wordplay that allows **which** to refer to **death,** so that the phrase would also describe medicine's operation against **death.**)
9. **past care:** i.e., (1) **past** caring (about my condition); (2) no longer taking **care** of me
10. **evermore:** i.e., constant
11. **discourse:** speech
12. **At random:** i.e., (varying) haphazardly; **vainly:** i.e., (and) senselessly, thoughtlessly
13–14. **fair, black, dark:** See notes to s. 127 and s. 131.13–14. **bright:** beautiful, splendid (a word often associated with Lucifer, brightest of the angels, who, when cast from heaven, became Satan)

147

My love is as a fever, longing still
For that which longer nurseth the disease,
Feeding on that which doth preserve the ill,
Th' uncertain sickly appetite to please.   4
My reason, the physician to my love,
Angry that his prescriptions are not kept,
Hath left me, and I desperate now approve
Desire is death, which physic did except.   8
Past cure I am, now reason is past care,
And, frantic-mad with evermore unrest,
My thoughts and my discourse as madmen's are,
At random from the truth vainly expressed.   12
   For I have sworn thee fair, and thought thee bright,
   Who art as black as hell, as dark as night.

The poet once again (as in ss. 113, 114, 137, and 141) questions his own eyesight. Here, he describes his eyes' image of his mistress as in conflict with his judgment and with the views of the world in general.

---

1. **eyes:** i.e., kind of **eyes; love:** Here, as throughout the sonnet, there is wordplay on **love** as (1) desire, affection; (2) Cupid or Venus; and, in l. 13, (3) the mistress.

4. **censures:** estimates, judges

5. **false:** deceitful, treacherous; **dote:** bestow excessive love

7. **denote:** indicate (that)

8. **eye:** with a pun on "ay" (Q's punctuation ["all mens: no,"] gives a reading of the line in which "no" means "no, it is not" and in which the pun almost disappears. Some editors retain Q's colon.)

10. **vexed with watching:** distressed by wakefulness

11. **though:** if; **mistake my view:** (1) i.e., see wrongly; (2) misinterpret what I see

12. **heaven clears:** i.e., the sky is free of clouds

148

O me, what eyes hath love put in my head,
Which have no correspondence with true sight!
Or if they have, where is my judgment fled,
That censures falsely what they see aright?   4
If that be fair whereon my false eyes dote,
What means the world to say it is not so?
If it be not, then love doth well denote
Love's eye is not so true as all men's "no."   8
How can it? O, how can love's eye be true,
That is so vexed with watching and with tears?
No marvel then though I mistake my view;
The sun itself sees not till heaven clears.   12
    O cunning love, with tears thou keep'st me blind,
    Lest eyes well-seeing thy foul faults should find.

The poet argues that he has proved his love for the lady by turning against himself when she turns against him.

---

2. **with thee partake:** i.e., take your side

3. **on:** i.e., about

3–4. **forgot . . . of:** i.e., have forgotten

7. **thou lour'st on:** i.e., you scowl at; **spend:** i.e., mete out, take (literally, expend, employ)

8. **present moan:** immediate suffering

10. **so proud . . . despise:** i.e., **so** arrogant or presumptuous as to **despise** being in your **service** (i.e., being the "servant" of Love or of the lady)

11. **defect:** insufficiency, imperfection

12. **Commanded:** controlled, dominated; **motion:** prompting, bidding

14. **blind:** i.e., blinded to the lady's faults (and, Evans suggests, hence of less interest to the lady than **those** who **can see,** and are thus more of a challenge)

149

Canst thou, O cruel, say I love thee not
When I against myself with thee partake?
Do I not think on thee when I forgot
Am of myself, all, tyrant, for thy sake? 4
Who hateth thee that I do call my friend?
On whom frown'st thou that I do fawn upon?
Nay, if thou lour'st on me, do I not spend
Revenge upon myself with present moan? 8
What merit do I in myself respect
That is so proud thy service to despise,
When all my best doth worship thy defect,
Commanded by the motion of thine eyes? 12
   But, love, hate on, for now I know thy mind;
   Those that can see thou lov'st, and I am blind.

The sonnet begins with the poet's questioning why he should love what he knows he should hate; it ends with his claim that this love of her unworthiness should cause the lady to love him.

2. **With insufficiency:** See s. 149.11.

3. **give . . . sight:** i.e., accuse **my true sight** of lying

4. **grace:** add splendor to, adorn

5. **becoming . . . things:** i.e., power of beautifying evil **things**

6. **refuse . . . deeds:** i.e., worst actions   **refuse:** scum, dregs, rubbish

7. **warrantise:** guarantee, assurance

12. **With . . . abhor:** i.e., you should not join **others** in loathing (Booth suggests, in **abhor,** wordplay on *whore* in both ll. 11 and 12.) **state:** condition (mental and emotional)

14. **worthy:** wordplay on (1) deserving of esteem (since I am magnanimous enough to love an unworthy person); (2) merited, fitting (since my love for an unworthy person shows my unworthiness)

150

O, from what power hast thou this powerful might
With insufficiency my heart to sway?
To make me give the lie to my true sight,
And swear that brightness doth not grace the day?   4
Whence hast thou this becoming of things ill,
That in the very refuse of thy deeds
There is such strength and warrantise of skill
That in my mind thy worst all best exceeds?   8
Who taught thee how to make me love thee more,
The more I hear and see just cause of hate?
O, though I love what others do abhor,
With others thou shouldst not abhor my state.   12
　　If thy unworthiness raised love in me,
　　More worthy I to be beloved of thee.

The poet displays the sexually obsessive nature of his love.

1–2. **Love . . . love:** wordplay on **love** as (1) the boy-god Cupid; (2) sexual passion; and on **conscience** as (1) the knowledge of right and wrong; (2) inward consciousness (Also at play are the Latin tag "Penis erectus non habet conscientiam" [i.e.,"an erection has no **conscience**"] and the platitude that love ennobles the lover.)

3. **cheater:** (1) deceiver; (2) escheator, or assessor, demanding forfeits from those who have defaulted from their obligations (Evans); **urge . . . amiss:** (1) i.e., do not charge me with misdeeds; (2) do not provoke me to commit misdeeds

5. **betraying me:** (1) revealing my faults; (2) seducing me

6. **nobler part:** i.e., mind or **soul** (l. 7); **gross:** sensual (though also "unrefined, coarse")

7. **he:** i.e., it

8. **stays:** i.e., awaits, waits for

9. **rising at thy name:** As Booth notes, the overt reference is to sexual erection, but the metaphor is that of conjuring spirits—i.e., compelling the spirit to rise through the repetition of names.

10. **his:** i.e., its; **Proud, pride:** Both **proud** and **pride** were used in relation to tumescence and lust.

11. **He:** i.e., it

(continued)

151

Love is too young to know what conscience is;
Yet who knows not conscience is born of love?
Then, gentle cheater, urge not my amiss,
Lest guilty of my faults thy sweet self prove.   4
For, thou betraying me, I do betray
My nobler part to my gross body's treason.
My soul doth tell my body that he may
Triumph in love; flesh stays no farther reason,   8
But, rising at thy name, doth point out thee
As his triumphant prize. Proud of this pride,
He is contented thy poor drudge to be,
To stand in thy affairs, fall by thy side.   12
   No want of conscience hold it that I call
   Her "love," for whose dear love I rise and fall.

12. **To . . . side:** The overt reference is sexual, but, as Booth notes, the metaphor is of the knight or soldier who stands beside his king or comrade and is ready to fight to the death (i.e., **fall by** the **side**) of the one he is protecting.

13. **want:** lack

"My mistress' eyes are nothing like the sun. . . ."
(s. 130)

151

Love is too young to know what conscience is;
Yet who knows not conscience is born of love?
Then, gentle cheater, urge not my amiss,
Lest guilty of my faults thy sweet self prove.　　　　4
For, thou betraying me, I do betray
My nobler part to my gross body's treason.
My soul doth tell my body that he may
Triumph in love; flesh stays no farther reason,　　　　8
But, rising at thy name, doth point out thee
As his triumphant prize. Proud of this pride,
He is contented thy poor drudge to be,
To stand in thy affairs, fall by thy side.　　　　12
　　No want of conscience hold it that I call
　　Her "love," for whose dear love I rise and fall.

The poet turns his accusations against the woman's inconstancy and oath-breaking against himself, accusing himself of deliberate blindness and perjury.

1. **I am forsworn:** I have broken an oath

3. **In act:** through action (specifically, sexual activity, as often in Shakespeare); **thy bed-vow broke:** i.e., having broken your marriage vow; **new faith torn:** i.e., having breached a **new** pledge or promise

4. **bearing:** entertaining, cherishing

6. **perjured:** forsworn, guilty of oath-breaking

7. **misuse:** This word could mean, among other things, "revile," "deceive," and "misrepresent." Lines 9–14 suggest that "misrepresent" is the primary meaning here.

8. **honest faith:** i.e., integrity; **in thee:** i.e., in (loving) you; because of you

9. **oaths of:** i.e., **oaths** asserting, affirming (as also in l. 10)

11. **enlighten thee:** i.e., to make you luminous (with wordplay on *light* as "fair" [and therefore as "beautiful"]); **eyes:** i.e., my **eyes**

12. **against the thing:** i.e., contrary to that which

13. **For . . . fair:** This repeats from s.147.13, which goes on to attack the lady; here, the poet instead attacks himself. **eye:** probable wordplay on *I* and *ay*

152

In loving thee thou know'st I am forsworn,
But thou art twice forsworn, to me love swearing;
In act thy bed-vow broke, and new faith torn
In vowing new hate after new love bearing.　　　4
But why of two oaths' breach do I accuse thee
When I break twenty? I am perjured most,
For all my vows are oaths but to misuse thee,
And all my honest faith in thee is lost.　　　8
For I have sworn deep oaths of thy deep kindness,
Oaths of thy love, thy truth, thy constancy;
And to enlighten thee gave eyes to blindness,
Or made them swear against the thing they see.　　　12
　　For I have sworn thee fair; more perjured eye,
　　To swear against the truth so foul a lie.

This sonnet uses an ancient parable to demonstrate that love's fire is unquenchable. It goes on to argue that only the mistress's eyes can cure the poet.

1–7. **Cupid . . . bath:** These lines retell a story (one that dates back to an ancient Greek poem) in which Diana's nymphs try to quench Cupid's torch in water but instead set the water on fire, turning the pool into a hot bath. The story is told again in s. 154.1–12.

1. **laid by his brand:** i.e., put down his torch

2. **maid of Dian's:** i.e., one of the virgin nymphs who serve Diana, the goddess of chastity (See picture, p. 220.) **advantage:** opportunity

4. **of that ground:** i.e., nearby

5. **Which:** i.e., the fountain; **Love:** i.e., Cupid

6. **dateless:** eternal; **still:** always

7. **grew:** i.e., became; **seething bath:** wordplay on (1) boiling spring or tub of water; (2) spring or tub of water suitable for soaking

7–8. **yet . . . cure:** i.e., **men** continue to show to be a potent remedy **against** extreme or unusual diseases (The **bath** may have a double reference to [1] hot mineral springs used for medicinal purposes and [2] sweating tubs used to treat venereal disease.)

9. **new fired:** i.e., ignited once again (For the **eye** as a source of rays, see note to s. 113.4.)

10. **for trial:** i.e., to test it; **needs would:** i.e., must

11. **withal:** i.e., with the touch of the **brand**

12. **hied:** hurried; **distempered:** disturbed; diseased

153

Cupid laid by his brand and fell asleep.
A maid of Dian's this advantage found,
And his love-kindling fire did quickly steep
In a cold valley-fountain of that ground,   4
Which borrowed from this holy fire of Love
A dateless lively heat, still to endure,
And grew a seething bath which yet men prove
Against strange maladies a sovereign cure.   8
But at my mistress' eye Love's brand new fired,
The boy for trial needs would touch my breast;
I, sick withal, the help of bath desired
And thither hied, a sad distempered guest,   12
    But found no cure. The bath for my help lies
    Where Cupid got new fire—my mistress' ⌜eyes.⌝

This sonnet, like s. 153, retells the parable of Cupid's torch turning a fountain into a hot bath, this time to argue that the poet's disease of love is incurable.

1–12. **The . . . diseased:** See note to s. 153.1–7.
2. **brand:** torch
5. **fairest votary:** i.e., most beautiful of the **nymphs** who had **vowed chaste life to keep** (l. 3)
7. **general:** (military) commander
9. **by:** nearby
11. **Growing:** i.e., becoming; **bath:** spring or tub of water (here, for medicinal purposes, as in note to s. 153.7–8)

Cupid with his torch. (s. 153, s. 154)

318

154

The little love-god, lying once asleep,
Laid by his side his heart-inflaming brand,
Whilst many nymphs that vowed chaste life to keep
Came tripping by; but in her maiden hand   4
The fairest votary took up that fire,
Which many legions of true hearts had warmed;
And so the general of hot desire
Was, sleeping, by a virgin hand disarmed.   8
This brand she quenchèd in a cool well by,
Which from Love's fire took heat perpetual,
Growing a bath and healthful remedy
For men diseased; but I, my mistress' thrall,   12
    Came there for cure, and this by that I prove:
    Love's fire heats water; water cools not love.

Two Sonnets from
The Passionate Pilgrim

The Passionate Pilgrime.
By W. Shakespeare.
London: for W. Iaggard, 1599.

These are the first versions of these two sonnets to be printed. See "An Introduction to This Text," p. xxxviii.

[138]

When my love swears that she is made of truth,
I do believe her, though I know she lies,
That she might think me some untutored youth,
Unskillful in the world's false forgeries.
Thus vainly thinking that she thinks me young,
Although I know my years be past the best,
I, smiling, credit her false-speaking tongue,
Outfacing faults in love with love's ill rest.
But wherefore says my love that she is young?
And wherefore say not I that I am old?
O, love's best habit is a soothing tongue,
And age in love loves not to have years told.
　　Therefore I'll lie with love, and love with me,
　　Since that our faults in love thus smothered be.

[sig. A 3]

[144]

Two loves I have, of comfort and despair,
That like two spirits do suggest me still.
My better angel is a man right fair,
My worser spirit a woman colored ill.
To win me soon to hell my female evil
Tempteth my better angel from my side,
And would corrupt my saint to be a devil,
Wooing his purity with her fair pride.
And whether that my angel be turned fiend
Suspect I may, yet not directly tell;
For being both to me, both to each friend,
I guess one angel in another's hell.
  The truth I shall not know, but live in doubt,
  Till my bad angel fire my good one out.

[sig. A 4]

Longer Notes

Sonnet 1.6 **Feed'st thy light's flame with self-substantial fuel:** While the image in this line is of a candle or other flame that lives by burning its own substance, it may also allude to the mythological story of Narcissus, the beautiful youth who destroys himself by falling in love with his own image. Ovid says of Narcissus, "He is the flame that sets on fire, and thing that burneth too" (*Metamorphoses* 3.356; trans. Arthur Golding, 1567).

Sonnet 13.1 **your self:** In the 1609 Quarto the words "your selfe" appear in ll. 1, 2, and 7 of s. 13; in l. 7, "your selfes" also appears. It was as rare for these words to be joined together as a single word in Shakespeare's day as it is for them to be separated today. Ordinarily, then, in this edition we print "yourself" and "yourself's." However, in ll. 1 and 7 of this sonnet, we follow some previous editors in retaining the Quarto's separation of "your" and "self" in order to call attention to the unusual use of the word *self* in these two instances. There is much wordplay in ll. 1 and 7; both lines are parts of apparent contradictions. The sonnet's opening lines, "O, that you were your self! But, love, you are / No longer yours than you yourself here live" (1–2), appear to tell the young man "you yourself are not your self." Similarly, ll. 6–7, "then you were / Your self again after yourself's decease," suggest to the young man "you can continue to be your self after you yourself are dead." These passages can be understood as paradoxes rather than contradictions only if we can find special meanings of the word *self* that allow a difference between "your self" and "yourself."

323

The sonnet suggests that the special sense of *self* must be associated with the young man's "sweet semblance" (4) and his "sweet form" (8), which he can pass on to his offspring in such a way that a *self* continues to endure even after he himself has died. Usually editors give the term *soul* for this special sense of *self*. There is evidence for the aptness of thinking of *self* as *soul* in a passage from *The Anatomy of Melancholy* (1621), a work by Shakespeare's near-contemporary Robert Burton. Discussing "the Rationall Soule," Burton presents an understanding of it that he identifies as deriving ultimately from the classical world and revived by recent writers. According to this view, sexual reproduction is reproduction of both body and soul, the body regarded as matter and the soul as form: "one man begets another, body and soule: or as a candle from a candle, to be produced from the seed: otherwise, they say, a man begets but halfe a man, and is worse then a beast that begets both matter and forme" (1.1.2.9). Another text that may bear on the sonnet's possible use of *self* in the special sense of *soul* or *form* is Aristotle's *Metaphysics*. There Aristotle provides the causes of "a man," including the "formal cause," usually explained by scholars as the "design" but called "the essence" by Aristotle, "essence" being another meaning of *soul:* "So whenever we inquire what the cause is, since there are causes in several senses, we must state all the possible causes. E.g., what is the material cause of a man? The menses. What is the moving cause? The semen. What is the formal cause? The essence. What is the final cause? The end" (1044a33–37).

But there are also difficulties with associating *self* in this sonnet with *soul* and *soul* with *form.* Burton, in the same subsection cited above, notes the contrary opinion of the great Fathers of the Church Jerome and Augustine that the soul is not conceived with the body: "The *Soule* is created of nothing, and so infused in the Childe or *Embrio* in his Mothers wombe, six moneths after the conception." Another difficulty in equating *self* with *soul* arises from the sonnet's strong implication that the *self* is mortal. If the self is to be thought of as the *soul*, then the sonnet implies that the *soul*, too, is mortal. While Burton records that there was in his time ongoing debate about the soul's immortality, he makes clear that any suggestion that the soul is not immortal is for him atheistic. In light of his repugnance toward this view, an attitude that may have been general at that time, it is hard to be sure that the sonnet should be read in terms of an equation of *self* and *soul*.

Sonnet 15.4. **Whereon . . . comment:** *Comment on* usually means "To make comments or remarks (*on, upon*). (Often implying unfavorable remarks)" (*Oxford English Dictionary*). In this instance, because the **influence** of the **stars** is in question, *comment on* may also have the unusual meaning of "control" or "make critical decisions about." Through the combination of these meanings, the stars may be represented as an audience observing and criticizing the human performance while secretly affecting the show's action through astrological influence. *Influence* is defined as "The supposed flowing or streaming from the stars or heavens of an etherial fluid acting upon the character and destiny of humans, and affecting sublunary things generally."

Sonnet 18.11. **shade:** The clearest reference in this line ("Nor shall Death brag thou wand'rest in his shade") is to walking through "the valley of the shadow of death" in Psalm 23. (The phrase **"shade** of death" was used interchangeably with "shadow of death.") In addition to this biblical allusion, however, the line also contains classical allusions, since "the shades," in classical mythology, is another name for Hades, the world of ghosts and disembodied spirits, and is also a way of referring to the darkness of that world; further, a **shade,** in classical mythology, is the ghost of a dead person, a disembodied spirit, or indeed any inhabitant of Hades.

Sonnet 35.8 **Excusing ... are**: Among the meanings for this line suggested by editors are the following: (1) "Excusing your sins to a greater extent than is warranted by the size of your sins"; (2) "(By) giving excessive exculpation for his friend's misconduct by reducing it, through his analogies (ll. 1–4), from a moral to a natural fault, his excuse for his friend's offense would be stretched so much wider than the offense itself that it would, if valid (which the poet knows it is not), exculpate all sins whatever"; (3) "(By) pleading excuses not only sufficient to cover your actual sins, but to cover them even if they were more (= greater)." The first is Booth's, the second Ingram and Redpath's; the third is quoted by Evans from an earlier editor.

Sonnet 36.5. **one respect:** This phrase is almost impossible to gloss; although **respect** has meanings that are vaguely appropriate, none is exactly right, and the meanings of the word that best fit the context are found only when the word appears as part of such phrases as "in respect to," "in respect of," "with respect to" or "to have respect to." (Booth, acknowledging the impossibility of adequately glossing this line, summarizes ll. 5–6 loosely as "In respect to our loves we are one, but in respect to our lives we are separate.") The word **respect** could mean "rank, standing, station in life," "consideration," "end, aim," "regard," "relationship," "reference," and "aspect"; any of these senses are worth considering in understanding ll. 5 and 6 of this sonnet.

Sonnet 43.4. **darkly bright:** This sonnet is filled with intricate wordplay, often involving paradox and oxymoron.

As Booth notes, "The recurring themes of this sonnet—things that are the opposite of what they would normally be expected to be, and the distinction between images or shadows of objects and the objects themselves—are played out stylistically in an intense display of antithesis and a range of rhetorical devices of repetition that make the language of the poem suggest mirror images."

Sonnet 46.3. **Mine eye my heart thy picture's sight would bar:** With the word **bar,** this sonnet begins introducing words with specific legal meanings as the sonnet brings the debate between the heart and the eyes into a court setting. The eyes would **bar** (i.e., arrest or stop [the heart] by ground of legal objection from enforcing its claim); the heart, in turn, **doth plead** (i.e., prosecutes its suit or action), presenting a **plea** (an argument or reason urged by a litigant in support of his case) that is in turn denied by the **defendant** (the eyes). A **quest** (a body of persons appointed to hold an inquiry, a jury) is **impaneled** (enrolled as jurors) to decide the **title** (i.e., who holds legal right to the possession of the property), and **their verdict** determines the **eyes' due** (i.e., that to which the eyes have a legal right) and the **heart's right** (i.e., its legal claim to the possession of property). This **verdict** leads, in s. 47, to a peaceful alliance between the eyes and the heart.

Sonnet 66.3: **needy nothing trimmed in jollity:** The literal meaning of these words would suggest that the poet is alluding to the poverty-stricken who use the money they beg to buy cheap finery. Most editors argue that Shakespeare is instead using "needy nothing" to mean (unusually) "worthless persons in need of nothing." There is no sure way to determine which meaning applies here. For an extensive argument for the more widely accepted editorial reading (i.e., "wealthy fops"), see Booth; for an answer to this argument, see Kerrigan.

Sonnet 86.5–11. **Was . . . boast:** These lines continue to intrigue scholars because they seem to suggest—through such words as "by spirits taught to write," "his compeers by night / Giving him aid," and "that affable familiar ghost / Which nightly gulls him with intelligence"—that the rival poet has dealings with supernatural spirits. Scholars and editors have pointed out that the lines can be read more innocently as alluding to books ("the spirits of dead writers as they appear in their writings") or to friends ("the lively spirits of companions"), but the hint of the occult continues to fascinate. Further, when taken together with certain hints in the poem's opening lines, ll. 5–11 also seem to give clues as to the identity of the rival poet. The lofty style, the appearance of learning, and the connection to night and to the helping presence of a ghostly forebear seem to many scholars to point most clearly to George Chapman, the first seven books of whose translation of *The Iliad* were published in 1598. For helpful discussions, see especially those in Ingram and Redpath, and in Evans.

Sonnet 96.13–14. **But . . . report:** When this couplet is used at the end of s. 36, the **do not so** urges the beloved to retain his honor, since he and the poet are one in their love and thus the beloved's good reputation (**report**) also honors the poet. In s. 96, the **do not so** instead urges the beloved not to lead others astray, since, the poet's love being so deep, any **report** (rumor or reputation) of the beloved will reflect on the poet. The repetition of the couplet may be authorial or may be a printing-house construction or error.

Sonnet 97.5–6. **summer's time, / The teeming autumn:** It is possible to see the relationship between **summer's time** and **autumn** in this poem in a variety of ways, any one of which is acceptable. Ingram and

Redpath suggest that we are to imagine the poem written in autumn as the poet looks back on summer. Booth suggests instead that the transition from summer to autumn in the poem is "fluid, like changes of season themselves." Evans sees the poet writing in summer and looking ahead to the "fecund *promise* of autumn." And Duncan-Jones explains the time of absence as the "whole period presided over by summer, which extends from spring to harvest."

Sonnet 99. There are many ways of accounting for this unusual fifteen-line sonnet. Some editors point to other sonnet sequences that include sonnets of that length, though they admit that such sonnets usually add the fifteenth line just before the concluding couplet. Other editors argue persuasively that the poem as it appears in the 1609 Quarto was in a draft state. They point to other signs of unfinished work, but note that while either l. 1 or l. 5 could be deleted and leave a quatrain that is complete in its rhyme scheme, both ll. 1 and 5 are necessary for the sense of the poem.

The poem is also unusual in that it comes close to duplicating a poem by Henry Constable published in 1592. (See Appendix, p. 353.) Editors assume that Shakespeare reworked the Constable poem. We know, however, that Shakespeare's sonnets were passed around in manuscript long before their printing in 1609 and that Shakespeare was working on his narrative poetry in the very early 1590s. It therefore seems difficult to determine which way the borrowing and reworking went.

Professor Steven May, editor of the forthcoming *Bibliography and First-Line Index of English Verse, 1559–1603*, suggests (in private communication) that the very similar Shakespeare and Constable poems might have been written in response to "a poetic competition or challenge such as the one that produced Sir Thomas

Heneage's response to Ralegh's 'Farewell false love' or Spenser's *Amoretti* 8," variants of which appear in poems by Dyer and Sidney. However the Shakespeare and Constable poems came to be, it is interesting to note their differences, Constable's being more in keeping with the traditional sonnet conventions.

Sonnet 119.1. **siren:** In classical mythology, the Sirens used their alluring songs to entice sailors to their deaths on the rocks near their island. In the most famous mythological encounter with the Sirens, Odysseus has himself tied to the mast of his ship (after stopping up the ears of his sailors with wax) so that he can safely hear the Sirens' songs as the sailors take the ship past their island (Homer's *Odyssey* 12). Although, as Booth notes, the adjective *siren* did not have to refer to women, Shakespeare's other uses of the word are clearly in reference to females. Further, scholars have also linked the sonnet's "**limbecks foul as hell within**" (l. 2) to female anatomy (with Evans, for example, noting that the alembic "has a long history as a slang term for the female pudendum") and to the kind of sexual nausea expressed in *King Lear* 4.6.142–46, where the female sexual parts are described as, in effect, "limbecks foul as hell": "beneath is all the fiend's. There's hell, there's darkness, there is the sulphurous pit; burning, scalding, stench, consumption!"

Sonnet 126. The 1609 Quarto prints, after l. 12, two sets of empty parentheses, as if to replace the missing ll. 13 and 14. It is possible that Shakespeare placed empty parentheses in his manuscript at the conclusion of the twelve-line poem; but editors generally agree that they were supplied by the Quarto's publisher or its printer, who, most editors argue, would have expected a full fourteen-line sonnet, and signaled with the parentheses that the lines had not been provided. (It has also been suggested that the publisher or the printer removed the final two lines because they contained information that pointed too directly to the identity of the "lovely boy.") Some editors today reproduce the two sets of empty parentheses.

Sonnet 134.2. **And I myself am mortgaged to thy will:** The word **mortgaged** begins a series of technical terms—**forfeit, surety-like, bond, statute, usurer, sue, debtor**—from property law, contracts, and finance. Vendler's explication of the relationship among these terms is helpful: "The speaker's new metaphor for himself is that he is a mortgaged debtor for whom the young man has stood surety, [the young man then] becoming himself forfeit. No matter how much the speaker wants to reverse the situation and forfeit himself instead, he is powerless. . . . Because the mistress now has two sources of repayment instead of one, she exacts the sexual debt from the young man, who pays." (The technical meaning of **surety** is "one who makes himself liable for the default or miscarriage of another, or for the performance of some act on his part [e.g., payment of a debt. . . " (*OED* 7)]. The person who stands as **surety** is **lost** as **forfeit** when, e.g., the contract is breached. Because the poet could not pay, the young man is lost.) Most editors read into ll. 7–8 and 11 a story in which the young man has wooed or interceded with the mistress on behalf of the poet and has then himself been captivated by her. Vendler's explication instead sees the sonnet as the poet's desperate attempt to construct a narrative that will put all the blame on the mistress. We recall that in s. 42 the poet attempted to excuse both the young man and the mistress, arguing first that they love each other only because of him, and then that since he and the young man are one, in loving the young man the woman actually loves the poet. In s. 134, instead of admitting that his strategies are merely "sweet

flattery" (s. 42.14), the poet remains caught in what
Vendler calls "this text of tangled anguish."

Sonnet 135.1. **will:** This line introduces the compli-
cated wordplay on the word **will** that constitutes s. 135
and s. 136 (and that reappears in the couplet of s. 143).
The wordplay finds its roots in the complexity of the
word and the concept itself, which ranges from the bibli-
cal (which sets God's **will** above man's) through the psy-
chological (which makes man's **will** a preeminent faculty
of the soul) to the bawdily physical (which uses the word
will as a slang term for both the penis and vagina)—with
an additional complication available when the poet's
name is William and he is called **Will.** Since the deter-
mination of the meanings in play in any particular line of
these sonnets is presented by the sonnet as a kind of puz-
zle to be solved and enjoyed, we will leave such determi-
nations to the reader, giving the following background
rather than attaching specific meanings in the notes to
the poems.

In the psychology of Shakespeare's day (known as
"faculty psychology"), **Will** and Understanding (or
Reason), the two faculties of the Rational Soul, are "the
two principal fountains of human action" (Richard
Hooker, *Laws of Ecclesiastical Polity* [1594–97], 1.7.2).
Understanding finds the good, and **Will** chooses that
good (or would do so had not man fallen as a conse-
quence of original sin). In theology and in faculty psy-
chology, **will** is supposed to govern man's appetites.
According to Hooker, "of one thing we must have special
care, as being a matter of no small moment, and that is,
how the **will** . . . differeth greatly from that inferior natu-
ral desire we call appetite. . . . [A]ppetite is the will's so-
licitor, and the will is the appetite's controller" (1.7.3). Or,
as Iago puts it: "Our bodies are our gardens, to the which
our **wills** are gardeners. So that if we will plant nettles or

sow lettuce, . . . the power and corrigible authority of this lies in our **wills**" (*Othello* 1.3.362–68).

Because **Will** (along with Reason) was corrupted at the Fall, the **will** is "prone to evil, . . . [is] egged on by our natural concupiscence," and "lust . . . we cannot resist" (Robert Burton, *Anatomy of Melancholy* [1621], 1.1.2.11). "The seat of our affections captivates and enforces our **will**. . . . Lust counsels one thing, reason another," and the "depraved **will**" often yields to passion (1.1.2.11). Again to quote Iago, the "lust of the blood" is often granted "the permission of the **will**" (1.3.377–78).

Sonnets 135 and 136 demonstrate the bawdy register of meanings attached to the word **will**, which in these poems means, variously, carnal desire, lust, intention, the penis, the vagina, the poet's name, perhaps the names of others named William (perhaps the young man, perhaps the woman's husband), and, at one point (s. 136.3), that faculty of the soul that governs volition. Vendler points out interestingly, and persuasively, that s. 136.5–10, taken as a freestanding poem, could be a religious poem addressed to God; in context, such a reading would, of course, be supremely blasphemous.

At several places in ss. 135, 136, and 143 the 1609 Quarto prints **will** in italic and with an uppercase *W*. We have printed all these appearances of "*Will*" (except for the final one in s. 136, where it is specifically the poet's name) in lowercase and in roman type. ("*Will*" is found at s. 135.1, 2 [twice], 11 [twice], 12 [the second instance], and 14 and s. 136.2, 5 [the first instance], and 14). We agree with Booth that "a modern reader's susceptibility to orthographical signals is so acute that Q's capitals and italics" can make it impossible for the full range of the wordplay to be effective.

Sonnet 145.13 **hate away:** In *Essays in Criticism* 21 (1971): 221–26, Andrew Gurr argued that **hate away** is

a pun on the name "Hathaway," supposed to be the name
of Shakespeare's wife. This argument has appealed to ed-
itors and readers who approach the *Sonnets* with a view
to coming closer to the poet Shakespeare. However, in
the surviving documents concerning Shakespeare's mar-
riage, the wife's name is given once as "Hathwey" and
once as "Whateley"; perhaps, then, Shakespeare's wife's
name was "Whateley" and not "Hathaway"; or, perhaps,
Elizabethan spelling being so variable, what appear to us
to be two different names are just different spellings of a
no-longer-determinable name. In light of the indetermi-
nacy surrounding the wife's name, certainty about a pun
on it is elusive.

Sonnet 146.2. **Pressed with these rebel powers
that thee array:** In the 1609 Quarto, the second line of
s. 146 opens with a repetition of the final three words of
l. 1. In other words, l. 2 in Q (modernized) reads "My sin-
ful earth these rebel powers that thee array." Some edi-
tors retain this line despite the repetition and despite its
being an unwieldy twelve syllables long. Most editors,
though, either replace "My sinful earth" with an ellipsis
to show something missing or substitute some two-
syllable word or phrase chosen from among a host that
have been proposed over the centuries. Among the more
familiar of these are "Fooled by," "Foiled by," "Thrall to,"
and "Feeding." We were persuaded by Stephen Booth's
conjecture: "If I had to offer my own no less arbitrary
preference, I would choose 'pressed with,' which partici-
pates in the phonetic pattern set in motion by the conso-
nants *Poor soul* and which pertains variously to the ideas
of weight, siege, and penalties that run through the whole
sonnet."

Textual Notes

The reading of the present text appears to the left of the square bracket. Unless otherwise noted, the reading to the left of the bracket is from **Q,** the Quarto text (upon which this edition is based). The *Sonnets* were published again by John Benson in 1640 as *POEMS: WRITTEN BY Wil. Shakespeare. Gent.*, a version which, while introducing many errors in reprinting sonnets from the 1609 Quarto, also corrected some errors printed in Q. **Ed.** indicates an earlier editor of the *Sonnets,* beginning with Gildon in 1710. No sources are given for emendations of punctuation or for corrections of obvious typographical errors, like turned letters that produce no known word. ***Uncorr.*** means the first or uncorrected state of the Quarto; ***corr.*** means the second or corrected state of the Quarto; ~ stands in place of a word already quoted before the square bracket; ʌ indicates the omission of a punctuation mark.

2	4. tattered] Q (totter'd)
	14. cold] Q (could)
6	1. ragged] Q (wragged)
10	10. lodged] Q (log'd)
11	6. this,] ~ʌ Q
12	4. all] Ed.; or Q
13	1. your self] Q
	7. Your self] Ed.; You selfe Q
15	8. wear] Q (were)
16	10. thisʌ . . . penʌ] ~ (. . . ~) Q
17	12. meter] Q (miter)
19	3. jaws] Ed.; yawes Q

20	2. Hast] Q (Haste)

20 2. Hast] Q (Haste)
22 3. furrows] Q (forrwes)
23 2. beside] Q (besides)
6. rite] Q (right)
14. with] Q (wit)
14. wit] wiht Q
24 1. stelled] Ed.; steeld Q
3. 'tis] ti's Q
26 11. tattered] Q (tottered)
12. thy] Ed.; their Q
27 1. haste] Q (hast)
2. travel] Q (trauaill)
6. thee,] Q *corr.;* ~; Q *uncorr.*
10. thy] Ed.; their Q
28 5. either's] Q (ethers)
12. gild'st the even] Ed.; guil'st th' eauen Q
31 8. thee] Ed.; there Q
32 8. height] Q (hight)
34 2. travel] Q (trauaile)
12. cross] Ed.; losse Q
35 8. thy] Ed.; their Q (twice)
37 7. thy] Ed.; their Q
38 2. breathe] Q (breath)
2. pour'st] Q (poor'st)
3. too] Q (to)
39 12. doth] Ed.; dost Q
40 7. thyself] Ed; this selfe Q
43 11. thy] Ed.; their Q
44 13. nought] Ed.; naughts Q
13. slow] Q (sloe)
45 9. life's] Q (liues)
12. thy] Ed.; their Q
46 3. thy] Ed.; their Q
8. thy] Ed.; their Q
9. 'cide] Ed.; side Q
13. thy] Ed.; their Q

14. thy] Ed.; their Q

47 10. Thyself] Q *corr.* (Thy selfe); thy seife Q *un-corr.*

11. no] Ed.; nor Q

50 6. dully] Ed.; duly Q

51 3. haste] Q (hast)

10. perfect'st] Ed.; perfects Q

55 1. monuments] Ed; monument Q

9. enmity] Q (emnity)

56 13. Or] Ed.; As Q

58 7. patience, tame∧ to sufferance,] Ed.; ~∧ ~, ~ ~∧ Q

59 6. hundred] Q (hundreth)

8. done,] ~. Q

11. whe'er] Q (where)

61 8. tenor] Q (tenure)

62 13. 'Tis] T'is Q

63 5. traveled] Q (trauaild)

65 12. of] Ed.; or Q

66 5. misplaced] Q (misplast)

9. tongue] Q (tung)

67 10. veins] Q (vaines)

68 7. second life] scond life Q

69 3. due] Ed.; end Q

5. Thy] Ed.; Their Q

14. soil] solye Q

70 1. art] Ed.; are Q

6. Thy] Ed.; Their Q

71 4. vilest] Q (vildest)

73 4. ruined] rn'wd Q

4. choirs] Q (quiers)

74 10. prey] Q (pray)

75 2. showers] Q (shewers)

76 4, 8. strange? . . . proceed?] *Question marks do not print in one copy of* Q

7. tell] Ed.; fel Q

77   1. wear] Q (were)
            10. blanks] Ed.; blacks Q
81   14. breathes] Q (breaths)
86   13. filled] Q (fild)
87   9. Thy self] Q
89   11. profane] Q *corr.* (prophane); proface Q *un-corr.*
90   11. shall] Ed.; stall Q
91   9. better] Ed.; bitter Q
92   6. end;] ~, Q
93   6. change.] ~, Q
94   4. cold] Q (could)
98   9. lily's] Q (Lillies)
            11. were] Q (weare)
99   4. dwells∧] ~? Q
              5. dyed] Q (died)
              7. marjoram] Q (marierom)
              9. One] Ed.; Our Q
101   2. dyed] Q (di'd)
102   11. bough] Q (bow)
106   12. skill] Ed.; still Q
110   6. Askance] Q (Asconce)
            10. grind] Q (grin'de)
111   1. with] Ed.; wish Q
112   14. methinks are] Ed; me thinkes y'are Q
113   6. latch] Ed.; lack Q
            13. more, replete] ~∧ ~, Q
            14. mine eye] Ed.; mine Q
116]   Q *corr.*; 119 Q *uncorr.*
116   8. height] Q (higth)
118   10. were∧ not,] ~, ~∧ Q
120   6. you've] Q (y'haue)
121   11. bevel;] ~∧ Q
122   1. Thy] TThy Q
123   12. haste] Q (hast)
125   4. waste] Q (wast)

	7. sweet∧] ~; Q
126	2. sickle∧] ~, Q
	3. show'st] Q (shou'st)
	5. mistress] Q (misteres)
	8. minutes] Ed.; mynuit Q
127	2. were] Q (weare)
	7. bower] Q (boure)
	9. mistress'] Q (Mistersse)
128	11. thy] Ed.; their Q
	11. gait] Q (gate)
	14. thy] Ed.; their Q
129	9. Mad] Ed.; Made Q
	10. quest∧ to have,] ~, ~ ~∧ Q
	11. proved a] Ed.; proud and Q
	12. Before, . . . proposed; behind,] ~∧ . . . ~∧ ~∧ Q
130	2. Coral] Q (Currall)
131	3. heart] Q (hart)
132	6. the east] Q (th'East)
	9. mourning] Q (morning)
133	3. Is 't] I'st Q
	10. bail] Q (bale)
134	12. lose] Q (loose)
136	6. Ay] Q (I)
137	8. tied] Q (tide)
138	12. to have] Q (t'haue)
140	3. Lest] Q (Least)
	5. were] Q (weare)
	13. belied] Q (be lyde)
143	12. part:] ~∧ Q
144	2. suggest] Q (sugiest)
	5. female] Q (femall)
	6. side] *Passionate Pilgrime,* Ed.; sight Q
	9. fiend] Q (finde)
145	7. doom] Q (dome)

146 2. Pressed with] This ed.; *Booth's conjecture*;
My sinfull earth Q
147 12. random] Q (randon)
148 8. men's "no."] mens: no, Q
14. Lest] Q (Least)
149 6. frown'st] Q (froun'st)
6. fawn] Q (faune)
7. lour'st] Q (lowrst)
150 6. deeds∧] deeds, Q *corr.*; deeds; Q *uncorr.*
151 4. Lest] Q (Least)
153 4. cold] Q (could)
14. eyes] Ed.; eye Q
154 3. vowed] Q (vou'd)

Appendix of Intertextual Material

From Ovid's *Metamorphoses,* trans. Arthur Golding (1567), book 15

(Line numbers correspond to the Golding translation. Spelling has been modernized.)

A. ll. 198–205 (Compare s. 60)
    Things ebb and flow, and every shape is made to pass
      away.
    The time itself continually is fleeting like a brook.
    For neither brook nor lightsome time can tarry still.
      But look
    As every wave drives other forth, and that that comes
      behind
    Both thrusteth and is thrust itself. Even so the times
      by kind
    Do fly and follow both at once, and evermore renew.
    For that that was before is left, and straight there
      doth ensue
    Another that was never erst.

B. ll. 206–7, 221–35 (Compare s. 73)
    We see that after day comes night and darks the sky,
    And after night the lightsome sun succeedeth
      orderly.
    . . . .
    What? Seest thou not how that the year as represent-
      ing plain
    The age of man, departs [i.e., parts] itself in quarters
      four? First bain [supple]

341

And tender in the spring it is even like a sucking babe.
Then green and void of strength, and lush, and foggy
    is the blade,
And cheers the husbandman with hope. Then all
    things flourish gay.
The earth with flowers of sundry hue then seemeth
    for to play,
And virtue small or none to herbs there doth as yet
    belong.
The year from springtide passing forth to summer,
    waxeth strong,
Becometh like a lusty youth. For in our life through-
    out,
There is no time more plentiful, more lusty hot and
    stout.
Then followeth harvest when the heat of youth grows
    somewhat cold,
Ripe, mild, disposed mean betwixt a young man and
    an old,
And somewhat sprent [sprinkled] with greyish hair.
    Then ugly winter last
Like age steals on with trembling steps, all bald or
    overcast
With shirl [rough] thin hair as white as snow.

C. ll. 235–51 (Compare s. 60)
                                        Our bodies also aye
Do alter still from time to time, and never stand at
    stay.
We shall not be the same we were today or yesterday.
The day hath been we were but seed and only hope
    of men,
And in our mother's womb we had our dwelling
    place as then,
Dame Nature put to cunning hand and suffered not
    that we

Within our mother's strained womb should aye dis-
    tressed be,
But brought us out to air, and from our prison set us
    free.
The child newborn lies void of strength. Within a
    season, though
He waxing four-footed learns like savage beasts to go.
Then somewhat falt'ring, and as yet not firm of foot,
    he stands
By getting somewhat for to help his sinews in his hands.
From that time growing strong and swift, he passeth
    forth the space
Of youth, and also wearing out his middle age apace,
Through drooping age's steepy path he runneth out
    his race.
This age doth undermine the strength of former
    years, and throws
It down.

D. ll. 287–95 (Compare s. 64)
    Even so have places oftentimes exchanged their
        estate.
    For I have seen it sea which was substantial ground
        alate [previously]
    Again where sea was, I have seen the same become
        dry land,
    And shells and scales of seafish far have lain from
        any strand,
    And in the tops of mountains high old anchors have
        been found.
    Deep valleys have by watershot [a sudden flood]
        been made of level ground,
    And hills by force of gulling [erosion] oft have into
        sea been worn.
    Hard gravel ground is sometime seen where marris
        [marsh] was before,

And that that erst did suffer drought becometh
   standing lakes.

E. ll. 984–95 (Compare s. 55)
   Now have I brought a work to end which neither
      Jove's fierce wrath,
   Nor sword, nor fire, nor fretting age with all the
      force it hath
   Are able to abolish quite. Let come that fatal hour
   Which (saving of [i.e., except for] this brittle flesh)
      hath over me no power,
   And at his pleasure make an end of mine uncertain
      time,
   Yet shall the better part of me assured be to climb
   Aloft above the starry sky. And all the world shall never
   Be able for to quench my name. For look how far so
      ever
   The Roman Empire by the right of conquest shall
      extend,
   So far shall all folk read this work. And time without
      all end
   (If poets as by prophecy about the truth may aim)
   My life shall everlastingly be lengthened still by fame.

The parable of the talents, Matthew 25.14–30

(Geneva Bible; spelling has been modernized.)
Compare s. 4.

14. For the kingdom of heaven is as a man that going
into a strange [i.e., foreign] country called his servants
and delivered to them his goods.
15. And unto one he gave five talents, and to another
two, and to another one, to every man after his own abil-
ity, and straightway went from home.

16.   Then he that had received the five talents went and occupied with them [i.e., put them out for interest, invested them], and gained other five talents.

17.   Likewise also he that received two, he also gained other two.

18.   But he that received that one went and digged it in the earth and hid his master's money.

19.   But after a long season, the master of those servants came and reckoned [i.e., settled accounts] with them.

20.   Then came he that had received five talents and brought other five talents, saying, "Master, thou deliveredst unto me five talents; behold, I have gained with them other five talents."

21.   Then his master said unto him, "It is well done, good servant and faithful. Thou hast been faithful in little, I will make thee ruler over much; enter in into thy master's joy."

22.   Also he that had received two talents came and said, "Master, thou deliveredst unto me two talents; behold, I have gained two other talents with them."

23.   His master said unto him "It is well done, good servant and faithful. Thou hast been faithful in little, I will make thee ruler over much; enter in into thy master's joy."

24.   Then he which had received the one talent came and said, "Master, I knew that thou wast an hard [i.e., tightfisted, stingy] man which reapest where thou sowedst not, and gatherest where thou strawedst [i.e., strewed, scattered] not.

25.   "I was therefore afraid, and went and hid thy talent in the earth. Behold, thou hast thine own."

26.   And his master answered, and said unto him, "Thou evil servant and slothful, thou knewest that I reap where I sowed not and gather where I strawed not.

27.   "Thou oughtest therefore to have put my money to the exchangers [i.e., money changers] and then at my

coming should I have received mine own with vantage [i.e., profit].

28. "Take, therefore, the talent from him, and give it unto him which hath ten talents.

29. "For unto every man that hath, it shall be given, and he shall have abundance; and from him that hath not, even that he hath shall be taken away.

30. "Cast therefore that unprofitable servant into utter darkness; there shall be weeping and gnashing of teeth."

Excerpts from Erasmus's "Encomium Matrimonii," in English translation from Thomas Wilson, *The Arte of Rhetorique* (1553), fols. 21v–34v.

An Epistle to persuade a young gentleman to marriage, devised by Erasmus in the behalf of his friend.

Albeit you are wise enough of yourself through that singular wisdom of yours (most loving cousin) and little needs the advice of others, yet either for that old friendship which hath been betwixt us and continued with our age even from our cradles, or for such your great good turns showed at all times towards me, or else for that fast kindred and alliance which is betwixt us, I thought myself thus much to owe unto you if I would be such a one indeed as you ever have taken me, that is to say a man both friendly and thankful, to tell you freely whatsoever I judged to appertain either to the safeguard or worship of you or any of yours and willingly to warn you of the same. . . . I have felt often your advice in mine own affairs, and I have found it to be as fortunate unto me as it was friendly. Now if you will likewise in your own matters follow my counsel, I trust it shall so come to pass that neither I shall repent me for that I have given you counsel, nor yet you shall forthink yourself, that you have obeyed and followed mine advice." [fol. 21v]

[Erasmus tells of learning from a mutual friend that the young gentleman's mother has died and his sister entered a convent.]

. . . [In] you only remaineth the hope of issue and maintenance of your stock, whereupon your friends with one consent have offered you in marriage a gentlewoman of a good house and much wealth, fair of body, very well brought up, and such a one as loveth you with all her heart. But you (either for your late sorrows which you have in fresh remembrance or else for religion sake) have so purposed to live a single life, that neither can you for love of your stock, neither for desire of issue, nor yet for any entreaty that your friends can make, either by praying or by weeping, be brought to change your mind. [fol. 22]

A. "Or who is he so fond will be the tomb / Of his self-love, to stop posterity?" (s. 3.7–8)

What is more right or meet than to give that unto the posterity the which we have received of our ancestors? . . . What is more unthankful than to deny that unto younglings the which (if thou hadst not received of thine elders) thou couldst not have been the man living, able to have denied it unto them? [fol. 22v]

Now again be it that others deserve worthy praise that seek to live a virgin's life, yet it must needs be a great fault in you. Others shall be thought to seek a pureness of life; you shall be counted a parricide or a murderer of your stock: that whereas you may by honest marriage increase your posterity, you suffer it to decay forever through your willful single life. . . . And now it mattereth nothing whether you kill or refuse to save that creature which you only might save and that with ease. [fol. 33v]

B. "Then, beauteous niggard, why dost thou abuse / The bounteous largess given thee to give?" (s. 4.5–6)

We do read that such as are in very deed chaste of their body and live a virgin's life have been praised, but the single life was never praised of itself. Now again the law of Moses accurseth the barrenness of married folk, and we do read that some were excommunicated for the same purpose and banished from the altar. And wherefore, I pray you? Marry, sir, because that they, like unprofitable persons and living only to themselves, did not increase the world with any issue. . . . A city is like to fall in ruin, except there be watchmen to defend it with armor. But assured destruction must here needs follow except men through the benefit of marriage supply issue, the which through mortality do from time to time decay. [fols. 23v–24]

C. "Then how, when nature calls thee to be gone, / What acceptable audit canst thou leave?" (s. 4.11–12)

And the wise founders of all laws [i.e., the Romans] give good reason why such favor was showed to married folk. For what is more blessful than to live ever? Now whereas nature hath denied this, matrimony doth give it by a certain sleight so much as may be. Who doth not desire to be bruited and live through fame among men hereafter? Now there is no building of pillars, no erecting of arches, no blazing of arms, that doth more set forth a man's name than doth the increase of children. [fols. 24v–25]

But what do we with these laws written? This is the law of nature, not written in the tables of brass but firmly printed in our minds, the which law, whosoever doth not obey, he is not worthy to be called a man, much less shall he be counted a citizen. For if to live well (as the Stoics wittily do dispute) is to follow the course of nature, what thing is so agreeing with nature as matrimony? For there is nothing so natural not only unto mankind but also unto all other living creatures as it is for every one of them to keep their own kind from decay and through increase of issue to make the whole kind immortal. The which thing, all men know, can never be done without wedlock and carnal copulation. It were a foul thing that brute beasts should obey the law of nature and men like giants should fight against nature, whose work if we would narrowly look upon, we shall perceive that in all things here upon earth, she would there should be a certain spice of marriage. [fol. 25v]

Hath not God so knit all things together with certain links that one ever seemeth to have need of another? What say you of the sky or firmament that is ever stirring with continual moving? Doth it not play the part of a husband while it puffeth up the earth, the mother of all things, and maketh it fruitful with casting seed (as a man would say) upon it? . . . And to what end are these things spoken? Marry, sir, because we might understand that through marriage, all things are, and do still continue, and without the same all things do decay and come to nought. . . . Thus we see plainly that such a one as hath no mind of marriage seemeth to be no man but rather a stone, an enemy to nature, a rebel to God himself, seeking through his own folly his last end and destruction. [fol. 26]

D. "For where is she so fair whose uneared womb / Disdains the tillage of thy husbandry?" (s. 3.5–6)

Therefore as he is counted no good gardener, that being content with things present, doth diligently prune his old trees and hath no regard either to imp or graft young sets, because the selfsame orchard (though it be never so well trimmed) must needs decay in time, and all the trees die within few years, so he is not to be counted half a diligent citizen that being content with the present multitude hath no regard to increase the number. Therefore there is no one man that ever hath been counted a worthy citizen who hath not labored to get children, and sought to bring them up in godliness. [fols. 26v–27]

Now I pray you, if a man had land that waxed very fat and fertile and suffered the same for lack of manuring forever to wax barren, should he not, or were he not worthy to be punished by the laws, considering it is for the commonweal's behoove, that every man should well and truly husband his own. If that man be punished who little heedeth the maintenance of his tillage, the which although it be never so well manured yet it yieldeth nothing else but wheat, barley, beans, and peas, what punishment is he worthy to suffer that refuseth to plow that land which being tilled yieldeth children? [fol. 29v]

E. "Who lets so fair a house fall to decay, / Which husbandry in honor might uphold . . . ?" (s. 13.9–10)

Now be it that others deserve great praise for their maidenhead, you notwithstanding cannot want great rebuke, seeing it lieth in your hands to keep that house from decay whereof you lineally descended and to continue still the name of your ancestors, who deserve most worthily to be known forever. . . . Will you suffer the hope of all your stock to decay, namely seeing there is none other of your name and stock but yourself alone to continue the posterity? [fol. 28v]

But whereas you . . . are like to have many children hereafter, seeing also you are a man of great lands and revenues by your ancestors, the house whereof you came being both right honorable and right ancient, so that you could not suffer it to perish without your great offence

and great harm to the commonweal: again seeing you are
of lusty years and very comely for your personage, . . . see-
ing also your friends desire you, your kinfolk weep to win
you, . . . the ashes of your ancestors from their graves
make hearty suit unto you, do you yet hold back, do you
still mind to live a single life? [fols. 34–34v]

F. "When your sweet issue your sweet form should
    bear. . . ." (s. 13.8)

What a joy shall this be unto you when your most fair
wife shall make you a father, in bringing forth a fair
child unto you, where you shall have a pretty little boy
running up and down your house, . . . such a one as
shall call you dad, with his sweet lisping words. . . . You
have them that shall comfort you in your latter days,
that shall close up your eyes when God shall call you,
that shall bury you and fulfill all things belonging to
your funeral, by whom you shall seem to be new born.
For so long as they shall live, you shall need never be
thought dead yourself. The goods and lands that you
have got go not to other heirs than to your own. So that
unto such as have fulfilled all things that belong unto
man's life, death itself cannot seem bitter. Old age
cometh upon us all, will we or nill we, and this way na-
ture provided for us, that we should wax young again in
our children. . . . For what man can be grieved that he
is old when he seeth his own countenance which he had
being a child to appear lively in his son? Death is or-
dained for all mankind, and yet by this means only na-
ture by her providence mindeth unto us a certain
immortality, while she increaseth one thing upon an-
other even as a young graft buddeth out when the old
tree is cut down. Neither can he seem to die that, when
God calleth him, leaveth a young child behind him.
[fol. 31]

G. "Then what could death do if thou shouldst depart, /
Leaving thee living in posterity?" (s. 6.11–12)

How many doth the plague destroy, how many do the seas
swallow, how many doth battle snatch up? For I will not
speak of the daily dying that is in all places. Death taketh
her flight everywhere round about, she runneth over them,
she catcheth them up, she hasteneth as much as she can
possible to destroy all mankind, and now do we so highly
commend single life and eschew marriage? [fol. 33]

From Christopher Marlowe, *Hero and Leander*

(Compare s. 4)

     Then treasure is abused
When misers keep it; being put to loan,
In time it will return us two for one.
. . . .
Who builds a palace and rams up the gate,
Shall see it ruinous and desolate.
. . . .
Less sins the poor rich man that starves himself
In heaping up a mass of drossy pelf,
Than such as you: his golden earth remains,
Which, after his decease, some other gains;
But this fair gem, sweet in the loss alone,
When you fleet hence, can be bequeathed to none.
. . . .
One is no number; maids are nothing, then,
Without the sweet society of men.
Wilt thou live single still? One shalt thou be,
Though never-singling Hymen couple thee.
. . . .
Base bullion for the stamp's sake we allow;
Even so for men's impression do we you[.]
                              (234–66)

Henry Constable,
Diana
"Sonnetto decissete"
(Compare s. 99)

My lady's presence makes the roses red,
Because to see her lips they blush for shame.
The lily's leaves, for envy, pale became,
And her white hands in them this envy bred.
The marigold abroad the leaves did spread,
Because the sun's and her power is the same.
The violet of purple color came,
Dyed with the blood she made my heart to shed.
In brief, all flowers from her their virtue take:
From her sweet breath their sweet smells do
        proceed;
The living heat which her eyebeams do make
Warmeth the ground and quick'neth the seed.
 The rain, wherewith she watereth these flowers,
 Falls from mine eyes, which she dissolves in showers.

Shakespeare's Sonnets:
A Modern Perspective

Lynne Magnusson

In the movie *Shakespeare in Love,* it is a conventionally beautiful woman of high social status and at least respectable morality who fires up Will Shakespeare's desire. If the filmmakers were taking their cues for a script about Shakespeare's passions from the *Sonnets,* one might have expected a less orthodox story. Most of the first 126 sonnets—if we can trust that the order in which the 154 sonnets were published in 1609 represents a planned sequence—evoke a poet's highly charged desire for a beautiful young *man* of high status. He is the one praised in Sonnet 18's "Shall I compare thee to a summer's day?," the famous romantic tribute that Will in the movie addresses to his lady. For the sonnet speaker, the fair young man is what grounds his idealizing imagination and his lyrical poetry, the trigger for complex emotions, and the object of sexual desire. The young man's face may be *like* a beautiful woman's, leading the poet to call him "the master mistress of my passion" (s. 20.2), but what is special in this relationship is between men. The reception of the sonnets has been colored by strategies for denying or downplaying this basic situation, allowing readers of scattered anthologized sonnets—like moviegoers—to slip very easily into the unchallenged assumption that the addressee to whom the speaker says "I love you so" (s. 71.6) is a woman like the fair and remote "she" of Petrarchan sonnet convention. Thus, before we come to the necessary qualifications about the sketchi-

355

ness of the sonnet story, it is important to be explicit about the primary relationship. Shakespeare transforms the conventional sonnet story by making his beloved a "he."

There is also a female lover in the sonnets, the focus of a secondary relationship treated in many of the last twenty-eight sonnets (127–54). But when attention turns to her, it is not to assert the normality of heterosexual romance. Things have gone downhill for the speaker, into an obsessive cycle of longing and loathing. By the conventional standards of the Petrarchan sonnet tradition, the woman in question lacks beauty and sexual virtue. Regularly referred to by sonnet readers as the "dark lady," she is described in the famous anti-Petrarchan poem "My mistress' eyes are nothing like the sun" (s. 130). It affords her ironic praise by inverting and undermining unrealistic sonnet compliments. The speaker's passion for the dark lady, set in contrast to his love for the fair young man, grounds his discourse in lies and equivocation, triggers out-of-control emotions and self-loathing, and tangles him in insatiable and shameful lust. The speaker deploys a playful satiric cleverness in some of these poems, as if to detach himself from strong emotions, but the savage self-loathing precipitated by dependence on this woman and even hints of misogyny break out. The speaker compares the dark lady's apparently promiscuous sexuality to a "bay where all men ride" (s. 137.6), and his punning imagination fantasizes a situation with his "will," or sexual member, only one among others filling her "full with wills" (s. 136.6). To top it all off, he turns the virtuosity of his poetic skill to excusing the ultimate degradation of the dark lady's sexual affair with his own male beloved.

Insofar as the sonnet sequence tells a story of passion, this sketch sets out some of its basic coordinates. Yet whether the *Sonnets* are telling any story that bears on

Shakespeare's life—or, indeed, any consistent story with a clear cast of characters at all—is a contentious issue. Are the *Sonnets* in any sense a record of events, evoking autobiographical reference or, more generally, particular sociohistorical contexts? Or are they exquisitely self-contained poems, to be valued primarily for their artistic play of words? Admirers of Shakespeare's *Sonnets* have tended to choose one approach or the other, often in an all-or-nothing way. This essay will argue for a middle course by suggesting how Shakespeare's verbal artistry is embedded in historical contexts. But let's first look briefly at the problems with the standoff.

Those seeking Shakespearean life events have cried "eureka" over identifications of the young man sparked by publisher Thomas Thorpe's inscription in the 1609 edition to a "Mr. W.H." Some, insisting the initials became somehow reversed, identify the young man as Henry Wriothesley, earl of Southampton, who was one of Shakespeare's earliest known patrons; others opt for another known patron, William Herbert, earl of Pembroke. Still others, adding cues from Shakespeare's wordplay, argue that puns on "will" and "hues" point to a Willie Hughes.[1] Scholars seeking to persuade readers of their various identifications of the mistress with, for example, an Elizabethan lady-in-waiting (Mary Fitton), a female poet (Emilia Lanier), or a London prostitute (Luce Negro), usually isolate the *Sonnets'* somewhat elusive characterization of her in terms of "blackness."[2] With varying interpretive ingenuity, they seek to apply this ideologically loaded descriptor to their candidate's eyes, deeds, hair, character, or complexion.

There are problems with reading the sonnets in this way. To begin with, there is simply too little information about Shakespeare's life on which to build arguments about his personal relationships or their intensity. Furthermore, reading to this end does little to open up the accomplishment of the sonnets: active interpretation of these complex and original poems is sacrificed to a narrow search for evidence. Finally, even if the poems were partly inspired by particular relations and circumstances, these are mediated by the sonnets' interplay with literary traditions and poetic intertexts. Shakespeare's choice of a male beloved is itself a good example, for what it signifies is closely tied to its surprising innovation on Petrarchan convention.

In the other camp, astute critics of lyric poetry such as Helen Vendler and Stephen Booth press readers to attend to the "sonnets as poems," not primarily because information about Shakespeare's life is scarce but because of their conviction about how poetic language works. In Vendler's view, the "true 'actors' in lyric are words," and the event or "drama of any lyric" has to do with innovations in words or "new stylistic arrangements."[3] It is undoubtedly true that the richest pleasures of the individual sonnets are to be gained through active reading. Such a reading process might profitably attend to the overall sonnet structure—to how the shape of the sentences and the trajectory of the thought cohere with or pull against the three quatrains and final couplet of the Shakespearean form. At a more detailed level, the reading might focus on rhetorical figures of speech. Part of the pleasure of a Shakespearean sonnet comes in recognizing its rhetorical play, both where repetitions of words and sounds (e.g., alliteration, assonance) make for rich resonances and where metaphor and wordplay trigger unexpected meanings in words.

Nonetheless, most readers would not accept that words are the only actors. The poems excite curiosity about the speaker's situation, and they powerfully express his emotions and private consciousness. If the lyric refers to or mimes anything outside the realm of words, Vendler claims, it is delimited to "the performance of mind in *solitary* speech." In her view, lyrical poetry typically "strips away most social specification (age, regional location, sex, class, even race)," so that the speaking "I" is "voiceable by anyone."[4] My contention is that to deny the relevance of social context is to misunderstand much of the innovation of Shakespeare's language. These sonnets are not the unaddressed speeches of an anonymous "I." They are utterances in which it matters who is speaking, to whom, and in what situation.

Shakespeare's use of pronouns gives a strong cue that direction of address and situational specifics matter. In other major sonnet sequences of his time, after the first-person pronoun "I," the third-person pronoun (i.e., "she," "her," or "him") occurs with greatest frequency. In Shakespeare, it is the second person of direct address, the "thou" or "you," and these pronouns occur almost as frequently as the speaking "I."[5] Shakespeare's speaker is not analyzing his inner experience in relation to the loved object, the "she" of most other Elizabethan sequences. Instead, the poems work like conversation, even if they get no direct answer. Most Shakespeare sonnets are less the isolated expression of an "I" than a social dialogue, albeit with only one speaker. As with any conversation or phone call overheard, they make a demand on the interpreter to imagine who would say *this* to whom, and in what situation. Speech is a social activity: what one says depends on whom one speaks to and in what context. Shakespeare, a dramatist turning his hand to lyric, innovates by creating the private thought of his speaker out of the materials of socially situated conversation. We as readers cannot come to know this "I" without making an active effort to figure out the context and follow the conversation. The rest of this essay will take a look at the opening movement of the sonnets as a changing "dialogue of one."[6]

Changing the Conversation

While the *Sonnets* as a whole are famous for giving a new intonation to inward feeling and private thought, the focus is not on the speaker's "I" from the outset. The sequence begins with seventeen sonnets often referred to as the pro-creation group. They advise a beautiful young man to marry and procreate so that his beauty will be replicated and preserved in his children against time's ruinous process of decay: "From fairest creatures we desire increase, / That thereby beauty's rose might never die" (s. 1.1–2). Who would speak this way, and in what situation? It is true that a conventional Petrarchan sonnet lover might use metaphors like "beauty's rose," but this speaker adopts a surprisingly public and authoritative stance. A first cue is the choice of "we" over "I," as if he is speaking for a larger group. In the first line, his vocabulary ("creatures . . . in-crease") seems to echo God's message in the scriptural cre-ation story, "Be fruitful and multiply" (Genesis 1.22, 28). Nonetheless, the voice that will eventually set up Nature and Time as the reigning forces in the sonnets' worldview sounds more secular than religious, more like a teacher than a preacher. The public role is reinforced in the cou-plet's directive not to pity a private lover but to "Pity the world" (s. 1.13). This directive raises curiosity about who the addressee can be to be so important that the world should care. Only the addressee's great beauty is given as an explicit reason in Sonnet 1, but soon the vocabulary, even where used metaphorically, comes to associate the addressee with the nobility. His imagined child is spoken of as an "heir" (s. 6.14) and in terms of "succession" (s. 2.12); he is spoken of as if in possession of a "legacy" (s. 4.2) and a "fair . . . house" (s. 13.9); and it is taken for granted he can afford liveried servants (s. 2.3) and the pompous splendor of a "tomb" (s. 3.7).

If the addressee is so important, in a society in which

power differences between nobles and commoners were strongly displayed and enforced, how is it that the speaker dares to criticize him? How can he accuse him, even with the indirection of a pun, of being "contracted" (i.e., *pledged* but also *shrunken*, as opposed to *increased*) to his "own bright eyes" (s. 1.5)? In Elizabethan English, power differences are strongly marked in use of pronouns: "you" is the usual address to a social superior, with "thou" tending to denote someone of lesser power or in an intimate relationship that is reciprocal.[7] How, then, is it that the speaker dares to "thou" the addressee throughout the first fifteen sonnets? The answer is in the historically specific social relationship signaled by the details of language: that of humanist poet-educator to youthful highborn patron.

How would an Elizabethan reader recognize this specialized relationship? The procreation group strongly echoes themes and metaphors from a famous letter written in Latin by the humanist educator Erasmus and circulated in English translation in Thomas Wilson's *Art of Rhetoric* as "An Epistle to Persuade a Young Gentleman to Marriage."[8] The letter is the source, for example, for the incredibly unromantic metaphor of plowing—"the tillage of thy husbandry" (s. 3.6)—used of what a man does when he has dutiful sex with a wife for the purpose of procreation.[9] This letter and other educational writings by Erasmus also modeled an interaction script recommended for educators instructing youthful prospective power-holders.[10] The vocation of Shakespeare's speaker is not, of course, tutor but poet. Renaissance poets, however, looked to the educational program of humanism to give an ethical grounding to the poet-patron relationships on which they depended for cash and other kinds of support.

Shakespeare had addressed and dedicated his first two published poems—*Venus and Adonis* and *The Rape of Lucrece*—to a patron, the earl of Southampton, in an opening epistle that is separated from the artistic compo-

sition. With the *Sonnets,* the address to an unnamed pa-
tron is assimilated into the composition, given extended
voicing in the compliments, advice giving, and boastful
offers to the young man of poetic longevity. The speaker
sounds like a humanist tutor instructing an aristocratic
youth in the duties of his class. Like Erasmus, whose
writings illustrate how instructors should use language
that is both forceful and familiar to influence their
charges, the speaker addresses the patron in ways that
half insult and half praise: "Unthrifty loveliness," he calls
him, and "Profitless usurer" (s. 4.1, 7). He dares to give
him orders, such as "Be not self-willed," and then, like a
schoolmaster, balances his reprimands and exhortations
with praise and encouragement: "for thou art much too
fair / To be death's conquest" (s. 6.13–14). Thus, to make
sense of the language in the opening sonnets is not to
strip away social specifications. Instead, it involves recog-
nizing the markers of sex, age, class, and vocation in the
dialogue script that Shakespeare develops to give initial
definition to the primary relationship.

The implied conversation is soon to change. Indeed,
Shakespeare constructs the unique love relationship of his
sonnets by situating it first as a poet-patron relation and
then displacing that relation—that is, changing the con-
versation. The private "I," withheld until Sonnet 10, begins
to make quiet intrusions into the safe and publicly ac-
countable language of instruction. In urging "Make thee
another self," the poet repeats his persuasion to "breed,"
but supplies a new motive: "for love of me" (s. 10.13). The
"I" assumes a greater prominence in Sonnets 12 to 15. The
speaker is no longer acting as spokesperson for the con-
ventional sexual politics of heterosexual marriage and
thereby effacing his own agency. He makes an intoxicating
claim to a self-important poetic role: "And, all in war with
Time for love of you, / As he takes from you, I engraft you
new" (s. 15.13–14). Surprisingly, this emerging "I" also

shifts his pronoun of address, at least temporarily, to the more deferential "you" (Sonnets 13, 15, 16, and 17). Why should the addressee now become "you"? I think it is because as the speaker's promise becomes more personal, he cannot hide behind the public role. The dutiful poet-teacher had kept his focus on the other and registered little consciousness of self. But the self-asserting poet-lover is suddenly also self-conscious. To be self-conscious is here to newly recognize what he is, not in himself but in relation to the elite and powerful other. The self-asserting "I" weighs himself in relation to "*your* most high deserts" (s. 17.2; emphasis added), and his status-conscious pronoun choice is an early register of a developing thematic concern with his own self-worth and deserts. If Shakespeare is inventing new language for private self-consciousness, what is fascinating here is how it shows itself in the verbal ballet of "thou" and "you," "we" and "I."

Then, in Sonnet 20, the authoritative script of humanist advice-giving is interrupted, never to be wholly resumed, by a confession—however guarded—of personal involvement, of an intimate love relationship. There has been endless debate about whether this sonnet supports or denies a physically enacted homosexual relationship in the overall sequence. Some readers imagine the debate is only an effect of the other side's intransigence, but it is almost certainly also an effect, at least in part, of the sonnet's language. The confessional speech act is indirect, ambiguous, and deniable—what linguists and politicians call "off-record." The sonnet distances self-revelation by telling a mythical story about how the beloved "master mistress" came to have the kind of beauty and attraction he has. Nature, intending to create a woman,

> as she wrought thee fell a-doting,
> And by addition me of thee defeated
> By adding one thing to my purpose nothing.

But since she pricked thee out for women's
    pleasure,
Mine be thy love, and thy love's use their treasure.
                            (s. 20.10–14)

Something, we must infer, happens in response to this
poem, or else between this poem and the next, for in
Sonnets 21 through 32 the discourse and the relationship
between the two men have been transformed. For the
speaker, the most salient fact is his certainty that
"I . . . love and am beloved" (s. 25.13). Now "thou"—
pretty clearly here the "thou" of intimacy—replaces the
"you" of deference,[11] even though in these poems the
overwhelming rapture and the emotional complexity of
the speaker's reciprocated affection are heightened and
given specific definition by an awareness of status differ-
ence. The other's social importance is in large measure
what makes the speaker "Unlooked for joy in that I honor
most" (s. 25.4). It makes the situation feel all the more
miraculous, as though something impossible has none-
theless happened. The speaker, like "an unperfect actor
on the stage" (s. 23.1), imagines himself speechless in the
face of what he can give in "recompense" for whatever
gesture of the beloved has gifted him with love's assur-
ance. He nonetheless knows he has at least one gift to put
in the balance—his writing: "O, let my books be then the
eloquence / And dumb presagers of my speaking breast"
(s. 23.9–10). On the one hand, the recognition of atten-
tion from his important friend brings on expressions of
unworthiness and self-deprecation: "Duty so great," he
imagines, is owed, "which wit so poor as mine / May
make seem bare" (s. 26.5–6). On the other hand, the gra-
cious recognition by the important other suggests poten-
tial worth in the self-deprecating speaker, putting
"apparel on my tattered loving / To show me worthy of
thy sweet respect" (s. 26.11–12).

It is important to see that the emotional contours of the speaker's happiness at "falling in love" are not blandly anonymous or universal. Unequal power relations complicate his speech and emotion. The introductory movement of the sonnet sequence has tracked an interruption in one kind of internalized conversation among unequals, the dutiful instruction by a humanist poet of an aristocratic patron. The interruption stages and enables the reader to follow a changed conversation and relationship, still historically specific but now unconventional and intimate. It is a relation for which Shakespeare has invented a new dialogue script, and hence a love relationship that escapes easy stereotyping. Furthermore, the "dialogue of one" in Shakespeare's *Sonnets* is artistically innovative partly because of the exciting way—long before novelists invented the artistic form of stream of consciousness narration—in which it adapts social conversation to put complex inward experience into words. Although the present discussion shows how the words and emotions grew out of their historical moment, they can nevertheless help illuminate the psychological processes of modern-day love relationships. Power imbalances and self-doubt, for example, still affect lovers today, who can recognize in the sonnets variations on their own situations and relational scripts without leveling all differences in such a manner as to colonize the speaker's "I."

I have illustrated a way to read the opening movement of Shakespeare's *Sonnets* that links lyric and history, the linguistic text and social context. Some qualifications are needed before extending this (or any other) interpretive strategy to the overall sequence. The interpretation above treats Sonnets 1 to 32 as a roughly sequential narrative built up out of the speaker's individual speech acts. This takes us back to the question of whether the sonnets can—in any sense—be read as a record of events. The answer is complicated by other unanswered questions.

Did Shakespeare authorize the publication in 1609 of his sonnets, many of which must have been written as early as the 1590s? Does their printed order reflect Shakespeare's plan, or could it be indebted to someone else—the publisher Thomas Thorpe, for example? If Shakespeare was writing individual sonnets over the course of many years, later gathered into the 1609 grouping, can we even be sure that the overall sequence has a consistent cast of characters, let alone a developing story line?

Internal evidence certainly casts doubt on any simple assumption that the sonnet order is chronological. Compare, for example, Sonnets 41 and 42 with Sonnets 133 and 134. Both early and late sonnet pairs treat a triangular relationship involving "me," "my sweet'st friend" (s. 133.4), and a mistress. Does the sonnet sequence treat two different triangular relationships separated by a period of time? Or—perhaps more likely—does it return, out of temporal sequence, to the same situation and the same set of characters? Sonnet pairs 57/58 and 153/154 pose a different but related problem as we consider the coherence of the sequence as a whole. Sonnet 58 reads like a rewrite of the situation in 57, with each poem giving vivid expression to the speaker's feeling of slavery at having to wait around until the powerful friend deigns to give him attention. Sonnet 154 replays the mythical anecdote in 153 of Diana's maid stealing Cupid's arrow and creating with its help an ineffective healing bath for diseased lovers like the poet-speaker. Do these twinned sonnets illustrate the Renaissance love of amplification, the art of elegantly varying a single theme? Or did Shakespeare's publisher fail to choose between a draft poem in Shakespeare's manuscript and its revision?

A cautious reader will regard the sonnet order as provisional; but need one go further, as some recent critics have suggested, and discard the overall sequence as contextual moorings for readings of individual sonnets?[12] That is, when we ask key questions—who is speaking? to whom? in what situation?—must we limit evidence to that individual sonnet? To make that argument would, in some cases, come close to reverting to Vendler's anonymous "I" and "thou" stripped of sex, rank, age, and other social specifications, since only about one-fifth of the sonnets specify even the sex of the beloved. But it would, in my view, be the wrong choice, if our aim is to gain insight into the rich psychology of the speaker or the exciting wordplay charging the language. In Sonnet 32, for example, what does Shakespeare's shadow-self mean by calling his own magnificent verse "poor rude lines" or by wittily recommending that his friend resolve: "Theirs for their *style* I'll read, his for his love" (ll. 4, 14; emphasis added)? It is not the false modesty of a great poet. Rather it is the internalized and perhaps inescapable doublespeak of someone living within a hierarchical culture and caught between two measures of self-worth: here, social status and poetic ability. If we are aware, from the context of surrounding sonnets, of the speaker's class consciousness, we will understand that the word choice of this utterance he imagines in his friend's mouth does not simply declare his own verse devoid of poetic style. Consider, for example, how Shakespeare's contemporary, William Cecil, announced his newly awarded peerage: "My *stile* is, Lord of Burghley."[13] In Shakespeare's sonnet, we should be able to hear the speaker's punning dig at his elite friend's snobbish value system: read theirs for their style (i.e., their social titles), mine for my love. It will help us see how the intense emotions arise within a unique relationship and a specific social context. We will better appreciate Shakespeare's poetic language and, through its innovative "dialogue of one" for expressing inward consciousness, something of how he might have felt.

My work on this essay was supported by a grant from the Social Sciences and Humanities Research Council of Canada and benefited from the advice of Barbara A. Mowat, Paul Stevens, and Paul Werstine.

---

1. Hyder Edward Rollins reviews conjectures up to the date of the New Variorum edition of *The Sonnets* (Philadelphia: J. B. Lippincott, 1944), 2:166–232. Katherine Duncan-Jones reviews recent views and opts for Pembroke in the Arden Third Series, *Shakespeare's Sonnets* (Walton-on-Thames: Thomas Nelson, 1997), pp. 49–69. Donald Foster has argued that the "begetter" of the sonnets referred to as "W.H." is a misprint for Shakespeare's own initials, "W.SH.," in "Master W.H., R.I.P.," *PMLA* 102 (1987): 42–54.

2. See reviews of "dark lady" candidates in Rollins, *The Sonnets*, 2:242–76; Duncan-Jones, *Shakespeare's Sonnets*, pp. 47–55; and S. Schoenbaum, *Shakespeare's Lives*, rev. ed. (Oxford: Clarendon Press, 1991), pp. 493–98.

3. Helen Vendler, *The Art of Shakespeare's Sonnets* (Cambridge, Mass.: Harvard University Press, Belknap Press, 1997), p. 3; for Stephen Booth's similar emphasis on poetic art as multiple verbal patterns, see *An Essay on Shakespeare's Sonnets* (New Haven: Yale University Press, 1969).

4. Vendler, *The Art of Shakespeare's Sonnets*, p. 2.

5. Giorgio Melchiori, *Shakespeare's Dramatic Meditations: An Experiment in Criticism* (Oxford: Clarendon Press, 1976), p. 15.

6. This is John Donne's phrase in his poem "The Ecstasy" (1633), but he uses it with a different sense to refer to the paradox of a communal speech by two persons so closely united as to be one.

7. On further complexities of second-person pronoun variation in early modern English, see Roger Lass,

"Phonology and Morphology," in *The Cambridge History of the English Language,* vol. 3, *1476–1776,* ed. Lass (Cambridge: Cambridge University Press, 1999), pp. 56–186, esp. 148–55.

8. Erasmus's letter was first published in 1518 and later circulated widely as an example of epistolary persuasion in *De conscribendis epistolis.* For a modern translation of the latter work, see "On the Writing of Letters," trans. Charles Fantazzi, in vol. 25 of *Collected Works of Erasmus,* ed. J. K. Sowards (Toronto: University of Toronto Press, 1985), pp. 10–254, esp. 129–45. See also Thomas Wilson, *The Art of Rhetoric* (1560), ed. Peter E. Medine (University Park: Pennsylvania State University Press, 1994), pp. 79–100. For excerpts from Erasmus's letter as translated by Wilson, see "Appendix of Intertextual Material," above, pp. 346–52.

9. Compare Wilson, *The Art of Rhetoric,* p. 92.

10. On this interaction script in Erasmus, see Lynne Magnusson, *Shakespeare and Social Dialogue: Dramatic Language and Elizabethan Letters* (Cambridge: Cambridge University Press, 1999), pp. 66–74.

11. This pronominal shift occurs gradually, with no second-person pronoun appearing in ss. 21, 23, or 25, and with s. 24 unusual for alternating between forms of "thou" and "you."

12. See, for example, Heather Dubrow's suggestions for reading strategies that reject the consistency of the standard sonnet story in " 'Incertainties now crown themselves assur'd': The Politics of Plotting Shakespeare's Sonnets," *Shakespeare Quarterly* 47 (1996): 291–305; rpt. in *Shakespeare's Sonnets: Critical Essays,* ed. James Schiffer (New York: Garland Publishing, 1999), pp. 113–33.

13. Lord Burghley to Nicholas White, 14 March 1570/1; in Thomas Wright, ed., *Queen Elizabeth and Her Times: A Series of Original Letters* (London: Henry Colburn, 1838), 1:391.

Further Reading

Shakespeare's Sonnets

Abbreviations: *Ant.* = *Antony and Cleopatra;* *AWW* = *All's Well That Ends Well;* *AYL* = *As You Like It;* *Ham.* = *Hamlet; Lear* = *King Lear; LLL* = *Love's Labor's Lost; Oth.* = *Othello; Rom.* = *Romeo and Juliet; Tro.* = *Troilus and Cressida; TN* = *Twelfth Night*

Booth, Stephen, ed. *Shakespeare's Sonnets, Edited with Analytic Commentary.* New Haven: Yale University Press, 1977.

Booth provides the text of the 1609 Quarto (Apsley imprint, the Huntington-Bridgewater copy) and his own edited text in parallel, followed by a detailed analytic commentary on each sonnet. What Booth thinks "a Renaissance reader would have thought" in progressing through a sequence felt "as both urgent and wanting" determines both text and commentary. The "pluralistically-committed" glosses reflect Booth's view that the poems are best thought about in terms of "both . . . and" rather than "either . . . or." In an appendix the editor briefly touches on matters relating to authenticity, dating, sources, arrangement, and biographical implications; addressing the question of Shakespeare's sexual preference, Booth observes: "William Shakespeare was almost certainly homosexual, bisexual, or heterosexual. The sonnets provide no evidence on the matter."

Cheney, Patrick. " 'O, Let My Books Be . . . Dumb Presagers': Poetry and Theater in Shakespeare's Sonnets." *Shakespeare Quarterly* 52 (2001): 222–54.

Cheney counters the commonplace view of Shakespeare as a "playwright and occasional poet." Noting frequent references to Shakespeare's theatrical career and the extensive use of theatrical metaphors and vocabulary (e.g., "show," "mask," "rehearse," "play," "part," "action," "actor," "shadow," "mock," and "dumb"), Cheney finds in the *Sonnets* "an unusual site" for exploring Shakespeare as "inextricably caught" in the rivalry between printed poetry and staged theater for cultural authority in early modern England. Cheney's examination of the intersection of poetic and theatrical discourses in several key sonnets (15, 29, 54, 108, 144, and especially 23) leads him to conclude that in these poems Shakespeare—the only prolific professional dramatist of the period to leave behind a sonnet sequence—resurrects and perfects a model of authorship tracing back to the celebrated Ovid, namely, the author as poet-playwright.

De Grazia, Margreta. "The Scandal of Shakespeare's Sonnets." *Shakespeare Survey* 46 (1994): 35–49. [Reprinted in Schiffer, pp. 89–112.]

De Grazia contends that editors and critics have erred in identifying the "scandal" of the *Sonnets* as Shakespeare's "desire for a boy," a desire that, in "upholding [the] social distinctions" essential to a patriarchal society, was really "quite conservative and safe." The real scandal lies in Shakespeare's "gynerastic longings for a black mistress"; these desires are "perverse and menacing, precisely because they threaten to raze the very distinctions his poems to the fair boy strain to preserve." Emphasizing psychosocial rather than psychosexual differences, De Grazia advocates a reclassification of the traditional reading of Shakespeare's "Two loves" that would replace post-eighteenth-century sexual categories of normalcy and abnormalcy with sixteenth-century social categories of hierarchy and anarchy—i.e., "of desired generation and abhorred miscegenation." Recent scholarship on early modern England's contact with Africa and on the cultural representations of that contact encourages an association of the Dark Lady's blackness with racial blackness.

Dubrow, Heather. " 'Incertainties now crown themselves assur'd': The Politics of Plotting Shakespeare's Sonnets." *Shakespeare Quarterly* 47 (1996): 291–305. [Reprinted in Schiffer, pp. 113–33.]

In her revisionist readings of the poems, Dubrow proposes switching the usually assumed addressee to his/her gendered opposite, thereby challenging critical claims based on a "map of misreading" that has characterized scholarship on the *Sonnets* since the end of the eighteenth century—most notably the bipartite division positing a male friend as the focus of the first 126 poems and a woman as the concern of the remaining 28. Also thrown into question is the widely held assumption of a linear plot involving the triangulated desires of Poet, Friend, and Dark Lady. If, for example, Sonnets 18 and 55 are read as addressing the woman, the sequence not only opens up a range of "contestatory images" imparting to her a Cleopatra-like infinite variety but also suggests a period of "idyllic happiness with *her* followed by disillusion." The 1609 Quarto's loose and rather arbitrary arrangement of the poems permits a reader "to construct any number of narratives."

Fineman, Joel. *Shakespeare's Perjured Eye: The Invention of Poetic Subjectivity in the Sonnets.* Berkeley: University of California Press, 1986.

In one of the twentieth century's most influential studies of the *Sonnets,* Fineman argues that "Shakespeare rewrites the poetry of praise by employing (implicitly in the sonnets addressed to the young man, explicitly in the sonnets addressed to the dark lady) in an unprecedentedly serious way the equally antique genre of the mock encomium," in the process inventing "the only kind of subjectivity that survives in the literature successive to the poetry of praise." Within this larger argument Fineman details the visual orientation of Shakespeare's rhetoric in the poet's praise of the young man and then explores how other sonnets in the sequence put into question such a rhetoric and thus how the "eye" is "perjured." Fineman's reading of the poems highlights, among other things, their privileging of their own textuality over visual media of representation. His dazzling critique and its indebtedness to the writings of the French psychoanalyst Jacques Lacan belong very much to the deconstructionist turn in twentieth-century criticism.

Herrnstein, Barbara, ed. *Discussions of Shakespeare's Sonnets.* Boston: D. C. Heath, 1964.

Herrnstein gathers nineteen items spanning the years 1640 to 1960 under the following headings: early commentary (the views of John Benson, George Steevens, Samuel Taylor Coleridge, John Keats, and Henry Hallam), speculation (Leslie Hotson's theory that most of the poems were written by 1589 and F. W. Bateson's retort), interpretation (Edward Hubler's "Shakespeare and the Unromantic Lady," Patrick Cruttwell's "Shakespeare's Sonnets and the 1590's," G. Wilson Knight's "Time and Eternity," and J. W. Lever's "The Poet in Absence" and "The Poet and His Rivals"), evaluation (negative assessments by John Crowe Ransom and Yvor Winters), and analysis (the Robert Graves/Laura Riding study of original punctuation and spelling in Sonnet 129, William Empson's focus on different types of ambiguity,

Arthur Mizener's rebuttal to Ransom's critique of Shakespeare's use of figurative language, and Winifred M. T. Nowottny's discussion of formal elements in ss. 1–6). In the volume's final selection, "The Sonnet as an Action," C. L. Barber claims that the "patterned movement of discourse [i.e., 'determinate rhythm and sound']," not the imagery, is the "main line" of the Shakespearean sonnet.

Hunter, G. K. "The Dramatic Technique of Shakespeare's Sonnets." *Essays in Criticism* 3 (1953): 152–64.

Hunter locates the "peculiar quality" of the poems' excellence in Shakespeare's "bias" toward the dramatic. What distinguishes Shakespeare's treatment of stock themes and use of rhetorical techniques like paradox and simile from that of Spenser, Sidney, Drayton, and Donne is an expressiveness that vividly defines the emotional tension in the "I-Thou" relationship of each sonnet, rendering it immediate, and thereby encouraging the reader to supply "from his imagination a complete dramatic situation." In Shakespeare's hands, "the Petrarchan instruments turn . . . into means of expressing and concentrating the great human emotions, desire, jealousy, fear, hope and despair, and of raising in the reader the dramatic reactions of pity and terror by his implication in the lives and fates of the persons depicted."

Lever, J. W. *The Elizabethan Love Sonnet.* 2nd ed. London: Methuen, 1966. [First published in 1956.]

Following chapters on the Petrarchan model, Wyatt, Surrey, Sidney, Spenser, and the late Elizabethan sonneteers, Lever turns his attention to Shakespeare's reworking of Petrarchan conventions. After a comparatively brief commentary on the sonnets addressed to the Mistress (the "subplot" of the sequence in which satire is the dominant mode), Lever discusses those concerned with the Friend under the following headings: "The Invitation to Marry," "The Poet in Absence," "The Friend's Fault," "The Poet and His Rivals," "The Poet's Error," and "Immortalization." For a full appreciation of Shakespeare's insights into human nature and his attitude toward various kinds of love, the reader needs to be aware of the "dual interpretation" at work in the sequence as a whole. The tension between the love sonnet's Petrarchan origins and a "distinctively English attitude" yields the main dynamic of development that commenced with Wyatt and culminated in Shakespeare.

Magnusson, Lynne. " 'Power to Hurt': Language and Service in Sidney Household Letters and Shakespeare's Sonnets." *ELH* 65 (1998): 799–824. [Incorporated into *Shakespeare and Social Dialogue: Dramatic Language and Elizabethan Letters,* pp. 35–57. Cambridge: Cambridge University Press, 1999.]

Magnusson uses ideas from discourse analysis and linguistic pragmatics, especially "politeness theory," to explore the rhetoric of social exchange in early modern England. Her analysis of the language of servitude in sample household letters of the Sidney family sheds light on how "social relations of power are figured" in several sonnets addressed to the young man, particularly Sonnet 58, which she reads "historically as the outward expression of a subservient social relation developed into the inner speech of the Poet-Servant's complicated desire." Stylistic resemblances between the interlocutory dynamic found in the letters and that in the sonnet—e.g., shared rhetorical strategies of nonpresumption, noncoercion, and self-disparagement on the part of the subordinate—demonstrate that Shakespeare's poetic language "derives something of its peculiar power" from everyday Elizabethan discourse.

Neely, Carol Thomas. "The Structure of English Renaissance Sonnet Sequences." *ELH* 45 (1978): 359–89.

Neely finds in the English Renaissance sonnet sequences a "characteristic overall structure" that is loose and elastic, and hence amenable to refining, reworking, and rearranging over time. This shared structure has several implications: (1) it confirms the indebtedness of the English sequences to those of Dante and Petrarch; (2) it validates the long-questioned standing order of the English sequences; and (3) it helps explain "the perplexing conclusions" of the major ones. The division into two unequal parts is the "primary structuring device" for developing the dichotomy between idealized love and sexual desire at the heart of the sonnet sequence genre. In its movement toward "mutual sexual passion" rather than "solitary sublimation and transcendence," the English sonnet sequence reconstructs rather than reproduces the Italian model.

Roberts, Sasha. "Textual Transmission and the Transformation of Desire: The *Sonnets, A Lover's Complaint,* and *The Passionate Pilgrim.*" In her *Reading Shakespeare's Poems in Early Modern England,* pp. 143–90. London: Palgrave, Macmillan, 2003.

Roberts points out that "perhaps because of their comparative scarcity in print," there are "more recorded transcriptions of Shakespeare's sonnets in manuscript than for any other of his works in the seventeenth century." There are, she writes, "some 24 manuscript copies of the sonnets largely dating from the 1620s and 1630s." Those who copied Shakespeare's sonnets felt free to alter the gender dynamics "so as to construct conventionally heterosexual love poems"; in copying, titles were also added and textual variants introduced. Sonnet 2 is particularly interesting in this context. It was "by far the most popular sonnet for transcription," and, in the context of

Caroline collections of amorous verse in which it appeared, it reads "more like a *carpe diem* lyric addressed to a female beloved," a reading "fostered by the addition of the title [in four of the manuscripts] 'To one that would die a maid.' "

Schalkwyk, David. *Speech and Performance in Shakespeare's Sonnets and Plays.* Cambridge: Cambridge University Press, 2002.

Drawing on the work of Ludwig Wittgenstein and J. L. Austin, Schalkwyk reads the *Sonnets* in relation to the Petrarchan discourses in a select group of plays to argue (in contrast to Fineman) that the language of the poems is essentially performative rather than descriptive. Like Magnusson, Schalkwyk argues that their "dialogic art" negotiates power relations between the interior and social worlds of "I" and "You." After an initial examination of the performative of praise (*Sonnets, Ant.,* and *AYL*), the author addresses such issues as embodiment and silencing (*Sonnets, LLL, Rom.,* and *TN*), interiority (*Sonnets, Ham.,* and *Lear*), and transformation (*Sonnets* and *AWW*). In his discussion of proper names and naming events in the *Sonnets, Rom., Tro.,* and *Oth.,* Schalkwyk reopens the autobiographical question, claiming that "it is precisely the peculiar absence of proper names in 'SHAKE-SPEARES SONNETS' that testifies to their autobiographical nature." [Earlier versions of chapters 1 and 2 appeared, respectively, in *Shakespeare Quarterly* 49 (1998): 251–58 ("What May Words Do? The Performative of Praise in Shakespeare's Sonnets") and in 45 (1994): 381–407 (" 'She never told her love': Embodiment, Textuality, and Silence in Shakespeare's Sonnets and Plays").]

Schiffer, James, ed. *Shakespeare's Sonnets: Critical Essays.* New York: Garland Publishing, 1999.

Schiffer's anthology of four reprinted essays and fifteen newly published ones offers a snapshot of critical theories and methodologies dominant in *Sonnets* scholarship of the 1990s. The reprinted essays are those by Peter Stallybrass, Margreta de Grazia, Heather Dubrow, and George T. Wright (see individual entries for annotations). Among the newly commissioned essays are Gordon Braden's revisiting of Shakespeare's Petrarchism; Naomi Miller's examination of the *Sonnets* in the context of early modern codes of maternity; Rebecca Laroche's reconsideration of Oscar Wilde's *The Portrait of Mr. W. H.;* Marvin Hunt's reading of the Dark Lady as "a sign of color"; Joyce Sutphen's discussion of memorializing strategies in the sequence's bipartite structure; Lisa Freinkel's "post-Reformation" reading of the poems' Christian "figurality"; Peter Herman's investigation of the language and imagery of usury in Sonnets 1–20; Bruce Smith's exploration of the sexual politics informing the pronominal interplay among "I," "you," "he," "she," and "we"; and Valerie Traub's examination of sodomy "as simultaneously a construction of and reaction to gender and erotic difference." In his extensive introductory survey of *Sonnets* criticism, Schiffer notes how Fineman's *Shakespeare's Perjured Eye* serves as a "leitmotif" throughout the volume.

Stallybrass, Peter. "Editing as Cultural Formation: The Sexing of Shakespeare's Sonnets." *Modern Language Quarterly* 54 (1993): 91–103. [Reprinted in Schiffer, pp. 75–88.]

In this cultural materialist study, Stallybrass argues that the *Sonnets,* assigned to the margins of the Shakespeare canon prior to Malone's 1780 edition, became in the editions and critical commentary of the nineteenth century a crucial site on which the "sexual identity" of the National Poet "was invented and contested." Out of the "cultural hysteria" prompted by the sexual implications of Malone's "narrative of characterological unity" linking the "I" of the poems to their author came the construction of "Shakespeare" as an interiorized heterosexual, a "back-formation" functioning as a "belated defense against sodomy." Consequently, the unified character of the author we as moderns know as "Shakespeare" is not "punctual"—i.e., is not a product of his own historical time—but rather retroactive, the creation of the nineteenth century's homophobic response to the *Sonnets*.

Willen, Gerald, and Victor B. Reed, eds. *A Casebook on Shakespeare's Sonnets*. New York: Thomas Y. Crowell, 1964.

Willen and Reed offer a newly edited text of the *Sonnets,* accompanied by six full-length essays and eight short explications of individual poems. The focus of the essays by Robert Graves and Laura Riding, L. C. Knights, John Crowe Ransom, Arthur Mizener, Edward Hubler, and G. Wilson Knight is on the poems themselves (their punctuation, structure, figurative language, and symbolism) rather than on "biographical puzzles." In the frequently anthologized "Shakespeare at Sonnets," Ransom faults the poems, with few exceptions, for their lack of logic and coherence, their "great violences" of idiom and syntax, and their "mixed effects." The Hubler piece, "Form and Matter," excerpted from his *The Sense of Shakespeare's Sonnets* (1952), examines Shakespeare's poetic practice to argue that the poet valued matter (the subject) over form (the means by which the subject finds expression); the homely image and the "vignettes of nature" are what we remember. The specific sonnets receiving explication are 57 and 58 (Hilton Landry), 71–74 (Carlisle Moore), 73 (R. M. Lumiansky and Edward Nolan), 129 (Karl F. Thompson and C. W. M. Johnson), 143 (Gordon Ross Smith), and 164 (Albert S. Gerard).

The appendices include a bibliography and a series of pedagogic exercises.

Wright, George T. "An Art of Small Differences: Shakespeare's *Sonnets.*" In his *Shakespeare's Metrical Art,* pp. 75–90. Berkeley: University of California Press, 1988.

Wright's focus here is on the contribution of the *Sonnets* to Shakespeare's dramatic verse art. It was in these poems, Wright notes, that "Shakespeare learned, presumably in the early 1590s, after he had written a few plays and the narrative poems, to fashion a reflective verse whose resonances would thereafter be heard in the speeches of his dramatic characters." Wright illustrates the ways in which the metrical art of the *Sonnets* "proceeds by way of small differences, quiet additions or withdrawals of emphasis," making the most "of small differences—of stress, of pattern, of feeling." The phrasing, he shows, is "extremely various," rising "to a height of expressive variation in one line and then [subsiding] in the next," but with the speech-tones "imitated in the sonnets . . . almost always those of quiet, intimate speech." Especially notable is the "softness and musical grace that result from [Shakespeare's] skillful use of pyrrhic feet [i.e., feet composed of two unstressed syllables]." The result is the "essentially quiet register" that characterizes the *Sonnets.*

Wright, George T. "The Silent Speech of Shakespeare's *Sonnets.*" In *Shakespeare and the Twentieth Century: The Selected Proceedings of the International Shakespeare Association World Congress, Los Angeles, 1996,* edited by Jonathan Bate, Jill A. Levinson, and Dieter Mehl, pp. 306–27. Newark: University of Delaware Press; London: Associated University Presses, 1998. [Reprinted in Schiffer, pp. 135–58.]

Noting how we usually read poetry in silence, Wright examines the *Sonnets* as silent meditations, "unvoiced, unsounded, unperformed," in which the phenomenon of silent speech functions as both theme and medium. The "ruminative" tone of the poems makes it easy to "take them to be not really spoken to anyone but as having been produced during 'sessions of sweet silent thought' " (s. 30). Wright connects this reflective quality, especially strong in the first 126 sonnets, to an emphasis on absence, separation, and silent waiting—themes that distinguish Shakespeare's sonnets from many others. The emergence of an inner voice has important implications for Shakespeare's development as a dramatist and for the development of the later English lyric.

Index to Illustrations

383

Index of First Lines